A Taste of

Old Cuba

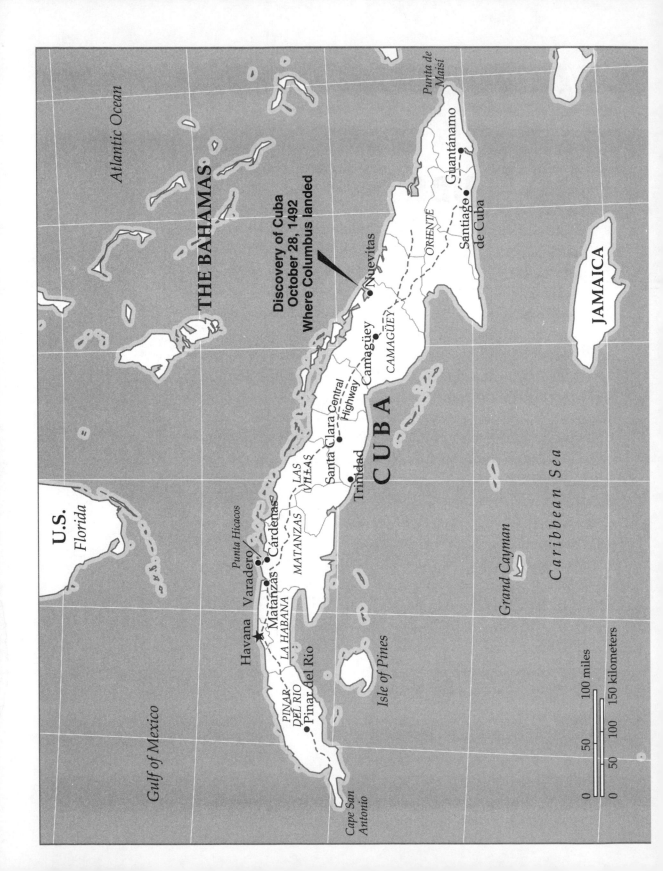

A Taste of Old Cuba

More Than 150 Recipes for Delicious, Authentic,
and Traditional Dishes Highlighted with
Reflections and Reminiscences

MARÍA JOSEFA LLURIÁ DE O'HIGGINS

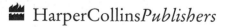 HarperCollins*Publishers*

HarperCollins books may be purchased for educational, business, or sales promotional use. For information please write: Special Markets Department, HarperCollins Publishers, Inc., 10 East 53rd Street, New York, NY 10022.

FIRST EDITION

Designed by Jessica Shatan

Library of Congress Cataloging-in-Publication Data

O'Higgins, María Josefa Lluriá de.
  A taste of old Cuba : more than 150 recipes for delicious, authentic, and traditional dishes highlighted with reflections and reminiscences / María Josefa Lluriá de O'Higgins. — 1st ed.
    p.   cm.
  Includes index.
  ISBN 0-06-016964-8
  1. Cookery, Cuban. 2. Cookery—Cuba. I. Title.
TX716. C8035   1994
641. 597291—dc20   94-10684

94 95 96 97 98 ❖/RRD 10 9 8 7 6 5 4 3

For Jack, who says that black beans are overrated but has been praising my cooking on five continents for fifty-four years, and for our five jewels:

Titi, Johnny, Mike, Jimmy, and Peggy

Cuba—This is the most beautiful land that human eyes have ever seen.

—CHRISTOPHER COLUMBUS,
October 28, 1492

CONTENTS

ACKNOWLEDGMENTS

My first thanks must go to the person who was the last to review this project: my competent and delightful editor, Kathy Martin, who so professionally organized my work of four years that at long last my book is a reality. I can never thank her enough.

Thanks to my children, Titi, Johnny, Mike, Jimmy, and Peggy, who gave me my first computer and have encouraged me to write since the days when I was writing my memoirs; to Mike and Donna, especially, who first "put the bug in my ear" about writing a Cuban cookbook. Thanks again, very especially to Peggy, who was my right hand in this project until its last year; and again to her husband, Robert Boyers, for their generous and loving hospitality during the summers when I attended New York State Summer Writers' Institute in Saratoga. And to Jimmy for finding for me my agent, Emilie Jacobson, who sold my project to HarperCollins Publishers.

Thanks to Katha Pollitt of the Summer Writers' Institute, for her teaching and guidance in the early stages of this book; and to David Rieff, also my mentor at the Institute, for his help and his enthusiasm for all things Cuban.

No thanks are sufficient for that saint, my *aplatanado* husband, for his unlimited patience throughout my struggles in this enterprise. Special thanks to my supportive brother, Pancho, for sharing our childhood memories and for his invaluable advice. Many thanks to my sisters, Ina and Sofy, who have sent me their recipes and family photographs; to my sisters-in-law, Isabelita La Rosa y Freire, Carmita Díaz y Díaz, and Noemí Miralles Poveda for variations of classic recipes. To my friend, Loló Torres, for her great recipes and for the photograph of Hotel Torres. I am also indebted to my cousin, Graciela Carol y Smith, for her delicious desserts and to her gourmet husband, Juan Diez Argüelles, for his recipes and his stories. Thanks to another great gourmet in our family, my nephew, Mikie Lluriá y Díaz, for his special recipes, and to his sister, Ronnie Lluriá y Díaz de Zúñiga, not only for her great recipes but also for those from her friends and relatives, María Elena Breton, Marilyn Calienes Fernández, and Dulce Zúñiga. Thanks also to Lucy Fiallo for her recipes and for her helpful suggestions, to Rafaelito Dalmau, the sole surviving son of Don Faustino, for his father's recipe of "the best sausages in the world," to my friend and neighbor, Norita Fernández Aramburo de Dalmau for the photo of the Hotel La Dominica and its owners, the elder Dalmaus, to another neighbor and friend, Tita Castro Muxó de Larrieu, for sharing the venerable classic, *Delicias de la Mesa* (Delights of the Table), by María A. de los Reyes Gavilán, and for enlightening me about the interesting story of *El Murciélago* (the bat), the mysterious trademark of Bacardí. To my cousin, Cuquita Sánchez Hernández de Aguirregaviria, for great recipes and to her daughter, Teresita Aguirregaviria y Sánchez de Dávalos, to Gelsys Martínez Milanés de Pascual, Nena Doy y Roselló de Sanabria, and Elinita Cora y Johnson, who gave me music, lyrics, and photographs of Varadero. Special thanks also to Dr. Gastón R. Jones y Diez Argüelles, for sharing his ancient book, *Our Islands and Their People,* and to José Esteban Fernández-Llebréz y Babot and his genteel wife, Lila Hernández y Hernández, for their helpful advice.

I must not forget the generosity of Juan Castro y Larrieu, who through the intercession of his wife, Christie Sabulé y Saladrigas, parted with the beautiful photograph of old Varadero's north beach, one of his precious possessions. Thanks also to François Larrieu y Vidal, for more photographs of old Varadero.

I especially want to thank Esperanza de Verona and Gladys Ramos who graciously helped me in my research at the Special Cuban Collection of the University of Miami Richter Library. And last of all, I wish to express my gratitude to my editors at HarperCollins, Susan Friedland, and her gracious assistant, Jennifer Griffin, who allowed me to bring this book to its completion.

A todos muchísimas gracias!

INTRODUCTION

*W*hen I was growing up in Cuba in the 1920s and '30s, there was always a fire burning in the massive charcoal stove of our huge kitchen. In the center of the kitchen was a big, crude wooden table, and along the tall white walls smaller tables were lined up like a counter. The broad, unscreened windows and gleaming tile floors added to the feeling of vastness. It might have seemed a forbidding place, especially to a child, were it not for the constant clutter of food and the friendly buzz of cooking.

I can still smell the sweet aromas that emanated from that kitchen, and from all the kitchens in our neighborhood. One could almost tell the time of day by them: The bracing blend of Cuban coffee brewing and raw milk boiling for *café con leche* meant that it was about 7:00 A.M., almost time *para desayunarse*, to eat breakfast. The pungent aroma of sautéing *sofrito*, the mixture of onion, garlic, and green bell pepper that is the base for so many Cuban dishes, meant that noon was near, time for *almuerzo*, the three-course midday meal. The delicate scent of a sour orange juice marinade bathing a piece of steak or chicken might signal the approach of *comida*, the formal evening meal.

Cubans have a vast and varied culinary inheritance: The Spanish who colonized the island, the Africans who were taken there as slaves, and the Chinese who came still later as laborers all brought their traditions to bear on Cuba's tropical abundance. It is an extraordinary combination.

For me Cuban cooking is home cooking, and home—the home of my heart—is the beautiful beach town of Varadero. I was born and spent the early part of my childhood in Cárdenas, a large port city in Matanzas province known as *la Ciudad Bandera,* the city of the flag, because it was the place where the flag of Cuba's independence from Spain first flew. My father's father, Miguel Lluriá Rosell, had built a fortune from shipbuilding and was a member of Cárdenas's elite. But the fortune was lost after his untimely death in 1916, and eventually the only home left to us was the "summer house" my mother's father had built at Varadero.

I was the oldest child, and by the time we moved to Varadero in 1925 I had three brothers, Lelén, Pili, and Pancho, and a baby sister, Ina. We were happy in our simple, almost wild life in Varadero. There was so much time for playing, for roaming in my grandfather Papabuelo's garden and plucking tamarinds from his trees. We swam in the ocean, we went fishing with Papá, and we took long walks on the beach to collect *conchas finas,* the finest sea shells I have ever seen. And we sneaked into the kitchen whenever possible to see what was going on in there, to discover what the cook was making that smelled so good.

When we were rich (until I was about five years old) we had many servants, and even when we were poor we had at least a cook. (My husband likes to tease that while other exiles brag about how rich their families were in Cuba, I brag about how poor mine was. In truth, though our financial circumstances fluctuated wildly, we were never truly impoverished.)

My mother, María Josefa Carol Aguirregaviria, was a lady who knew a lot about good food and how it should be prepared and served. She only cooked when the cook was away—never for more than a day or two—but the *picadillo* (savory ground beef) and *ropa vieja* (special beef hash) she made were the best we ever had. And when she made garlic soup, we children (Cheo, Peggy, and Sofi had made eight of us by then) would tell her that it was even better than Chicha's.

Chicha, María Wencesla Rosell, was our great-grandmother on my father's side. She was a cantankerous *Catalana* (a woman from Catalonia, a province in northeastern Spain) who presided over much that had to do with meal preparation and the running of our household. She was forever shuffling about the house fussing with the servants, who sometimes quit rather than submit to her intransigent supervision. My mother had taken Chicha into our home when she was 80, little suspecting that she would live to be 103 and hold onto the reins of power almost until the day she died!

Besides Mamá and Chicha, the person who most shaped my culinary sensibilities was my father, Pedro Lluriá García. What he lacked as a businessman my father made up for in swashbuckling charm and joie de vivre. He was a brilliant fisherman and hunter, and an epicure beyond compare. It was he who set the exacting standards for food in our home, and on those rare occasions when he would make us his special paella or *pisto* (scrambled eggs), he proved himself to be a brilliant cook as well.

I never did any cooking as a child, but I watched! What I saw, smelled, and tasted, I reproduced as a grown woman in my own kitchen. My marriage to Jack O'Higgins—an Irish-American whom I met while attending convent school in Philadelphia—took me all over the world as he pursued his career with a variety of oil companies. With our five children—Titi, Johnny, Mike, Jimmy, and Peggy—we lived in Venezuela for fourteen years, spending the summers in my beloved Varadero. That idyll ended in 1959, when Fidel Castro put Cuba under Communist rule.

In the succeeding years, Jack's job took us to the Far East, Africa, Europe, and back to South America. Along the way I gained a deeper appreciation for the international influences on Cuban cuisine, and I honed my culinary skills by entertaining family and friends. Today, in retirement, Jack and I live in Miami, where so much of Cuban life and culture flourishes.

Cuban cuisine has assumed a crucial role in preserving the culture of our homeland outside the island to which so many of us may never return. Indeed, the richness, variety, and vitality of our food reflect the very qualities of Cuban life that have been celebrated by so many writers, artists, and musicians. I invite you to partake of this world of sunshine and music, of laughter and dance. We Cubans have always found joy and friendship in our kitchens and around our tables. May you find the same in yours.

My maternal grandmother, María Aguirregaviria y Aramberry. Mamaía, as we called her, was a concert pianist. In our family she was famous for her Bacalao al Pil-Pil and Basque rice pudding. Cárdenas, circa 1923. *Author's collection*

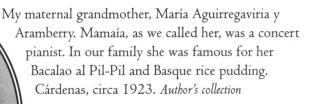

Me with my maternal grandfather, Cipriano Carol y Sicard, whom I called Papabuelo, in front of his garden. Varadero, 1930. *Author's collection*

GLOSSARY

AGUACATE: Avocado. Cuban avocados, like those grown in Florida, are large and meaty. The smaller California variety may be substituted. Used in salads, appetizers, and dips, the avocado, once cut, must be stored in the refrigerator with its seed and sealed with plastic wrap so that it does not turn black. In Cuba, a large slice of aguacate was often served in soup instead of croutons.

ALMENDRAS: Almonds. A part of the Arabian inheritance passed on to Cuba from Spain, almonds are used in many Cuban entrées, desserts, and drinks. Fresh, unpeeled almonds must be soaked in hot water to loosen their skins. Once peeled, they can be toasted in the oven or a skillet.

ALMÍBAR: A homemade sugar-based syrup used in many Cuban desserts.

ALMUERZO: Lunch. Served at midday, almuerzo was a full, three-course meal served between noon and 2:00 P.M., the time when most businesses were closed. As a rule, almuerzo was not as formal as the evening meal, or *comida.*

ANONES: Custard apples. This tropical fruit, which is also found in the south of Spain, bears little resemblance to the apple. Anones are always green, even when ripe. Their inedible shell looks as if it were made of many tiny beads fused together. The glossy white interior sections, which are sweet and succulent, are marred only by the presence of black seeds that resemble small watermelon seeds both in their abundance and bothersomeness. Anones are used to make ice cream, sherbet, and *batidos* (shakes). In some Latin markets, one can purchase the seed-free pulp frozen.

AZAFRÁN: Saffron, a spice made from the stigma of the crocus and imported from Spain. Saffron was used to add color, aroma, and flavor to many Cuban dishes. Some cooks substitute other coloring substances such as bijol (a blend of cumin, corn flour, and food coloring), but saffron's taste is irreplaceable.

To toast saffron, place the strands in a 300-degree oven or in a dry skillet over medium heat for about 30 seconds, until they lose their moisture and can be crumbled into a powder.

BACALAO: Salted codfish, imported from northern waters, mostly Scandinavian. Some of Cubans' favorite Spanish dishes are made with bacalao.

BATIDOS: Luscious tropical milkshakes made with a variety of fruits including guanábana, mango, mamey, and papaya.

BONIATOS: White Cuban sweet potatoes. Although they look and taste different from their North American counterparts, boniatos can be prepared in much the same way. Boniatos are used in stews such as *ajiaco* and desserts such as *boniatillo* and *buñuelos.*

BUTIFARRAS: A spicy pork sausage from the Catalonian region of Spain.

CALABAZA: Cuban pumpkin. This squash is used in side dishes, salads, and entrées. The tougher the skin, the better the calabaza; ideally, you should not be able to pierce it with your fingernail. Also a deep, orange color is important.

CAMARONES SECOS: Dried shrimp. Brought to Cuba by the Chinese, dried shrimp is used almost exclusively as a condiment, and adds a distinctive flavor to dishes. It is available in some American markets (certainly in Miami), as well as in Oriental food markets.

CASABE: The bread that the native Siboneyes Indians made from the cassava or yucca root.

CHAYOTE: A pear-shaped, tropical squash with pale green skin and a large avocadolike seed. If it were possible to cross-breed zucchini and avocados, perhaps their offspring would resemble chayote. Always in season, chayotes grow on vines in Central America and throughout the Caribbean. Chayotes have a delicate flavor and can be cooked in ways similar to American squash. Favorite ways to serve them are as an entrée stuffed with *picadillo,* and as a dessert with bread pudding. They can be purchased in Latin markets and some supermarkets.

CHORIZO: Spicy Spanish sausage. This paprika-rich pork sausage is used in a variety of Cuban dishes, especially in stews of Spanish origin. It is a flavorful addition to paella, and can transform an omelet in an instant.

COCO SECO: Dry coconut. This is the ripened dark brown variety of coconut found in the produce section of grocery stores in America. It is used mainly for its white meat. Although it is called "dry," it does have some liquid inside. Shake each coconut before buying it to be sure that it contains liquid; if it doesn't, it is likely to be spoiled. The shell is very hard and must be opened with a hatchet or machete.

COCO VERDE: Green coconut. This is the unripened counterpart to coco seco. While dry coconuts, used for their meat, fall from the trees of their own accord, green coconuts are picked from the trees and used for the liquid inside them. To obtain the liquid, cut the coconut open at the top or poke holes in the "eyes" with an ice pick or screwdriver.

COMIDA: Dinner. Although the word comida literally means "meal" in Cuba it referred to the evening meal. Comida was taken earlier than the Spanish *cena,* but was nevertheless a dressy affair in most Cuban homes, regardless of the social status of the family. Every day, adults returned from work and children came home from school and play to bathe and dress in fresh clothes for dinner, which was served at 7:00 or 8:00 P.M. The ladies of leisure in my time dressed in their fashionable everyday clothes. But in the days of my grandparents, ladies wore *batas,* long white linen dresses, usually hand-embroidered, with ruffles and lace down to their ankles.

The food served for comida was generally lighter than that served for almuerzo, but it was nevertheless rather elaborate, consisting of three courses. Cubans living in America nowadays do not generally distinguish much between dishes appropriate for cena or almuerzo. Most have adopted the American custom of having a single large meal in the evening, at which any dish can be served.

CORDERO: Lamb.

DESAYUNO: Breakfast. Breakfast in Cuba was not a ceremonious occasion. Short and to the point, it consisted of café con leche (coffee with milk), plain café (Cuban coffee), or, in some homes, heavy Spanish-style hot chocolate. The hot drink of choice was accompanied by something bready and dunkable such as *sube y bajas* (literally "raises and lowers"), toasted bread cut in long strips.

FALDA: Brisket. This meat was used in soups and stews, and to make such signature Cuban dishes as ropa vieja and vaca frita.

FRUTA BOMBA: Papaya. Well known for its exotic though bland flavor, papaya was thought to aid digestion and to make an effective diuretic. Practitioners of *Santería* (Cuban black magic) believed it could cure insanity.

GRANO: Dried beans. Garbanzos (chick-peas), *chícharos* (whole dry green peas), *lentejas* (lentils), *frijoles de carita* (black-eyed peas), and, of course, *frijoles negros, blancos,* and *colorados* (black, white, and red beans) are the basis for many popular Cuban dishes.

GUANÁBANA: Large custard apple. The guanábana looks like a large anón, but its taste is dramatically different. Guanábana is best in *champola,* a refreshing drink, and is also good in ice cream and in batidos. In some Latin markets one can buy its juice in cans and its pulp in frozen form.

GUAYABA: Guava. This tropical fruit, about the size of a plum, is pale yellow-green on the outside and light red on the inside. Although it is rife with tiny seeds, it is eaten raw by many who like its tart taste. Mostly it is used to make jams, jellies, and desserts, the most famous of which is *casquitos de guayaba.*

HICACOS: Cocoplums. These small, plumlike fruit grow on trees that proliferate along the seashore in Cuba and other tropical locales. They are used to make desserts.

JAMÓN DE COCINAR: Cooking ham. The ham used for cooking in Cuba was cured raw ham known as *jamón serrano* in Spain and *prosciutto crudo* in Italy. In America it is generally known by its shortened Italian name, prosciutto, and can be purchased in most international food markets. In Latin markets it is known as jamón de cocinar. It is sold by the slab or in chunks, but butchers will usually slice it for you.

JAMÓN EN DULCE: Sweet ham. This glazed ham has a very distinctive flavor, unlike the familiar American version found at deli counters. It is sold in Latin markets, and is used mostly for sandwiches and *saladitos* (appetizers).

LIMÓN: Lime. Not to be mistaken for lemons, which are known in Cuba as *limones franceses* (French lemons) and are rarely used, the limes most often used in Cuban cooking are the Persian limes found in any American supermarket. They are indispensable to Cuban cooking. *Limones criolles* are small, very juicy limes known in America as Key limes.

MALANGA AMARILLA: Yellow malanga. Quite different from its white sister, this tuber has a tough yellow interior and a strong flavor. It must be consumed as soon as it is cooked or it will harden and become inedible.

MALANGA BLANCA: White malanga. Also known in Cuba as *guaguí*, this starchy tuber can be cooked as you would a potato. It probably came to Cuba from Nigeria, the country from which most of the African slaves of Cuba hailed. There it was known as "cocoa yam," an apt name given its shaggy brown exterior and soft, yamlike interior.

MAMEY COLORADO: Red mamey, a very delicate, rare tropical fruit. The mamey has a rough brown skin that resembles sandpaper, but inside it is smooth and creamy like an avocado. The flesh is orange-red, and the seed in the center is large, black, and glossy. Mamey can be cut in half and eaten directly from the shell, or can be made into rich desserts, ice cream, and batidos. Another variety, *mamey de santo domingo* (Dominican mamey), is yellow and bland.

MANGOS: One of the most delicious foods cultivated in the tropics, mangos are sold all over the world. They are low in calories and sodium, and high in potassium and vitamins A and C. In Florida as in Cuba, mangos are in season from May to August. One can get them at other times throughout the year but these tend to be of lesser quality. Mangos vary in color from red to yellow to deep orange to green. Ripe mangoes produce a rich, fruity scent. Generally, it is best to buy them firm and blemish-free, and allow them to ripen at home. But they are at their sweetest best when they fall ripe from the tree. Although the rich taste of a plain mango is impossible to improve upon, mangos can be used successfully in a variety of recipes, especially as a replacement for peaches. Mangos can be preserved easily—canned or frozen—and are wonderful in ice cream and batidos. I do not recommend using them in fruit salad, because the mango overwhelms the other fruit flavors.

MOJO: A sauce made of garlic, oil, and citrus, mojo is almost always served with certain vegetables, like yucca and ñame. The bottled variety sold in Latin markets is a poor substitute for freshly made mojo.

MOROS: Though it literally means Moors, on Cuban restaurant menus it generally refers to *moros y cristianos*, a mixture of black beans and white rice.

ÑAME: African white yam. Another tuber of African origin, ñame is loved by Cubans. It is prepared and eaten in exactly the same ways as its cousins, the two malangas. It is widely available in Latin grocery stores, and occasionally can be found with other "exotic" produce in regular supermarkets.

NARANJA AGRIA: Sour orange. As indispensable as that of the lime, the juice of the sour orange is used in marinating meats and in the preparation of many other foods. When it is not available, substitute a 50–50 mixture of sweet orange juice and lime juice.

OIL: In general, olive oil is used in seafood dishes and in dishes of Spanish origin. I use vegetable oil (canola is my favorite) in place of the lard traditionally used in other Cuban recipes.

PAN CUBANO: Cuban bread. It is similar in shape, texture, and taste to French or Italian bread. At home in Cuba I never saw anyone making bread; we had a *panadero* or bread man who would deliver fresh loaves to us every morning. In American cities with a large Cuban population, Cuban bread can be purchased in Cuban bakeries and grocery stores.

PETIT POIS: Tiny canned peas. Because they were imported, and therefore rare and expensive, petit pois were used as a garnish in many Cuban dishes. Tiny frozen peas are a more flavorful and attractive modern substitute.

PICADILLO: A savory dish made of ground beef and a tasty sofrito (sautéed onion, green bell pepper, garlic, and tomato sauce) to which other ingredients are added at the cook's discretion: raisins, olives, almonds, capers, and cubed potatoes.

PLÁTANOS: Plantains. These members of the banana family are loved by Cubans at all stages of their growth—green, semiripe, and ripe to the point of blackness. In all their forms they are the perfect prelude, accompaniment, or ending to any Cuban meal.

PLÁTANOS BURROS: Donkey plantains. Although these short, broad plantains have a different appearance and a milder taste than regular plantains, they are prepared in exactly the same ways. They are especially good in *tostones,* twice fried plantain patties.

PLÁTANOS MANZANOS: Apple *plantains.* This squat, roundish fruit is more akin to bananas (called *plátanos Johnson* by Cubans) than plantains, and is eaten as bananas are.

QUIMBOMBÓ: Okra. These fresh green pods with their tiny pink seeds are used in a number of Afro-Cuban dishes.

SALADITOS: Appetizers, akin to the Spanish tapas.

SOFRITO: A combination of lightly sautéed vegetables that is the foundation of many Cuban dishes. The combination must include at least two of the three most essential ingredients: onion, garlic, and green bell peppers. Tomatoes are frequently added, as well as herbs and spices such as parsley, oregano, and cumin.

TASAJO: Jerked beef. This dried, salty meat was produced in abundance in Cuba in colonial times, and is still used in a number of traditional recipes.

TOSTONES: Twice-fried green plantain patties. Tostones that have been fried just once are available in the frozen-food section of Latin markets, ready for a second frying at home.

VIANDAS: Starchy vegetables such as malanga, boniato, yucca, ñame, and potatoes.

YUCA: Yucca or cassava. This root vegetable was one of the staple foods that nourished Cuba's native Siboneyes Indians. It is found fresh in the exotic produce section of many grocery stores as well as in Latin markets, but I highly recommend frozen yucca, which is peeled, cleaned, and ready to boil. Neither the flavor nor the texture suffers from being frozen. Yucca is most often boiled and served with mojo.

$\mathcal{S}$ALADITOS (Appetizers)

Bocaditos (Little Party Sandwiches) 5

Empanaditas (Little Spanish Turnovers) 6

Cangrejitos (Little Pastry Crabs) 7

SALADITOS (Appetizers)

Saladitos are served mainly at parties and sometimes are ordered as hors d'oeuvres at restaurants. They are festive treats that are never seen at the typical daily main meal. Nevertheless, since the lives of most Cubans are filled with special occasions such as weddings, christenings, *quinces* (girls' fifteenth birthday parties), and frequent gatherings at which extended families come together to celebrate the simple fact of being related, saladitos are well known to the Cuban palate. Many saladitos are indistinguishable from their Spanish ancestors, tapas, but some, such as tiny tamales or fritters made with tropical tubers, are uniquely Cuban.

Other Saladitos

Some recipes for entrées and side dishes can be adapted for use as saladitos by altering in size and shape to make them easy to handle. Here are some examples: Camarones al Ajillo (page 56); Serrucho en Escabeche (page 58); Frituras (all varieties) (page 175); and Tortilla Española Clásica (page 171).

Saladitos can also be improvised from any number of foods according to one's imagination and what happens to be in one's cupboard or refrigerator. Here are some suggestions:

Anchoas (anchovies)
Chorizos
Aceitunas (black or green
    olives)
Pimientos
Mariquitas (plantain chips)

Yuquitas (yucca chips)
Quesos (cheeses)
Almendras (almonds)
Maní (peanuts)
Rositas de maíz (popcorn)

The Carol quinta, the house where my mother and her seven brothers grew up. Her father sold it and it was converted to a school called La Progresiva. Cárdenas, circa 1920. *Author's collection*

Bocaditos are literally "little mouthfuls," tiny sandwiches that take only two or three bites to consume. They are served as hors d'oeuvres at practically every Cuban gathering. Traditionally, they are made with little round rolls sold expressly for this purpose at Cuban bakeries, but they can also be made by cutting other types of bread down to size. What is distinctive about bocaditos is not the bread but the filling. I have included several of my favorites.

Filling of your choice (recipes follow)
24 little rolls (see Note)

Split open the little rolls and spread the filling lightly on the inside. Arrange them on a tray with a variety of bocaditos.

NOTE: If you don't have access to a Cuban bakery, you may substitute any party-size bread, or simply cut pieces of bread into 2-inch circles and sandwich the filling between pairs of them.

Relleno de Jamón y Queso (Ham and Cheese Filling)

½ pound sweet Cuban ham, diced (see Note)
1 tablespoon Dijon mustard
2 tablespoons finely chopped parsley

½ pound Swiss cheese, thinly sliced and cut into pieces the size of the bread

1. Place the ham, mustard and parsley in a mixing bowl and mix with a fork until well blended.
2. After spreading this filling lightly on one side of each roll, top it with a slice of cheese and close the roll.

NOTE: If Cuban sweet ham, called *jamón en dulce*, is not available, substitute plain baked or boiled ham.

Relleno de Atún (Tuna Filling)

Two 7-ounce cans white tuna, drained
4 scallions, chopped

¾ cup mayonnaise
½ cup chopped parsley

Relleno de Huevos (Egg Filling)

8 hard-boiled eggs, chopped
¼ cup mayonnaise

2 teaspoons onion salt
1 teaspoon paprika

Combine all the ingredients for the filling of your choice in a food processor. Pulse until well blended.

EMPANADITAS
(LITTLE SPANISH TURNOVERS)

About 24 turnovers

Empanadas and their diminutive version, empanaditas, are ours by way of Spain, probably through the Moors, who gave us so many delicacies. The Cuban influence can be tasted in the variety of fillings we use for these party favorites. Like croquettes and fritters, empanaditas are a great use for leftover meat and fish.

2 cups all-purpose flour
1 teaspoon salt
1 tablespoon sugar
½ cup lard or butter

2 eggs
¼ cup dry white wine
1½ cups filling (see Note)
1½ to 2 cups vegetable oil

1. Sift the flour, salt, and sugar into a large mixing bowl.

2. Using a pastry blender or two knives crossed scissors fashion, cut in the lard until the mixture resembles crumbs.

3. In a separate bowl, beat the eggs together with the wine. Make a well in the center of the flour mixture and pour in the liquid. Knead the dough until well mixed.

4. Roll out the dough on a floured surface to a thickness of about ⅛ of an inch and cut it into circles about 2 inches in diameter.

5. Place a tablespoon of filling in the center of each circle, then

fold it in half and seal the edges with the tines of a fork. (Moisten the fork with water so it does not stick.)

6. In a large, deep skillet or deep fryer, heat the oil until fragrant, about 375 degrees. Fry the empanaditas, no more than 4 at a time, until golden. Drain them on paper towels. If they are not to be served immediately, you may keep them in a warm oven for a short time.

NOTE: Typical fillings include Picadillo Clásico (page 71), cooked fish or shellfish, guava preserves, and cheese.

CANGREJITOS
(LITTLE PASTRY CRABS)

Named for the crabs they resemble, these light, delicate pastries are served with a variety of fillings, but most often with ground ham. Make the filling while the dough is chilling.

About 30 pastries

2 cups all-purpose flour, sifted
I teaspoon salt
8 tablespoons (I stick) butter, cut
    into pieces
8 ounces cream cheese
2 cups filling (recipe follows)
I egg yolk
I tablespoon milk

I. Sift the flour with the salt into a large mixing bowl.

2. Using a pastry blender or two knives crossed scissors fashion, cut in the butter until the mixture resembles crumbs. Add the cream cheese in the same manner.

3. Divide the dough into 4 or 5 balls, and refrigerate them in a covered container for about I hour.

4. Preheat the oven to 400 degrees.

5. Put each of the chilled dough balls between two pieces of waxed paper and roll it out, as you would a pie crust, to a thickness of about ⅛ inch.

6. Cut the dough into 4-inch squares, and cut each square into 2 triangles. You will have about 30 triangles.

7. Place a tablespoonful of filling in the center of each triangle. Starting with the longest side of the triangle closest to you, fold the

top corner down so that the point is in the middle of the triangle. Then fold the lefthand corner over the center of the dough and the righthand corner over that, so that it resembles a little crab. Seal the dough with your fingers.

8. Beat the egg yolk with the milk and brush the tops of the pastries with this mixture. Place them on a cookie sheet and bake them for about 20 minutes, until they are golden. Serve warm.

RELLENO PARA CANGREJITOS

(FILLING FOR LITTLE PASTRY CRABS)

RELLENO DE JAMÓN (Ham Filling)

2 cups sweet Cuban ham (or baked
    ham), coarsely chopped
4 teaspoons Dijon mustard

Combine all the ingredients in a food processor. Pulse until well blended.

Sopas y Guisos

(Soups, Stews, and Pottages)

Caldo de Res (Beef Broth) 13

Sopa de Puré de Plátanos (Puréed Plantain Soup) 14

Sopa de Plátanos Para Uno (Plantain Soup for One) 14

Munyeta Catalana (Dry Bean Pottage Catalonian Style) 15

Munyeta Moderna (Modern Bean Pottage) 16

La Sopa de Ajos Auténtica (The Authentic Garlic Soup) 18

Migas de Gato (Dry Garlic "Soup") 19

Jigote Cubano (Ground Chicken Soup) 20

Puré de Vegetales de Mamaía (Mother's Purée of Vegetables Soup) 21

Carne con Papas (Meat and Potato Stew) 22

Cocido (Boiled Dinner from Spain) 23

Ajiaco (Vegetable and Meat Stew) 25

Fabada Asturiana (Asturian Bean Stew) 27

Caldo Gallego (Soup from Galicia) 28

Montería (Pork and Plantain Stew) 29

Sopas y Guisos (Soups, Stews, and Pottages)

*I*n Cuba, despite our warm climate, hot soup was served almost every day. A delicious, rich soup was usually served at the beginning of almuerzo, the leisurely midday meal, when businesses and shops closed and everyone went home to eat and take a siesta or relax with the family. When a stew like *cocido* or *ajiaco* was served, it was a meal unto itself, served with crusty bread and, in our house, a salad.

The key to a good soup is a good *caldo* or broth. In my youth, homemade broth was considered a basic necessity of cooking. I still consider it so today.

Broth-making was an ongoing project in our kitchen years ago; the broth was always being replenished and varied from day to day. The cook, who was in charge of buying the day's provisions, arrived from the market early each morning. She (or he, for we had a few male cooks over the years) began by putting beef bones, chicken parts, or fish heads in a large pot filled with cold water. (If Ropa Vieja or Vaca Frita was to be served, the broth would be based on a large piece of brisket.) What else the cook put in the soup pot depended upon what she was making. As she prepared the day's food, she added ingredients to the soup pot—a bit of onion, a scrap of carrot, whatever was on hand. The soup kettle always went on the charcoal jet of the big kitchen stove, the one that burned continuously to heat the hot water tank.

It's the rare home today where cooking is an all-day process, and I have provided recipes here that approximate the broths that were improvised by our cooks. I believe that a new broth is created every time water is used to boil or steam vegetables, meats, fowl, or fish, but I realize this perspective is not shared by many modern cooks. For the convenience-minded, bouillon cubes are handy substitutes for homemade broth, and there are many good canned broths as well. (These products tend to contain great quantities of salt, and the salt measure of the recipe should be reduced accordingly.) Nonetheless, you owe it to yourself to make broth from scratch at least once so you can taste the delicious difference it makes.

Broth can be stored in the refrigerator for three days without spoiling. If you plan to keep it longer, take it out and bring it to a boil every third day. I like to freeze broth in ice-cube trays and store the cubes (each is about 2 tablespoons) in a double-strength plastic bag for later use.

2 pounds beef brisket
2 pounds beef bones
2 onions, peeled and coarsely
    chopped
6 garlic cloves, peeled and coarsely
    chopped
2 large green bell peppers, cored,
    seeded, and coarsely chopped

5 plum tomatoes,
    coarsely chopped
I tablespoon salt
6 peppercorns
2 sprigs parsley
I bay leaf
12 cups water

CALDO DE RES
(BEEF BROTH)

About 10 cups

I. Put all the ingredients in a large soup pot.

2. Bring the water to a boil. Reduce the heat and simmer, partially covered, for at least 2 hours. (I often use a crockpot for this stage.)

3. Strain the broth. Save the boiled brisket for use in Ropa Vieja (page 73) or Vaca Frita (page 74). Discard the remaining contents of the strainer.

VARIATIONS

Caldo de Pollo (Chicken Broth): Substitute 8 pounds of chicken necks, backs, and wings for the beef bones and meat. (When I cook whole chickens, I always save the backs and necks in the freezer until I have enough for broth.) After straining the broth, pick out the morsels of chicken meat and save them for Chicken and Pineapple Salad (page 219).

Caldo de Pescado (Fish Broth): Substitute 2 fish heads, preferably grouper, for the brisket and beef bones. (Whenever buying a whole fish, ask your fishmonger to remove but include the head, and freeze it until you have enough for broth.) Cut the heads into quarters, and add 1½ teaspoons dry leaf oregano with the other aromatics.

SOPA DE PURÉ DE PLÁTANOS

(PURÉED PLANTAIN SOUP)

6 to 8 servings

This rich, creamy soup is as Cuban as the Royal palm trees.

3 large green plantains
¼ cup lime juice
2 quarts Chicken Broth (page 13)

2 slices toasted Cuban or French
   bread
Salt

1. With a sharp knife, slash the skin of each plantain once lengthwise. Cut the plantains into 1½-inch pieces. Take the skin off each piece by opening it away from the center as if you were taking off a coat. Discard the skins. Sprinkle the pieces with ¼ cup of the lime juice to prevent discoloration.

2. Bring the broth to a boil in a large saucepan and add the plantains. Reduce the heat, cover, and simmer for about 30 minutes, until they are very tender. Remove them from the heat.

3. With a slotted spoon, transfer the plantains to a food processor. Pulse them, gradually adding enough of the broth to form a smooth paste. Crumble the bread into the processor bowl and pulse just until smooth. (Be careful not to overprocess.)

4. Whisk the plantain mixture into the remaining broth and heat it, stirring constantly, until the soup is thick and hot. Add salt to taste.

SOPA DE PLÁTANOS PARA UNO

(PLANTAIN SOUP FOR ONE)

1 serving

If you have plantain chips and tostones on hand—standard supplies in many Cuban households and any Latin market—this soup can be put together in minutes. Tostones, fried green plantain patties, are sold frozen. You may also make your own with the recipe on page 189, or omit them. This recipe for one is ideal for a quick lunch; it can, of course, be multiplied as many times as you like.

1 cup Chicken Broth (page 13)
1 cup salted plantain chips (see
   Note)

2 tostones, fried only once
   (optional)
1 lime wedge

1. Bring the broth to boil in a small saucepan.

2. Meanwhile, in a food processor, grind the plantain chips into fine crumbs.

3. Whisk the ground plantain chips into the boiling broth, making sure not to let it get lumpy.

4. Drop the tostones into the boiling soup, reduce the heat, and simmer, covered, for 20 minutes.

5. Garnish with a lime wedge for squeezing into the soup.

NOTE: If using bouillon rather than homemade broth, be sure to buy the unsalted variety of plantain chips.

MUNYETA CATALANA
(DRY BEAN POTTAGE CATALONIAN STYLE)

8 servings

Here is a taste of old Cataluña, home of my father's paternal ancestors. Cuban cooking is heavily influenced by the cooking of Spain because Cuba was, of all the Spanish American colonies, the last one to be liberated from the mother country. For many years the monarchs of Spain referred to Cuba as "The Ever Faithful Island," and to keep it that way, encouraged a tremendous flow of Spaniards to migrate to Cuba. Munyeta was a favorite of my great-grandmother, Chicha, a real *Catalana.* It is typically served as a side dish or as a first course instead of soup.

12 ounces dried white kidney beans (cannellini)
½ cup olive oil
2 medium onions, peeled and chopped
2 butifarras or 3 small chorizos, skinned and thinly sliced (see Note)

4 garlic cloves, peeled and minced
¼ cup crushed tomatoes
½ teaspoon salt
¼ teaspoon freshly ground pepper

1. Clean the beans of any impurities. Place them in a large soup pot, cover them with water, and soak them for at least 8 hours.

2. Drain and rinse the beans, cover them with fresh water, and bring them to a boil. Reduce the heat to medium and cook, without salt, until very tender, 45 minutes to an hour.

3. Meanwhile, heat the oil in a large skillet and sauté the onions with the sliced sausages for about 3 minutes, until the onion is translucent. Stir in the garlic and cook for another 2 minutes. Stir in the tomatoes and cook for 5 more minutes.

4. Drain the cooked beans, reserving ¼ cup of the liquid. Stir the beans, liquid, salt, and pepper into the sausage mixture.

5. Cook, uncovered, over very low heat for about 1½ hours, until the mixture is dry and resembles an omelet.

6. Once the munyeta has achieved this consistency, treat it like a Spanish omelet: Slide it gently onto a plate and then flip it back into the skillet so the other side can brown. Cut it into wedges to serve.

NOTE: Munyeta can also be baked, uncovered, in a well-greased quiche dish at 200 degrees for 5 to 6 hours. That way one avoids the tricky flipping action and is assured of an attractive result. Once the munyeta is as dry as a Spanish omelet, it can be served right from the quiche dish. If you cannot find butifarras, a type of pork sausage, consider making your own. The recipe is on page 95.

MUNYETA MODERNA

(MODERN BEAN POTTAGE)

6 to 8 servings

My nephew, the fifth Miguel Lluriá, whom we call Mikie, lives in Key Biscayne, Florida, with his wife, Ana Vilar, and their son, Miguel Lluriá VI. There is no one in our family who is more like his grandfather, especially in his culinary talent. Like the true YUCA (Young, Upscale Cuban-American) that he is, Mikie has adapted many traditional recipes, including this one, to his modern life-style.

⅓ cup cubed salt pork
3 tablespoons finely chopped onion
1 medium chorizo, skinned and thinly sliced

Two 19-ounce cans cannellini (white kidney beans), rinsed and drained

1. Rinse the pork under running water to remove extra salt. Set it aside to drain on paper towels.

2. In a medium-size skillet, heat some oil over medium heat and sauté the pork until most of its fat has melted. Add the onion and sauté until it is translucent, about 3 minutes. Stir in the chorizo and cook about 2 minutes more.

3. Stir in the beans, reduce the heat to low, and gently simmer, uncovered, for about 1 hour, until the mixture resembles a Spanish omelet. Slide it onto a plate and flip it back into the pan to allow the other side to brown.

4. Cut the munyeta into wedges and serve.

Jack and I vacationing with our five children. Varadero, 1956. *Author's collection*

Garlic Soup

Of all the soups served with our noonday meal, sopa de ajos was our favorite, and we children firmly believed that our great-grandmother, Chicha, had invented it. (Years later I realized why. Garlic soup was of such fundamental importance that if you wanted to say that someone was especially clever, you would say, "He invented garlic soup!" We must have heard this expression applied so often to our ingenious great-grandmother that we came to believe it was the literal truth.) In our home, as in many others, this easy-to-digest soup was the elixir of choice for ailing children and old people. Despite its medicinal use, we regarded it as a wonderful treat.

This association of garlic soup with comfort and curing stayed with me into my adult years. When I was pregnant with my first child in faraway Coatesville, Pennsylvania, it was only thanks to garlic soup that I survived the first few months of morning sickness. Ever since I have thanked the memory of our Spanish ancestors for this great and absolutely essential soup.

LA SOPA DE AJOS AUTÉNTICA

(THE AUTHENTIC GARLIC SOUP)

I serving

This recipe for one may be multiplied as many times as you like.

5 garlic cloves
I tablespoon Spanish olive oil
I cup water or chicken broth
½ chicken bouillon cube or
    ¼ teaspoon salt

3 slices day-old Cuban or French
    bread
I egg (optional)

I. Press the garlic cloves with a fork or the flat side of a knife to soften them; leave them whole and unpeeled.

2. Heat the oil in a skillet over medium-high heat and fry the garlic cloves until dark brown but not burned. Remove the pan from the heat.

3. Put the water or broth on to boil in a small saucepan. If using water, add the bouillon cube or salt.

4. With a slotted spoon, remove the garlic from the oil and drop

it into the boiling water. Remove the saucepan from the heat and set the broth aside to steep for a few minutes.

5. Place the bread in the skillet, in the now-cooled oil. Strain the water into the skillet and bring it to a boil again. Discard the garlic. Lower the heat and simmer for about 5 minutes.

6. If you desire a thicker, richer soup, beat the egg slightly and stir it in just before serving. (Or you may poach the egg in the simmering soup.)

MIGAS DE GATO
(DRY GARLIC "SOUP")

4 servings

In Spain, migas is a dish of bread, garlic, and olive oil that is often served with ham or salt pork and fried eggs. The Cuban migas de gato (literally "cat's crumbs") is a poor-man's version that is a legacy of Cuba's devastating war for independence from Spain. During that war, which lasted thirty long years until 1898, food was scarce and people ate what they could. Old, hard bread was never discarded, and it was one of the few foods that was plentiful. From this plenty was born this humble but delicious dish.

When I was growing up, we enjoyed migas de gato no matter what our circumstances, but there were those who considered themselves above such low-class fare. Once, the mother of a wealthy neighbor asked me what I ate that made me so *linda y gordita* (pretty and plump). I replied without hesitation that I had become so by eating migas de gato. The lady was very surprised that a friend of her daughter's should announce without embarrassment that such humble food was a staple of her diet.

16 garlic cloves
¼ cup Spanish olive oil
2 cups water

12 thin slices of day-old Cuban or
   French bread
Salt

I. Using a meat mallet or the flat side of a knife, mash the unpeeled garlic slightly. Heat the oil in a heavy skillet over medium-high heat, and fry the garlic until it is almost black but not burned. Remove the skillet from the heat.

2. While the oil cools, measure the water into a saucepan and bring it to a boil. With a slotted spoon, remove the garlic cloves from the oil and put them into the boiling water. Remove the water from the heat.

3. Crumble the bread into the oil. Pour the water through a sieve onto the bread. Discard the garlic.

4. Simmer the soup over low heat until it reduces to a porridge-like consistency. Stir in salt to taste.

JIGOTE CUBANO
(GROUND CHICKEN SOUP)

6 servings

Only a bit less declasé than migas de gato, this soup was another humble but tasty staple of my childhood. Sometimes it was made with beef broth and beef instead of chicken. To make a jigote, one needed a meat grinder, and they were standard equipment in most kitchens years ago. Today, of course, meat grinders are all but obsolete outside of butcher shops, but a food processor does the job nicely. The hard-boiled egg is an untraditional but attractive and nourishing garnish.

2 cups boiled, roughly chopped chicken meat (from which broth has been made)
6 cups Chicken Broth (page 13)
¼ cup vegetable oil
1 large onion, peeled and chopped
3 garlic cloves, peeled and minced

4 slices of day-old Cuban or French bread, ground into crumbs
1 teaspoon salt
½ teaspoon freshly ground pepper
3 hard-boiled eggs, finely chopped

1. In a food processor, grind the chicken and ½ cup broth into a fine paste.

2. Put the rest of the broth in a saucepan to boil.

3. Meanwhile, heat the oil in a large skillet over medium heat and sauté the onion until translucent, about 3 minutes. Add the garlic and sauté 2 more minutes.

4. Stir the chicken, the onion mixture, and the bread crumbs into the boiling broth. Lower the heat and simmer for about 15 minutes. Stir in the salt and pepper.

5. Ladle the soup into bowls, and sprinkle each serving with chopped egg.

PURÉ DE VEGETALES DE MAMAÍA

(MOTHER'S PURÉE OF VEGETABLES SOUP)

6 to 8 servings

Mamaía is what we children called our maternal grandmother. Later, when we had children of our own and Mamaía had died, my mother inherited the name. She remained Mamaía to all her many dear friends and relatives as long as she lived.

While in exile in Miami, she made many a batch of this simple, delicate, and mellow soup, and it became known in our extended family as Mamaía's soup. Even though we had an "Osterizer" blender, she used the old-fashioned method of puréeing the vegetables by pushing them through a fine, cone-shaped colander with a large pestle.

Easy to digest, this soup is especially comforting when one is feeling under the weather.

6 cups Chicken Broth (page 13)
1 pound potatoes, peeled and cubed
1 pound calabaza, peeled and cubed (see Note)
2 pounds white malanga, peeled and sliced (see Note)
4 carrots, peeled and cut into chunks

1 large onion, peeled and chopped
2 garlic cloves, peeled and lightly crushed
1 small green bell pepper, cored, seeded, and chopped
¼ cup crushed tomatoes
Salt

1. In a large soup pot, combine the broth, potatoes, calabaza, malanga, carrots, onion, garlic, green pepper, and tomatoes. Bring to a boil, reduce the heat, and simmer, covered, for about 45 minutes, until all the vegetables are tender.

2. Purée the vegetables with the broth in a food processor or blender. (You will need to do this in batches.)

3. Reheat the soup if necessary, add salt to taste, and serve.

NOTE: You may substitute pumpkin and turnip for calabaza and malanga for an entirely different but still delicious soup.

CARNE CON PAPAS

(MEAT AND POTATO STEW)

🌿

6 servings

In Ernest Hemingway's *The Old Man and the Sea*, it is carne con papas that the boy uses to revive the exhausted old man. Hemingway understood that this nourishing and economical dish was one that the boy was likely to have ready at hand.

Perhaps the only "person" ever to have resisted the charms of carne con papas was the comic strip character Ramona. "Pancho y Ramona" was the Cuban version of "Maggie and Jigs," a popular American cartoon of the 1930s. Like Jigs, who invariably would choose corned beef and cabbage over caviar, Pancho always preferred sneaking out to eat carne con papas with his rough friends to participating in the fancy dinners that his wife insisted on arranging. The dish was much too déclassé for his social-climbing wife, Ramona.

Save for the caper and wine flourishes, this is the version served in my home while I was growing up.

½ cup vegetable oil
2 pounds stew meat or chuck, cut into 1½-inch cubes
1 large onion, chopped
1 green bell pepper, chopped
3 garlic cloves, peeled and minced
¼ cup tomato sauce
1 cup water

1 cup dry white wine
½ teaspoon salt
⅛ teaspoon sugar
1 teaspoon paprika
1 bay leaf
2 pounds potatoes, peeled and cubed
1 cup capers (optional)

1. Heat the oil in a large dutch oven over medium heat and brown the meat.

2. Add the onion and green pepper, and sauté for about 3 minutes, until the onion is translucent. Add the garlic and cook 2 minutes more.

3. Add the tomato sauce, water, wine, salt, sugar, paprika, and bay leaf. Reduce the heat and simmer, covered, for 45 minutes.

4. Stir in the potatoes and optional capers. Add more water if necessary to keep the stew from drying up. Cover and simmer 30 minutes more, until the meat is tender and the potatoes are cooked.

COCIDO
(BOILED DINNER FROM SPAIN)

12 servings

In the Varadero of my youth, the best-known version of cocido was served at Manuel el Gallego's house. His wife, Aurora, was an expert at preparing this very Spanish dish, and she made it for a spectacular party they threw each New Year's day, which was also her husband's feast day. (It's a Spanish custom to celebrate your feast day—the day on which the saint for whom you were named ascended to heaven—as though it were a second birthday.) No matter how many *gallegos* (natives of Galicia, a province in northwestern Spain) might be around, Manuel was *the* Gallego. A fisherman, handyman, and local politician, he was everybody's friend.

El Santo de Manuel el Gallego was the most festive occasion of the quiet winter season; he celebrated it *echando la casa por la ventana* (literally, "throwing the house out the window"). Our family and the few others from Cárdenas who stayed in Varadero year-round were always invited to the picnic-style feast in the Gallegos's yard. There we would rub elbows with the entire winter population of our beautiful beach, from fishmongers to charcoal vendors to the likes of our intellectual neighbor and friend, Dr. Antonio Garcia Maceda, who always attended with his wife, Clara Matilde, and their baby daughters, Nenela and Mayi.

1 pound chick-peas
1 ham hock
¼ pound salt pork
1 pound beef brisket
2 chorizos
2 pounds chicken pieces (breasts, legs, and thighs)
1 pound potatoes, peeled and cubed
1 medium turnip, peeled and cubed
1 leek, white and tender green only, coarsely chopped
1 large onion, peeled and coarsely chopped
1 medium green bell pepper, cored, seeded, and coarsely chopped
1 small cabbage, cut into thin wedges
1 tablespoon salt
¼ pound angel hair pasta or other very thin noodles

1. Clean the chick-peas of any impurities and soak them in water for at least 8 hours.

2. Drain and rinse the chick-peas and put them in a large pot. Add the ham hock and cover with about 6 quarts of water. Bring to a boil, reduce the heat, and simmer, covered, for 15 minutes.

3. Meanwhile, cut the pork and brisket into 1½-inch cubes and the chorizo into 1½-inch rounds. Add this meat, along with the chicken, to the simmering stew.

4. Add the potatoes, turnip, leek, onion, green pepper, and cabbage and continue cooking for 30 minutes, or until the vegetables are tender.

5. Strain the broth into another large pot, add the salt, and bring it to a boil again. Meanwhile, put the meats in one covered casserole and the vegetables in another, and place them in a warm oven.

6. When the broth is boiling rapidly, drop in the noodles and cook them until just tender, about 5 minutes.

7. Serve the broth and noodles as a first course and the meats and vegetables as a second course.

Cuban ajiaco, fashioned after the Spanish cocido, is distinctive for its combination of Caribbean, Spanish, and African influences. It has been said that the name comes from the *ajíes* or peppers used in the sofrito, the vegetable sauté that is an essential part of so many Cuban dishes. If so, the name is misleading, for some ajiacos from other countries have no peppers at all. (In Colombia, for example, ajiaco is a delicate chicken stew made with three kinds of potatoes.) Cuban Ajiaco is made principally with *viandas*, or root vegetables. It was created by African slaves for their Spanish masters using local roots that were like African tubers, combined with meats available in Cuba, especially the precious jerked beef, tasajo. A meal in itself, ajiaco usually was served in Cuba for almuerzo (lunch) because it was too heavy for the evening meal. Like all recipes containing tasajo, this one requires planning ahead because the jerked beef must be soaked and desalted.

AJIACO

(VEGETABLE AND MEAT STEW)

12 servings

FOR THE BROTH:

½ pound tasajo (jerked beef), cut into 2-inch chunks

1 pound pork meat, cut into 2-inch chunks

1 pound beef brisket, cut into 2-inch chunks

1 bay leaf

FOR THE SOFRITO:

¼ cup vegetable oil

2 large onions, peeled and chopped

1 medium green bell pepper, cored, seeded, and chopped

3 garlic cloves, peeled and minced

1 teaspoon freshly ground pepper

½ teaspoon ground cumin

1 cup crushed tomatoes (canned are fine)

TO COMPLETE THE STEW:

½ pound (1 medium) yellow malanga

1 pound (2 medium) white malanga

1 pound (2 medium) boniato

½ pound (½ medium) ñame

1 pound (2 medium) yucca

1 pound (½ medium) calabaza

2 ears of corn, husked

2 green plantains

¼ cup fresh lime juice

2 semiripe (yellow) plantains

1 ripe (almost black) plantain

MAKE THE BROTH:

I. Cover the tasajo with cold water and soak it for at least 8 hours. (There is no need to refrigerate it.) Change the water and continue soaking for another hour. Drain again and rinse under cold running water.

2. Put the tasajo in a large, heavy pot and add about 6 quarts of water. Bring to a boil, reduce the heat, and simmer, covered, for I hour.

3. Add the pork, beef brisket, and bay leaf, and let the three meats cook together until tender.

4. Remove the pot from the heat and skim as much fat as possible from the broth. (If you have time, the best way is to refrigerate the broth overnight until the fat solidifies and then remove it.)

MAKE THE SOFRITO:

I. Heat the oil in a skillet over medium heat and sauté the onions and green pepper until the onions are translucent, about 3 minutes. Add the garlic and cook 2 minutes more. Add the pepper, cumin, and tomatoes and cook for another 2 minutes.

2. Add the sofrito to the broth and simmer, covered, while you prepare the vegetables.

COMPLETE THE DISH:

I. Peel the malanga, boniato, ñame, yucca, and calabaza and cube them. Cut the corn into I½-inch rounds. Add the root vegetables and corn to the simmering stew.

2. With a sharp knife, slash the skin of each green plantain once lengthwise and cut them into I½-inch peices. Take the skin off each piece by opening it away from the center as if you were taking off a coat. Sprinkle the plantain pieces with the lime juice. Slit the semiripe and ripe plantains lengthwise and slice them crosswise into I½-inch rounds. Do not remove their skins or they will distintegrate in the stew.

3. Add the green plantains to the simmering stew. After about I5

minutes, add the semiripe plantains. After another 15 minutes, add the ripe plantains and let them simmer for about 10 minutes.

4. Serve hot in soup plates or, cocido-style, with the meats, vegetables, and broth in separate dishes. (Each diner removes the skin from the semiripe and ripe plantains himself.)

FABADA ASTURIANA

(ASTURIAN BEAN STEW)

6 servings

Fabada is the best-known dish of the Spanish province of Asturias. Every year in Cárdenas, as in many cities in Cuba, there was a great celebration at the Centro Asturiano on the feast of Our Lady of Covadonga, the patron Saint of Asturias. As a young girl, I was often invited to attend the festivities by my friend Oliva Alvarez, whose parents were Asturian. It was a memorable all-day affair with Asturian music, folk dancing, and wonderful food. Still, the fabada was unquestionably the main attraction.

1½ pounds large white dried navy beans
2 pounds beef brisket
½ pound salt pork
4 morcillas or chorizos (about 16 ounces; see Note)

2 tablespoons Spanish olive oil
1 large onion, peeled and chopped
2 garlic cloves, peeled and minced
Salt

1. Clean the beans of any impurities. Place them in a large pot, cover them with water, and soak them for at least 8 hours.

2. Drain and rinse the beans, return them to the pot, and cover them with 4 quarts of fresh water. Bring to a boil, lower the heat, and simmer, covered, for 20 minutes.

3. Cut the brisket and salt pork into chunks. Add the meat to the stew, cover the pot, and continue cooking gently for 20 minutes more.

4. Slice the morcillas into 3-inch pieces and add to the stew.

5. In a large skillet, warm the oil over medium heat and sauté the onion until translucent, about 3 minutes. Add the garlic and cook 2 more minutes.

6. Stir this sofrito into the stew and cook for 20 minutes more, or until it has thickened. Taste the broth and add salt if desired.

NOTE: Morcillas, spicy blood sausages from Spain, are very hard to find in this country. Do not bother buying the canned or Latin American varieties, which are inferior. You are better off substituting chorizos, in which case you will not have a true fabada, but you will have a delicious stew.

CALDO GALLEGO
(SOUP FROM GALICIA)

8 servings

Though none of my ancestors came from the Spanish province of Galicia, this rich soup was often served in our home at the midday meal. It is highly popular among Cubans in exile; most Cuban restaurants have it on their menus, and one can even buy it in cans, ready to heat and serve. But there is nothing so wonderful as caldo gallego lovingly made at home.

I pound dried white beans
I medium ham hock (about I pound)
I small piece of pork fat (¼ pound)
I medium chorizo (about 4 ounces), peeled and cut into I-inch chunks
I large onion, peeled and chopped

I½ pounds potatoes, peeled and cubed
4 turnips, peeled and cubed
I cabbage, coarsely chopped
½ pound kale, coarsely chopped
I teaspoon salt
½ teaspoon freshly ground pepper

1. Clean the beans of any impurities. Cover them with water and soak them for at least 8 hours.

2. Drain and rinse the beans. Place them in a large pot with the ham hock and pork fat and add about 5 quarts of water. Bring it to a boil, reduce the heat, and simmer, covered, for 30 minutes.

3. Add the chorizo, onion, potatoes, turnip, cabbage, kale, salt, and pepper. Simmer for about 30 minutes more, until the vegetables are tender.

In Spanish, *monteria* is the term for the hunt for wild boar. In Cuba, however, it refers to an old Afro-Cuban dish typically made the day after Christmas with leftovers from the *lechón asado* (roasted suckling pig). It is just as delicious made with leftover turkey. We used to look forward to it almost as much as to the lechón itself. Like most Cuban dishes, this one is served with fluffy white rice.

MONTERÍA

(PORK AND PLANTAIN STEW)

6 to 8 servings

½ cup pork lard or vegetable oil
2 medium onions, peeled and finely chopped
1 large green pepper, cored, seeded, and chopped
4 garlic cloves, peeled and minced
3 to 4 pounds leftover roast pork, cut into chunks
1 teaspoon salt
½ teaspoon freshly ground pepper
¼ teaspoon ground cumin
1 cup dry white wine
1 cup tomato sauce
1 cup Chicken Broth (page 13)
½ cup capers
12 to 16 tostones (plantains) that have been fried only once (see Note)

1. In a large dutch oven, heat the lard over medium heat. Sauté the onions and green pepper until the onions are translucent, about 3 minutes. Stir in the garlic and cook for 2 minutes more.

2. Add the pork, salt, pepper, cumin, wine, tomato sauce, broth, and capers. Bring to a boil and cook for 3 minutes.

3. Reduce the heat to low and place the tostones carefully in the pot, making sure they do not break. Spoon the pan juices over the tostones, covering them completely. Simmer, covered, for 20 minutes.

NOTE: The classic monteria calls for once-fried tostones, but some Cuban cooks prefer twice-fried ones because they do not lose their shape or texture in the stew. The recipe for tostones is on page 189.

CONEJO EN SALSA SABROSA

(RABBIT IN PIQUANT SAUCE)

6 servings

My great-grandmother, Chicha, was a capricious old lady. She refused to eat rabbit because she said rabbits reminded her of *jutías,* the little animals eaten by Cuba's first inhabitants, the Siboneyes. When she was very old, Chicha did eat rabbit when it was presented to her as chicken. Today, I consider rabbit a delicacy, and find that it tastes better than all but farm-fresh chicken.

One 3-pound rabbit, skinned, cleaned, and cut into serving pieces (see Note)
½ cup flour
I teaspoon salt
I teaspoon freshly ground pepper
I teaspoon paprika
½ cup Spanish olive oil
I garlic clove, peeled

I large onion, peeled and chopped
I cup Beef Broth (page 13)
I cup red wine
I carrot, peeled and cut into chunks
I sprig parsley, chopped
¼ cup capers
4 salted anchovies
I bay leaf

I. Wash the rabbit meat under cold running water and pat it dry with paper towels.

2. Mix the flour, salt, pepper, and paprika together and dredge the meat in the mixture.

3. In a large dutch oven, heat the olive oil over medium heat until fragrant. Brown the garlic clove until almost burned; remove and discard it. Brown the meat well on all sides and remove it from the pan. Sauté the onion until translucent, about 3 minutes.

4. Return the meat to the pan. Add the broth, wine, carrot, parsley, capers, anchovies, and bay leaf. Cover the pan, raise the heat, and bring to a boil. Lower the heat to medium-low and simmer, covered until the meat is tender, about I hour. Transfer the meat to a serving dish and cover it with foil.

5. Remove the bay leaf, pour the sauce into a blender, and purée it. (Add more broth if a thinner sauce is desired.)

6. Return the sauce to the pan and heat it just until warmed through. Pour it over the meat and serve.

NOTE: Rabbit, like chicken, should be cut into serving pieces at the joints. Ask your butcher to do this for you.

When I was a child, this stew was cooked gently in a heavy iron pot over medium-gray coals on the charcoal stove. Today, I sometimes make it in the pressure cooker, which takes only 10 minutes, or, if time permits, in the crockpot, where it simmers for 10 hours.

ESTOFADO DE CONEJO

(RABBIT STEW)

℮

6 servings

One 3-pound rabbit, skinned, cleaned, and cut into serving pieces (see Note)
2 cups dry white wine
¼ cup sour orange juice (or a 50–50 mixture of sweet orange juice and lime juice)
¼ cup chopped parsley
4 garlic cloves, peeled and minced
1 teaspoon dry leaf oregano
6 peppercorns

1 bay leaf
½ pound bacon
2 large onions, peeled and chopped
3 carrots, peeled and sliced into ¼-inch rounds
3 tablespoons vegetable oil
½ teaspoon salt
2 slices toasted Cuban or French bread, grated (or ¼ cup bread crumbs)

1. Rinse the rabbit meat under cold running water and place it in a container suitable for marinating.

2. Stir together the wine, orange juice, parsley, garlic, oregano, peppercorns, and bay leaf. Pour this marinade over the meat, cover, and refrigerate for about 12 hours.

3. About 2 hours before serving, fry the bacon in a large, heavy skillet over medium heat until crisp. Drain it on paper towels and set aside.

4. Remove all but about 2 tablespoons of the bacon grease from the pan. Sauté the onions in the remaining grease until translucent, about 3 minutes. Stir in the carrots and remove from the heat.

5. Remove the rabbit pieces from the marinade and pat them dry on paper towels. Reserve the marinade.

6. Heat the oil in a large dutch oven over medium heat until fragrant. Brown each piece of the rabbit on both sides.

7. Stir in the onion mixture and the reserved marinade. Raise the heat, bring it just to a boil, reduce the heat to low, and simmer, covered, until the rabbit is tender, about 1 hour.

8. Transfer the rabbit to a casserole. Crumble the bacon over it and cover it with foil.

9. Stir the bread crumbs into the pan juices and cook gently until the juices thicken. Pour this sauce over the rabbit and serve.

NOTE: Rabbit, like chicken, should be cut into serving pieces at the joints. Ask your butcher to do this for you.

CHIVO O CARNERO GUISADO CON VEGETALES

(STEWED GOAT OR LAMB WITH VEGETABLES)

6 to 8 servings

This recipe came from Agustina, our old cook, who could make a perfect *chilindrón*. Goat was eaten much more often than lamb in our house; it was plentiful and quite economical. Agustina was the only servant we had when times were difficult in the 1930s, and she stayed on without pay to help my mother when Mamá went to work as a schoolteacher.

Whenever Agustina made this dish with lamb rather than goat, she would trim off the fat and store it in the pantry—not for cooking, but to remedy various ailments such as arthritis. It so happens that in those days, no one in my family had arthritis, but Agustina seemed to believe it was important to have *cebo de carnero* on hand just in case. It smelled bad, and so served as a repellent for little children who might otherwise spend more time than was healthy snooping in the pantry to see what mischief could be made or what treats could be nabbed in that inviting place.

2 pounds goat or lamb shanks, cut into chunks, fat removed
1 cup sour orange juice (or a 50–50 mixture of sweet orange juice and lime juice)
3 garlic cloves, peeled and minced
¾ cup lard or vegetable oil
1 large onion, peeled and sliced into thin rounds
1 green bell pepper, cored, seeded, and chopped
1½ cups tomato sauce
¾ cup dry white wine
1 cup Beef Broth (page 13)
1 teaspoon salt
½ teaspoon freshly ground pepper
2 carrots, peeled and sliced into thin rounds
12 new potatoes, scrubbed
1 cup cubed calabaza (optional)
One 8-ounce can petit pois (tiny peas), drained, or small frozen peas, thawed

1. Place the meat in a nonreactive container suitable for marinating. Stir together the orange juice and garlic. Pour this marinade over the meat, cover, and refrigerate for 2 hours.

2. Remove the meat and drain it on paper towels. Reserve the marinade.

3. In a large dutch oven, warm the lard over medium heat. Add the meat and brown it lightly.

4. Add the onion and green pepper and sauté until the onion is translucent, about 3 minutes.

5. Add the tomato sauce, wine, broth, salt, pepper, carrots, potatoes, and optional calabaza. Bring to a boil, reduce the heat to low, cover, and simmer, until the meat is tender and the vegetables are cooked, about 30 minutes.

6. Stir in the peas just before serving.

CORDERO ANDALUZ

(ANDALUSIAN LAMB)

❧

10 to 12 servings

De la mar, el mero y de la tierra, el cordero. (From the sea, the grouper, and from the land, the lamb.) —SPANISH PROVERB

Unlike Andalusians, who would never think of serving this delectable dish with anything but bread, Cubans accompany it with white rice.

2 cups Spanish olive oil
10 garlic cloves, peeled and
   crushed
Six 1-pound shanks of young lamb,
   cleaned of all fat
1 large onion, peeled and chopped
¼ cup dried rosemary
3 cups tomato sauce
4 carrots, peeled and thinly sliced
   on the diagonal

1 cup Spanish brandy
6 cups red wine
4 cups Beef Broth (page 13)
1 teaspoon salt
6 whole peppercorns
1 bay leaf
1 cup pitted green olives
1 cup diced dry bread

1. In a large dutch oven, heat the oil over medium heat until fragrant. Brown the garlic until it is almost burned; remove and discard it. Brown the lamb lightly.

2. Stir in the onion and rosemary and sauté until the onion is limp, about 2 minutes. Add the tomato sauce and cook 2 minutes more.

3. Add the carrots, brandy, wine, broth, salt, peppercorns, and bay leaf. Bring just to a boil, reduce the heat, cover, and simmer until the lamb is tender, about 2 hours. (Or cook for 10 minutes in the pressure cooker.)

4. Stir in the olives and dry bread. Simmer just until the sauce has thickened, and serve.

PESCADOS Y MARISCOS (SEAFOOD)

Pargo Asado a lo Varadero (Baked Red Snapper Varadero Style) 39

Pescado Asado a lo Andaluz (Baked Fish Andalusian Style) 40

Pescado en Sobreuso (Recycled Fish) 41

Lisa Frita (Fried Black Mullet) 42

Pescado en Salsa Verde (Fish in Green Sauce) 44

Pudin de Bonito (Tuna Fish Pudding) 45

Poached Whole Fish 46

Pescado Frío con Salsa de Aguacate (Cold Fish with Avocado Sauce) 47

Pescado Frío a la Jardinera (Cold Fish Garden Style) 47

Bacalao (Salted Codfish) 48

Bacalao a la Vizcaina (Salted Codfish Vizcaya Style) 49

Bacalao al Pil Pil (Codfish in a Special Garlic Sauce) 50

Langostas Enchiladas (Lobster in Savory Sauce) 53

Harina con Jaibas (Cornmeal with Crabs) 55

Camarones al Ajillo (Shrimp in Garlic Sauce) 56

The old Club Náutico with the pier from which we fished. Varadero, circa 1920. *François Larrieu*

Pescados y Mariscos (Seafood)

$\mathcal{T}$hough our family's fortunes rose and fell, we had the abiding luxury of a home in Varadero, the loveliest spot on Cuba's glorious two-thousand-mile coastline. In time its alabaster white sands and crystal blue waters transformed it into an elite international beach retreat, but in the 1920s Varadero was still a quiet resort town on the Península de Hicacos enjoyed almost exclusively by the people of Cárdenas. It was a fisherman's paradise—indeed, our family's paradise, for daily the almost miraculous bounty of the sea graced our dinner table. To this day I can think of nothing better than fish fresh from the sea, fried crisp in olive oil or baked to perfection in a rich Spanish sauce.

In *alta mar*, the deep sea off Varadero, my father and his friends set out to catch the coveted *pargo del alto* or deep-sea red snapper in his yacht, *El Tiburón* (The Shark). This graceful vessel had both sails and motor as well as a spacious cabin, but its best feature was hidden below the deck: a *vivero*, a wooden tank with openings to let the seawater in and out. It was there that the day's catch was kept, alive, until it was delivered to our kitchen. And when Papá caught more fish than we could eat or give away, the vivero is where the remainder would stay until needed, a sort of floating fish pantry as close as the pier of the old Club Náutico behind our house.

For smaller fish, Papá had an array of *atarrayas* or fish nets of various weights and strengths. When we saw him take out his finest net, we children knew he was going to catch *majuas* (tiny sardines), and we followed him to the beach to watch the mesmerizing process: Slowly, he waded barefoot into the shallows, standing motionless until he spotted a school of fish silvering the clear blue water. Then suddenly, graceful as a *torero*, he swung his net around and cast it out, snagging hundreds of majuas. Over and over he cast his net and poured its sparkling contents into a basket. When the basket was full we all walked home together triumphantly, sharing in his prowess. He poured the tiny fish into the kitchen sink and the cook rinsed, floured, and fried them so that we could eat them in crispy bites, bones and all.

The most memorable fish are, of course, the ones you catch yourself, and I have fond memories of fishing experiences we children shared with our father. Though we went no farther than the pier behind our house and caught nothing more exotic than *ronquitos* (grunts), Papá had a way of surrounding these outings with ritual and mystery. He awakened us in the *madrugada*, the time just before dawn, and the four oldest children—Lelén, Pili, Pancho, and I—quietly put on our fishing uniforms: the blue Indianhead overalls that Mamá and Chicha made, our old leather sandals, and the special fishing hats Papá fashioned from brown paper bags. (We had to cover our little heads for protection from the *sereno*, the "moonlight dew," for it was believed to cause colds.)

We grabbed our fishing gear—string-wrapped sticks, sinkers, and fish hooks—and slipped away with him while everyone else slept. Once at the pier, we sat at the edge, our little legs dangling over the shallow water. Papá helped us bait our hooks with pieces of raw lobster and cast out our short lines. Then, when we felt the tug of a ronquito, we would squeal, *"Ya me está picando!"* (I already have a bite!) and pull the line in. At expedition's end we marched to the kitchen with our baskets of grunting ronquitos, for they never stopped grunting until they were in our cook's clutches.

I cannot relive those treasured experiences, but I have re-created for you in the pages ahead some of the treasured tastes of the sea that I knew in the Cuba of my youth.

In the waters around Florida and other Gulf Coast states, red snapper is almost as plentiful as it was in Cuba. In other parts of this country, I have been able to order it at fish markets.

One 6-pound red snapper, cleaned and scaled, with head removed

⅓ cup freshly squeezed lime juice

3 small red potatoes, peeled and thinly sliced

5 garlic cloves, peeled

2 teaspoons salt

1 teaspoon dry leaf oregano

1 cup Spanish olive oil

1 large onion, peeled and thinly sliced

1 large green bell pepper, cored, seeded, and thinly sliced

4 bay leaves

¼ teaspoon freshly ground black pepper

2 tablespoons white wine vinegar

1 cup tomato purée

1 cup dry white wine

Parsley sprigs

1. Rinse the fish under cold running water and pat it dry. Make 3 diagonal slits on each side.

2. Place it in a large glass or ceramic container (a serving platter works well), pour the lime juice over it, and set it aside.

3. In a small saucepan, cover the potato slices with water and bring to a boil. Reduce the heat and cook until barely tender, about 3 minutes. Drain and set aside.

4. While the potatoes are cooking, mash the garlic, salt, and oregano into a paste. (A mortar and pestle works best, but you may mince the garlic finely or put it through a garlic press and mash the seasonings in with a fork.)

5. Rub the garlic paste into the cavity of the fish.

6. Preheat the oven to 350 degrees.

7. Drizzle 2 tablespoons of the olive oil into a glass or ceramic baking dish that is large enough to hold the fish. Cover the bottom of the dish with the potato slices. Layer on half the onion slices and half the green pepper strips. Crush 2 of the bay leaves and sprinkle over the vegetables. Drizzle on 2 more tablespoons of olive oil and add half of the black pepper.

8. Place the fish in the baking dish and tuck a little of the remaining onion and green pepper into the slits and cavity. Stir the vinegar into the tomato purée and pour it over the fish. Arrange the remaining onion slices and green pepper strips on top. Crush the remaining 2 bay leaves and sprinkle them over the vegetables. Pour on the remaining ¾ cup of the olive oil, the wine, and the remaining ⅛ teaspoon black pepper.

9. Cover the dish loosely with foil and bake for about 35 minutes. Remove the foil and bake for 10 minutes more, or until the fish flakes when pierced with a fork.

10. Garnish with parsley and serve.

PESCADO ASADO A LO ANDALUZ

(BAKED FISH ANDALUSIAN STYLE)

6 servings

Many Cubans came from Andalusia in southern Spain, bringing with them a taste for almonds inherited from the Arabs, or Moors, who ruled that region of Spain for some 700 years until the time of Columbus.

¾ cup whole blanched almonds
½ cup Spanish olive oil
2 large peeled onions, 1 chopped and 1 sliced into thin rings
2 tablespoons chopped parsley, plus sprigs for garnish
12 garlic cloves, peeled and minced
1 cup Fish Broth (page 13)
¼ teaspoon salt (optional)

2 small bay leaves, crushed
One 6-pound red snapper or grouper, cleaned and scaled, with head removed
6 tablespoons freshly squeezed lime juice
½ teaspoon freshly ground pepper
1 cup dry white wine

1. Toast the almonds by spreading them in a shallow pan and baking them at 300 degrees, stirring often, until they are lightly browned, about 15 minutes. Place the almonds in a food processor or blender and process them until pulverized.

2. In a medium-size skillet, heat 3 tablespoons of the olive oil over medium heat. Add the chopped onion and chopped parsley, and sauté until the onion is are translucent, about 3 minutes. Stir in the

garlic and cook for 2 minutes more. Stir in the almonds and fish broth. Check the seasonings, adding the salt if necessary. Remove the mixture from the heat.

3. Preheat the oven to 350 degrees.

4. Coat the bottom of a large glass or ceramic baking dish with the remaining olive oil. Spread the onion rings over the oil and sprinkle with the crushed bay leaf.

5. Rinse the fish under cold running water and pat it dry. Place the fish in the baking dish; pour on the lime juice and sprinkle on the pepper. Spread the almond mixture over the fish, leaving only the tail exposed. Pour the wine over all.

6. Cover the fish loosely with foil and bake for about 35 minutes. Remove the foil and bake for 10 minutes more, or until the fish flakes when pierced with a fork.

7. Garnish with parsley sprigs and serve.

PESCADO EN SOBREUSO
(RECYCLED FISH)

6 servings

The next time you fry or bake fish fillets, make extra so that you can enjoy the leftovers *en sobreuso*—literally "reused"—the next day. Serve this dish with fluffy white rice, fried ripe plantains, black beans, and an avocado salad for a quintessential Cuban meal.

¾ cup Spanish olive oil
1 large onion, peeled and chopped
½ medium green bell pepper, cored, seeded, and chopped
2 tablespoons chopped parsley
3 garlic cloves, peeled and minced
¼ cup tomato sauce

1 small bay leaf
¼ teaspoon salt
¼ teaspoon freshly ground pepper
¼ cup dry white wine
6 servings of leftover cooked fish fillets (about 2 pounds uncooked weight)

1. In a medium-size saucepan, warm the oil over medium heat. Add the onion, green pepper, and parsley. Sauté, stirring occasionally, until the onion is translucent, about 3 minutes. Stir in the garlic and cook 2 more minutes. Add the tomato sauce, and bring the sauce to a boil. Lower the heat and simmer it, stirring, for a few minutes more.

2. Stir in the bay leaf, salt, pepper, and wine. Bring the sauce back to a boil, then lower the heat to a simmer and cook, stirring occasionally, for about 5 minutes.

3. *Stovetop Method:* Arrange the fish in a medium-size skillet. Pour the sauce evenly over the fish, cover, and cook over low heat until warmed through, about 10 minutes.

4. *Oven Method:* Preheat the oven to 350 degrees. Arrange the fish in a medium-size glass or ceramic baking dish. Pour the sauce evenly over the fish, cover tightly with a lid or aluminum foil, and bake until warmed through, about 15 minutes.

LISA FRITA
(FRIED BLACK MULLET)

6 to 8 servings

Lisa, or black mullet, is a flaky-fleshed river fish that came down the Canímar River to the salt waters of Varadero in great avalanches only three times a year, and then only under a full moon. When word came in the night that they were running, true fish lovers like my father would rush to the beach with their nets and haul in the precious lisas by the dozens. We would feast on them almost to the point of gluttony and would enjoy their prized roe as an appetizer. The remaining lisas would be salted and stored in little wooden boxes in our pantry to be used later like salted codfish.

Black mullet is not the coveted fish in this country that it was in Cuba, but it is delicious nonetheless. Here in Miami, I buy black mullet that is caught off the Gulf Coast. It is lovely cooked in this simple, traditional manner.

2 mullets (about 4 pounds total), cleaned, scaled, and cut into 1-inch rounds	1 teaspoon freshly ground pepper
	½ cup flour
½ tablespoon salt	½ cup Spanish olive oil
	3 limes, cut into wedges

1. Rinse the fish under cold running water and pat dry. Mix together the salt, pepper, and flour in a broad dish. In a large, heavy skillet, warm the oil over medium-high heat.

2. Dredge the fish in the flour mixture and shake off the excess.

Place the fish, about 4 pieces at a time, in the skillet and fry until crisp around the edges, about 5 minutes. Turn and fry for 3 or 4 more minutes, until the other side is crisp and the fish flakes when pierced with a fork.

3. Remove the pieces from the skillet and place them on several thicknesses of paper towels to absorb the extra oil. Flour and fry the next batch, placing the fried fish in a warm oven until you are done.

4. Garnish with juicy lime wedges and serve.

Victorian houses along the beach in Varadero, circa 1920. *François Larrieu*

PESCADO EN SALSA VERDE

(FISH IN GREEN SAUCE)

🦐

6 servings

This simplified version of a venerable Spanish dish was popular in Cuba in the 1940s and '50s after electric blenders were introduced. Many Cubans learned the recipe from Nitza Villapol, the hostess of a highly popular television show in the 1950s called "Cocina al Minuto" ("Minute Cooking"). It can be prepared in 30 minutes and should be served with plenty of white rice and crusty bread to soak up the savory sauce.

6 to 8 fillets of grouper, red snapper, or other white-fleshed fish
  (about 2 pounds total)
¼ cup Spanish olive oil
¾ cup canola oil
¾ cup dry white wine
2 tablespoons white wine vinegar

1 cup roughly chopped parsley
1 small onion, peeled and coarsely
  chopped
2 garlic cloves, peeled and coarsely
  chopped
1 teaspoon salt
½ teaspoon freshly ground pepper

1. Blot the fillets on paper towels. (Be sure to dry them thoroughly or your sauce will be watery.) Set them aside.

2. In a blender or food processor, combine the olive oil, canola oil, wine, vinegar, parsley, onion, garlic, salt, and pepper, and process on high until smooth. Set aside.

3. *Stovetop Method:* In a large skillet, arrange the fish in a single snug layer and pour the sauce evenly over the fish. If the fish will not fit in a single layer, place one layer of fillets in the bottom of the pan, cover them with half the sauce, add a second layer of fish, and cover with the rest of the sauce. Bring the sauce to a boil over high heat. Immediately reduce the heat to low, partially cover the pan, and gently simmer the fish for 15 to 20 minutes or until it flakes when pierced with a fork.

4. *Oven Method:* Preheat the oven to 350 degrees. In a large ceramic or glass baking dish, arrange the fish in a single snug layer and pour the sauce evenly over the fish. If the fish will not fit in a single layer, place a one layer of fillets in the bottom of the pan, cover them with half the sauce, add a second layer of fish, and cover with the rest of the sauce. Cover the dish loosely with aluminum foil and bake for 15 to 20 minutes, or until the fish flakes when pierced with a fork.

Imagine eating canned tuna fish when fresh fish was so abundant! But this simple recipe was one of my mother's favorites, and it rekindles warm memories of home for me. Mamá liked to have it served often for lunch—too often as far as my father was concerned. He was highly exacting when it came to food, and insisted on variety in our menus. If anything was served more than once a month, he would threaten to eat at El Hotel Torres down the street!

Serve this Cuban "comfort food" with lime wedges and a side dish of mayonnaise (homemade if possible) spiked with garlic.

PUDIN DE BONITO

(TUNA FISH PUDDING)

6 servings

4 slices white bread, cut into pieces
½ cup milk
¼ cup Spanish olive oil
1 large onion, peeled and chopped
4 eggs, beaten
¼ teaspoon freshly ground pepper

¼ teaspoon salt (optional)
⅛ teaspoon ground cumin
Two 6-ounce cans tuna, drained and flaked
Butter
1 lime, cut into wedges

1. Place the bread in a mixing bowl and pour the milk over it.

2. In a small skillet, warm the oil over medium heat and sauté the onion until translucent, about 3 minutes.

3. Stir the eggs into the bread mixture. Add the onion, pepper, salt, cumin, and tuna, and stir the mixture just enough to combine it.

4. Preheat the oven to 350 degrees.

5. Grease a 2-quart casserole with butter and fill it with the tuna batter. Bake for 30 minutes or until a knife inserted in the middle comes out clean.

6. Allow the pudding to cool to room temperature, and unmold it onto a serving dish. Serve with the lime wedges on the side.

POACHED WHOLE FISH

6 servings

This somewhat involved but highly rewarding recipe is the basis for Pescado Frío con Salsa de Aguacate (page 47) and Pescado Frío a la Jardinera (page 47), two beautiful cold entrées that are perfect for the buffet table. As a bonus, the poaching process yields delicious fish broth that can be refrigerated or frozen for later use. To simplify preparation, you may poach the fish up to a day before serving. Note that you need cheesecloth for wrapping the fish.

I cup diced carrots
¼ cup chopped parsley
I large onion, peeled and chopped
½ small green bell pepper, cored, seeded, and chopped
I large bay leaf
½ teaspoon dry leaf oregano

I cup fresh lime juice
½ teaspoon whole peppercorns
I½ teaspoons salt
About 4 quarts water
One 6-pound red snapper or grouper, cleaned and scaled, with head removed

I. Place the carrots, parsley, onion, green pepper, bay leaf, oregano, lime juice, peppercorns, salt, and water in a fish poacher or a large roasting pan with a rack and lid. Bring to a boil, reduce the heat, cover, and simmer for 30 minutes. Remove the pan from the heat and let the liquid cool until it is lukewarm.

2. While the poaching liquid is cooling, rinse the fish under cold running water and pat it dry. Wrap it in a double thickness of cheese-cloth, allowing the cloth to extend about 6 inches beyond each end of the fish. Tie the ends of the cloth with kitchen string.

3. Grasping the tied ends, lower the fish into the poaching liquid. (If using a roasting pan, tie the ends of the cheesecloth to the handles of the pan.) The liquid should just cover the fish; add more water if necessary.

4. Place the pan over high heat. When the liquid shows the first sign of boiling, lower the heat, cover the pan, and allow the fish to simmer for 45 minutes.

5. Remove the pan from the heat and uncover it. When it is cool enough to handle, lift the fish by the ends of the cheesecloth and lay it on a serving platter. (Save the poaching liquid to use as broth.)

6. Cut open the cheesecloth and, with a sharp knife, lightly slash the fish lengthwise. Pull off the skin in strips and discard. Grasping the ends of the cheesecloth, turn the fish over and skin the other side, leaving the tail intact. Discard the cheesecloth. Cover the fish loosely with plastic wrap and refrigerate until chilled.

PESCADO FRÍO CON SALSA DE AGUACATE

(COLD FISH WITH AVOCADO SAUCE)

6 servings

2 large or 4 small ripe avocados
1 teaspoon salt
¼ teaspoon freshly ground pepper
¼ cup freshly squeezed lime juice
¼ cup Spanish olive oil
6 lettuce leaves or 1 cup watercress leaves, rinsed and dried

1 chilled Poached Whole Fish (page 46)
One 6-ounce jar pimientos, drained and sliced
½ cup pitted green olives, sliced
2 hard-boiled eggs, sliced

1. Cut the avocados in half and remove but do not discard the seeds. Scoop out the pulp and place in the container of a blender or food processor.

2. Add the salt, pepper, and lime juice. Turn the machine on high and slowly pour in the oil, processing until well blended. Place the avocado seeds in the sauce to prevent discoloration; cover and refrigerate it.

3. At serving time, arrange a bed of lettuce or watercress leaves on a serving platter and place the fish on it. Remove the avocado seeds and spread the sauce over the fish, covering all but the tail. Arrange the pimientos, olives, and eggs on the fish in a festive pattern.

PESCADO FRÍO A LA JARDINERA

(COLD FISH GARDEN STYLE)

6 servings

¼ pound green beans, sliced into ½-inch pieces
2 large carrots, peeled and cubed
1 Poached Whole Fish, chilled (page 46)
3 small beets, peeled and coarsely chopped
1 cup canned petit pois (tiny peas),

drained, or small frozen peas, thawed
4 hard-boiled eggs, coarsely chopped
¼ cup Spanish olive oil
¼ cup white vinegar
½ cup mayonnaise (homemade if possible)

1. In a small saucepan, cover the green beans and carrots with water. Bring to a boil, then reduce heat, cover, and simmer until barely tender, about 5 minutes. Drain them and refrigerate until chilled.

2. At serving time, place the fish on a platter. Arrange small mounds of beans, carrots, beets, peas, and eggs on top of the fish. Stir together the olive oil and vinegar and drizzle it over the garnishes.

3. Place the mayonnaise in a small bowl and serve alongside the fish.

BACALAO
(SALTED CODFISH)

"Te conozco bacalao, aunque vengas disfrazao." (I would know you, codfish, even if you came in masquerade.)

—An old saying used to tell someone that you will not be deceived

If you have not been initiated into the delights of bacalao you may wonder, "Why waste a delicious sauce on dried, salted codfish when you could use fresh fish?" To that question I can only answer, "Taste it." You will immediately appreciate its distinctive qualities. The flaky texture of bacalao is as alive and appealing as that of the freshest fish, but the flavor has a full-fledged personality of its own. The results of these somewhat elaborate recipes will well repay your labors.

Bacalao is available in most Latin markets. At least 12 hours and two water changes are needed for soaking the codfish, so these recipes require planning ahead.

Soaking Procedure

1. At least 12 hours before you plan to cook the bacalao (the day before is best), place it in a large pot and cover it with cold water. Soak for 2 hours. (There is no need to refrigerate it.)

2. Drain the fish, cover it with fresh water, and soak for 10 more hours or overnight.

3. Drain the fish again. Remove any bones and skin, and cut it into 3-inch squares.

This variation of a famous Basque dish was one of the most popular codfish dishes in Cuba. The Spanish original uses *pimientos choriceros* (dry pimientos), and though it is delicious, I am partial to the Cuban version which calls for canned pimientos.

BACALAO A LA VIZCAINA

(SALTED CODFISH VIZCAYA STYLE)

8 servings

1 ½ pounds Salted Codfish, prepared as described on page 48
⅔ cup Spanish olive oil
1 pound potatoes, peeled and sliced into ¼-inch rounds
1 cup tomato purée
1 large green bell pepper, cored, seeded, and sliced into thin rounds

2 large onions, peeled and sliced into thin rounds
4 garlic cloves, peeled and minced
One 6-ounce jar pimientos, undrained
1 tablespoon white vinegar
¼ cup dry white wine
8 to 10 slices Cuban or French bread

1. Place the fish in a large pot, cover it with cold water, and bring to a boil. Lower the heat and simmer, uncovered, until the fish is tender, about ½ hour. Drain the fish, reserving ⅓ cup of the cooking liquid.

2. Coat the bottom of a large skillet with 1 tablespoon of the oil and arrange the potato slices in it. Add ½ cup of the tomato purée. Layer the codfish, green pepper, onions, and garlic. Mix the remaining ½ cup of tomato purée with the reserved ⅓ cup of cooking liquid and pour it on top.

3. Drain the pimiento liquid into a blender or food processor. Add half the pimientos, the vinegar, wine, and ⅓ cup of the olive oil. Process it until smooth and pour it over the fish mixture.

4. Bring the contents of the skillet to a boil, immediately reduce the heat to low, and simmer, partially covered, for about 1 hour, until the potatoes are tender.

5. Meanwhile, heat the remaining olive oil in a large skillet over medium-high heat and fry the bread slices on both sides until golden brown. Slice the remaining pimientos into strips.

6. Serve the bacalao hot, garnished with the fried bread and pimiento strips.

BACALAO AL PIL PIL

(CODFISH IN
A SPECIAL
GARLIC SAUCE)

4 servings

This dish, as Basque as jai-alai, was a favorite of my maternal grand-mother, María Aguirregaviria y Aramberry. Its name comes from the Basque word *pilpiliar,* "to shake." Serve it with lots of fresh bread for mopping up the plentiful, pungent gravy.

1½ pounds Salted Codfish, prepared as described on page 48

2 cups Spanish olive oil
20 garlic cloves, peeled and cut into slivers

1. Place the codfish pieces in a 4- to 6-quart pot, cover with cold water, and bring to a boil. Lower the heat and simmer, uncovered, until the fish is tender, about ½ hour. Drain the fish, reserving 1 cup of the cooking liquid.

2. In a large pan at least 4 inches deep, with two sturdy handles, heat the olive oil over medium heat and sauté the garlic until golden but not brown. Remove the garlic with a slotted spoon and set it aside. Allow the oil to cool in the pan for about 1 hour.

3. Place the fish in the cool oil, turn the heat to medium-low, and rhythmically shake the pan as the fish fries. Do not stop shaking ("*pilpiliando,*" as the Basques say) for 20 minutes, or until the oil has turned somewhat milky. With a slotted spoon, remove the fish to a large casserole (an earthenware one is typical).

4. Pour the cooked oil into a container with a spout (a gravy sep-arator works best) and let it cool until the milky substance has settled to the bottom. Carefully pour the oil into another container, reserv-ing the milky substance.

5. Preheat the oven to 325 degrees.

6. Place the milky substance in a blender or food processor and process it at low speed. With the machine running, pour in the oil in a slow, steady stream; the mixture will thicken like mayonnaise. With the blender still running, pour in enough of the reserved cooking liq-uid so that the sauce is thin enough to pour.

7. Scatter the garlic slivers over the fish and pour the sauce over

all. Cover the casserole and warm it in a the oven for about 20 minutes. (You may instead warm it in the microwave at a medium setting for about 5 minutes.)

LANGOSTAS (Lobsters)

It was at the end of summer, after the vacationers had left, that the lobsters came to Varadero Beach. Their arrival was one of the most spectacular phenomena of each year. With the first north winds, a huge army of small brown creatures in rank and file—about six across and perhaps a mile long—marched across the sand bar just off the beach. We might take a walk to the beach early one morning and discover hundreds of lobsters solemnly crawling along in an almost religious procession.

We raced home to call Papá, and he grabbed his heaviest fish net and ran back to the beach with us. He climbed into a rowboat he kept there, cast out his net, and quickly snagged enough lobsters to fill the boat. In the meantime, we children would have the pleasure of catching langostas with our bare hands. (Unlike their Maine cousins, Cuban lobsters have no claws, so it was safe to do so.) At other times of the year, Papá would catch lobsters in deep water with his *nasas*, large straw traps with funnellike bottoms that the lobsters would enter, never to exit.

Lobsters were always cooked as soon as they were caught, or kept alive until needed in the vivero, the seawater tank in Papá's yacht. They were so abundant we even used them for fish bait.

Langostas are known here as Florida lobster. (Though some people call them crawfish, they are not to be confused with that freshwater crustacean.) You may substitute Maine lobster in these recipes.

How to Boil and Clean a Lobster

At home, boiled lobster was generally served cold with homemade mayonnaise or used in salads or croquettes. These dishes often were made from the meat of the lobster body that was set aside when making Langostas Enchiladas (page 53). Other times, the whole lobster was boiled in the manner described here. If using only the lobster body, begin with Step 2.

1. Soak the live lobster for at least 1 hour in a solution made with 4 quarts water and 1 pound salt. This spares the lobster any unnecessary suffering by numbing it and insures that its meat is tender.

2. Fill a large pot with water, add a tablespoon of salt, and bring to a boil. Plunge the lobster into the rapidly boiling water. Lower the heat and simmer for 5 minutes, or until the lobster is red. Drain it in a colander and set aside until it is cool enough to handle.

3. Pry open the shell. Remove the greenish liver (tomalley) and, in females, the red ovary (coral roe; see Note). Scrape the body cavity, removing and discarding the spongy lungs and the stomach ("lady"). Remove all the white meat from the shell.

4. Pull the tail meat from the body's shell in one piece. Remove and discard the intestinal vein that runs down the center of the tail. If using a Maine lobster, crack open the claws and remove the meat. Cut the meat into pieces of the desired size.

NOTE: The liver and ovaries are edible and can be used to enrich sauces. The lungs, while edible, are tough and not particularly flavorful and should be discarded. The stomach is *not* edible and must be thrown out.

This recipe captures all the flavor the lobster has to give by leaving the shell on during the cooking process. It's easier to eat than you might imagine; the medallions of cooked meat are easily separated from the tail sections with a knife and fork.

The festive variation, Langostas con Chocolate, from my cousin Cuquita Aguirregaviria, never fails to intrigue one's guests. Few will identify chocolate as the source of its unusual flavor. As you will note from the second variation, a delicious version of this dish can be made with crab. Whichever version you choose, serve it with white rice.

LANGOSTAS ENCHILADAS

(LOBSTER IN SAVORY SAUCE)

6 servings

4 Florida lobster tails, 2 ½ to 3
   pounds total (raw or frozen;
   see Note)
½ cup Spanish olive oil
I large onion, peeled and chopped
I large green bell pepper, cored,
   seeded, and chopped
3 garlic cloves, peeled and minced
I teaspoon salt
½ teaspoon freshly ground pepper
½ teaspoon sugar
¼ teaspoon Tabasco sauce
I cup tomato sauce
¾ cup dry white wine
2 tablespoons white wine vinegar
I bay leaf
½ cup chopped parsley

I. Using a sharp knife, cut the lobster tails at each joint, dividing them, shell and all, into their natural sections. Remove the small reddish vein that runs down the center of the tail by pushing a toothpick through the center of each section.

2. In a large dutch oven, heat the oil over medium heat and sauté the lobster sections until the shells turn red.

3. Add the onion and green pepper and sauté until the onion is translucent, about 3 minutes. Stir in the garlic and cook for 2 minutes more. Stir in the salt, pepper, sugar, Tabasco sauce, tomato sauce, wine, vinegar, bay leaf, and parsley. Cover the pan, reduce the heat, and cook gently for about 30 minutes.

4. Remove the bay leaf and transfer to a serving dish.

NOTE: If starting with whole lobsters, cut the bodies off and refrigerate immediately. Since lobster is extremely perishable, you should cook it within a few hours (see directions on page 51–52). The cooked meat from the body can then be used for salads or croquettes, or may be frozen.

VARIATIONS

Langostas con Chocolate (Lobster with Chocolate): Prepare Langostas Enchiladas as directed and allow it to simmer for about 20 minutes. In a double boiler, melt one 1-ounce square of sweet or semisweet chocolate per section of lobster tail being cooked. Add the melted chocolate to the lobster, stirring gently until all the sections are covered and the chocolate is well blended into the sauce. Simmer another 5 minutes and serve. Garnish with toasted, slivered almonds if desired.

Cangrejos Enchilados (Crabs in Savory Sauce): Substitute 5 or 6 crabs, about 6 pounds total, for the lobster. To prepare the crabs for cooking, scrub them with a brush under hot running water. Pull the claws to loosen them and hit the crabs several times with a hammer to break the shells for easier eating. Heat the oil in a large dutch oven and proceed as directed above.

CANGREJOS Y JAIBAS
(Crabs Big and Small)

Crabs were so abundant in Cárdenas, where I was born, that the natives were called *cangrejeros* (crab vendors or, as I prefer, crab lovers). Crabs were just as plentiful in Varadero, and we children used to fish for them from the pier of the old Club Náutico on the south beach, or chase the tiny ones as they ran backward on the north beach where we went swimming. We followed their feathery tracks and caught them just before they disappeared under the sand. Those crabs had hardly any meat at all on their tiny bodies, so we just played with them and put them back in the sea, right where the waves on a calm day would caress them into the water.

At the entrance of the Península de Hicacos, just before one reached Varadero proper, there was a special place that was a crab lover's paradise. It was called *Paso Malo* (Bad Pass) for a rickety old bridge that had long since been rebuilt. I never fished there; somehow it was not for girls. But my brother Pancho remembers that with just a baited piece of string suspended from a stick he would catch flat, blue crabs there by the dozen.

There were many land crabs at Paso Malo as well, the large, bluish gray *cangrejos de la tierra.* Pancho and his friends caught them at night, sometimes with their bare hands. Waving their lanterns, they skulked along the low brush by the water, poking the bushes where the crabs hid. When the crabs emerged, startled, the boys nabbed them and tossed them into their sacks.

My favorite crab dishes, Cangrejos Enchilados (page 54) and Harina con Jaibas, can be made with any kind of crab.

HARINA CON JAIBAS

(CORNMEAL WITH CRABS)

8 to 10 servings

This scrumptious but inelegant dish was usually served at informal family meals. There is no neat way to get the precious meat from the crabs. It's best to make a mess of things, licking the saucy cornmeal and nibbling every last morsel from the shells. Be sure to have plenty of paper napkins at hand and, if you are serving guests, provide finger bowls as well. Serve this dish with a crisp green salad.

10 small crabs, 4 to 5 pounds total
⅔ cup Spanish olive oil
3 medium onions, peeled and
    chopped
1 large green bell pepper, cored,
    seeded, and chopped
6 garlic cloves, peeled and minced

1½ cups tomato purée
2 tablespoons vinegar
1½ tablespoons salt
½ teaspoon freshly ground pepper
5 quarts water
4 cups coarse yellow cornmeal

1. Under hot running water, thoroughly wash the crabs, scrubbing them with a brush. (Hot water anesthetizes crabs so they are easier to handle and do not suffer when they are cooked.) Pull the claws to loosen them and hit each crab with a hammer several times to break the shell for easier eating. Refrigerate.

2. In a large, heavy pot (at least 8 quarts), warm the oil over medium heat. Sauté the onions and green pepper until the onions are translucent, about 3 minutes. Stir in the garlic and cook for 2 minutes more. Stir in the tomato purée and vinegar and cook for a few minutes longer.

3. Add the salt, pepper, water, and cornmeal. Bring to a boil, stirring constantly so that the cornmeal does not form lumps. When the cornmeal begins to thicken, lower the heat, add the crabs, cover, and simmer for about 1 hour, stirring occasionally, until the cornmeal is thick and has absorbed the crabs' delicious flavor.

CAMARONES AL AJILLO
(SHRIMP IN GARLIC SAUCE)

4 servings

This simple recipe is very Spanish, but while in Spain shrimp is generally served with its shell on, in Cuba it was most often peeled and deveined before cooking. Serve it with white rice.

1 cup Spanish olive oil
16 large shrimp, shelled and deveined
10 garlic cloves, peeled and cut into thick slices
¼ cup freshly squeezed lime juice
1¼ teaspoons salt
½ teaspoon freshly ground pepper
2 tablespoons chopped parsley

1. Heat the oil in a large, heavy skillet over medium-high heat until it is fragrant. Add the shrimp and garlic and sauté until the shrimp turns pink, about 3 minutes.

2. Add the lime juice, salt, and pepper. Sauté for about 2 minutes more, being careful not to overcook the shrimp.

3. Transfer the shrimp to a serving dish and sprinkle them with chopped parsley.

Everyone compliments me on my shrimp creole, but I must admit that this recipe, from my cousin Juan Diez Argüelles, is even more delectable. You must plan ahead for this dish to allow time for the shrimp to marinate. Black beans, fried ripe plantains, and plenty of white rice are delicious accompaniments.

4 pounds fresh, large shrimp, shelled and deveined
¼ cup freshly squeezed lime juice
I teaspoon salt
I teaspoon freshly ground pepper
½ cup Spanish olive oil
I large red onion, peeled and chopped
I large green bell pepper, cored, seeded, and chopped

4 garlic cloves, peeled and chopped
One 8-ounce can tomato sauce
One 6-ounce jar pimientos, chopped and the liquid reserved
I teaspoon ketchup
I teaspoon Tabasco sauce
I teaspoon lemon pepper
¼ cup chopped parsley
½ cup dry white wine

I. Place the shrimp in a large glass or ceramic container. Add the lime juice, salt, and pepper. Cover and refrigerate the mixture for at least 2 hours. Drain the shrimp, reserving the lime juice.

2. In a large, deep skillet, heat the oil over medium-high heat until fragrant and sauté the shrimp just until they turn pink. With a slotted spoon, remove the shrimp.

3. In the same oil, sauté the onion and green pepper until the onion is translucent, about 3 minutes. Add the garlic and cook 2 more minutes.

4. Reduce the heat to low, return the shrimp to the skillet, and cook for 5 minutes. Add the tomato sauce, pimientoes and their liquid, ketchup, Tabasco sauce, lemon pepper, parsley, wine, and the reserved lime juice. Cook just until warmed through.

SERRUCHO EN ESCABECHE

(PICKLED SWORDFISH)

❧

12 servings

In the pantry at home, there was always a large glass or terra cotta container of pickled swordfish to be taken on picnics or served as a special treat to guests. The pickling process preserves the fish and there is no need to refrigerate it. Escabeche must be prepared at least a week ahead of serving time.

Serve the escabeche at room temperature with crusty Cuban or French bread.

1 cup Spanish olive oil, plus enough to cover the fish
1 cup flour
1 teaspoon salt
4 pounds (about 6) swordfish steaks, 1 inch thick (kingfish and scrod steaks may be substituted)
3 large onions, peeled and sliced into ¼-inch rings

2 large green bell peppers, cored, seeded, and sliced into ¼-inch rings
4 bay leaves
1 tablespoon peppercorns
½ teaspoon paprika
1¼ cups pitted Spanish green olives
¾ cup capers
white wine vinegar

1. Warm the oil in a large, heavy skillet over medium heat. Combine the flour and salt in a broad dish.

2. Dredge the fish steaks in the flour mixture, shake off the excess, and fry them until golden on both sides. Transfer the fish to a deep glass or terra cotta container.

3. In the same skillet, sauté the onions and green peppers with the bay leaves until the onions are translucent, about 3 minutes. Remove the pan from the heat and stir in the bay leaves, peppercorns, paprika, olives, and capers. Pour this mixture over the fish.

4. Pour equal amounts of vinegar and olive oil into the container until the contents are covered.

5. Seal the container with 4 layers of cheesecloth tied securely with string. Store it in a cool, dry place for at least a week.

El Centro Vasco, a great Cuban restaurant in Miami, serves the best calamares en su tinta I've eaten in this country. Juan Saizarbitoria founded the restaurant in Havana in the 1920s and later transplanted it to these shores. He has passed away, but his son, Juanito, still runs El Centro Vasco in high style, and was generous enough to share this recipe, which is much like the one I've used for years. Serve it the Cuban way with white rice, or Basque-style with fresh, crusty white bread.

CALAMARES EN SU TINTA

(SQUID IN THEIR OWN INK)

8 servings

3 pounds fresh squid (see Note)
3 large onions, peeled and finely
   chopped (about 3 cups total)
1 cup Spanish olive oil
1 cup red wine
1 teaspoon red wine vinegar
½ teaspoon salt
Fresh bread crumbs
   (optional)

1. One by one, hold each squid firmly in one hand and with the other hand pull off the tentacles; the head, eyes, and inner organs will come with them. (Be careful not to burst the delicate sacs of bluish-black ink behind the tentacles; gently remove the ink sacs and save them in a small bowl.) Cut off and discard the organs, including the eyes and the bony mouth. Reserve the tentacles.

2. Remove and discard the thin, slimy membrane that covers the body and wash the squid under cold running water. Turn the body inside out as you would a sock, removing and discarding the two flat little bones or cartilages as you do so. Wash the squid again under cold running water until all gelatinous material has been removed.

3. Finely chop the reserved tentacles and stir them together with the chopped onions. Push the mixture firmly into the body of each squid.

4. Heat the oil over medium-high heat in a large dutch oven or a fire-resistant earthenware casserole. Sauté the stuffed squid until lightly golden on all sides.

5. While the squid are sautéing, put the ink sacks, red wine, vinegar, and salt in a blender or food processor and process on high until well blended. Strain the liquid through a colander over the squid. It should just cover them.

6. When the liquid begins to boil, reduce the heat to low and simmer, covered, for about 1 hour if the squid are small (under 3 inches) and fresh. If they are large and/or frozen, it may take up to 2 hours. The squid is done when it is tender enough to cut with a fork.

7. If you like, thicken the sauce with tiny bread crumbs plucked by hand from a fresh loaf.

NOTE: If fresh squid is unavailable, you may substitute frozen. Though the dish will taste almost as good, the ink from the frozen squid is brownish and less plentiful. You may supplement it as the chef at El Centro Vasco does and use packets of squid ink, called *chipirón,* that are imported from Spain. (You may write to the supplier, R.G.S., at 12786/SS, Pasajes, Guipúzcoa, Spain.)

Carne de Res (Beef)

CARNE DE RES (Beef)

*S*eafood was king in our home, thanks to my father's passion for fishing, but beef was the most popular entrée in most Cuban homes of my youth. It had been from ancient days: Beef, in the form of tasajo or jerked beef, was among the provisions carried by the crews of La Pinta, La Niña and La Santa María when they landed on the island in 1492. The cattle Columbus brought on those same ships thrived on the verdant island, and eventually spawned an export industry: The meat was salted in order to preserve it, and ships carrying treasure back to Spain from South America stopped in Cuba to buy jerked beef for the long journey home. The African slaves the Spanish brought to Cuba in the seventeenth, eighteenth, and nineteenth centuries had known beef in their homeland, and we have them to thank for the Afro-Cuba beef dishes we now treasure such as ropa vieja, which turns humble brisket into something splendid with long, slow simmering and the addition of a distinctly Cuban sofrito (sautéed onion, green bell pepper, and garlic). Another very Cuban touch is the marinade of sour orange juice and garlic that adds tenderness and flavor to beef dishes such as palomilla steak and boliche mechado (stuffed eye of round) and to many pork and chicken dishes in the chapters ahead as well.

Thin, well-pounded steak such as this was an everyday dish in most Cuban homes of old.

2 garlic cloves, peeled
½ teaspoon salt
¼ teaspoon freshly ground pepper
½ cup sour orange juice (or a 50-50 mixture of sweet orange juice and lime juice)
1 pound flank or sirloin steak, about ½ inch thick

2 eggs
1 cup dry bread crumbs
2 to 3 tablespoons vegetable oil
4 parsley springs
4 lime wedges

BISTEC EMPANIZADO
(BREADED BEEF STEAK)

4 servings

I. Mash the garlic, ¼ teaspoon of the salt, and the pepper into a paste. (A mortar and pestle works best, but you may mince the garlic finely with a knife or put it through a garlic press and mash the seasonings in with a fork.) Combine the garlic paste with the orange juice in a container suitable for marinating the steak.

2. Pound the steak with a meat hammer until it is about ¼ inch thick and cut it into 4 pieces.

3. Place the meat in the marinade, cover, and refrigerate for 15 to 20 minutes. Remove the steaks and blot them with paper towels. Discard the marinade.

4. In a flat dish such as a pie pan, beat the eggs with the remaining ¼ teaspoon of salt. Put the bread crumbs in another flat dish. Dip the steaks one by one in the egg and then the bread crumbs, repeating until they are well breaded on all sides.

5. Heat the oil over medium-high heat in a large, heavy skillet and fry the steaks for a few minutes on each side, until golden brown.

6. Garnish with parsley sprigs and lime wedges.

BISTEC DE PALOMILLA

(FRIED TOP
SIRLOIN STEAK)

❦

4 servings

Like bistec empanizado, palomilla steak was a favorite in most Cuban households of my youth. Today, you will find it on the menu of virtually every Cuban restaurant in Miami.

3 garlic cloves, peeled
¼ teaspoon salt
¼ teaspoon freshly ground pepper
2 tablespoons sour orange juice (or a 50-50 mixture of sweet orange juice and lime juice)

I pound top sirloin
¼ cup vegetable oil
¼ cup finely chopped onion
¼ cup finely chopped fresh parsley

I. Mash the garlic, salt, and pepper into a paste. (A mortar and pestle works best, but you may mince the garlic finely with a knife or put it through a garlic press and mash the seasonings in with a fork.) Combine the garlic paste with the orange juice in a container suitable for marinating the steak.

2. Pound the steak lightly with a meat hammer and cut it into 4 pieces. Place the meat in the marinade, cover, and refrigerate for at least 30 minutes. Blot the steaks on paper towels. Reserve the marinade.

3. Heat the oil over medium-high heat in a large, heavy skillet and fry the steaks for a few minutes on each side, until golden brown. Transfer the meat to a serving platter.

4. Stir the marinade into the pan juices and heat it through. Drizzle this sauce onto the steaks. Top each with about I tablespoon of onion and I tablespoon of parsley.

This version of Cuban "Swiss" steak is from my paternal grand-mother, Abuela Carmela. With its olives and raisins, it is another delicious dish that shows the Arab influence on Spanish and in turn Cuban cuisine.

3 garlic cloves, peeled
½ teaspoon salt
¼ teaspoon freshly ground pepper
¼ teaspoon dry leaf oregano
⅓ cup sour orange juice (or a 50-50 mixture of sweet orange juice and lime juice)
2½ pounds top round steak, cut into 8 pieces
I large onion, peeled and cut into thin rings

I medium green bell pepper, cored, seeded, and cut into thin rings
3 tablespoons vegetable oil
½ cup Beef Broth, (page 13)
¾ cup red wine
½ cup pitted green olives
½ cup raisins
3 tablespoons cold water
2 tablespoons cornstarch

1. Mash the garlic, salt, pepper, and oregano into a paste. (A mortar and pestle works best, but you may mince the garlic finely with a knife or put it through a garlic press and mash the seasonings in with a fork.)

2. Combine the garlic paste with the orange juice in a container suitable for marinating the steaks.

3. Place the meat in the marinade, and top it with the onion and green pepper rings. Cover and refrigerate for I hour.

4. Blot the steaks on paper towels. Reserve the marinade and onion and green pepper rings.

5. Heat the oil in a large dutch oven over medium-high heat and brown the steaks on both sides.

6. Add the marinade, onion and green pepper rings, broth, and wine. Bring the liquid just to a boil, then reduce the heat to medium-low, cover, and simmer for I hour.

7. Add the olives and raisins and simmer for 30 minutes more.

8. Transfer the steaks to a serving dish and cover to keep them warm.

9. Combine the water and cornstarch and add the mixture to the pan juices. Stir over low heat until the sauce thickens. Pour it over the steaks and serve immediately.

CARNE ENROLLADA
(CUBAN-STYLE BEEF ROULADE)

12 servings

When this stuffed, rolled beef roast was served in our house, we children called it *brazo gitano de carne*, inspired, no doubt by *brazo gitano*, the Spanish name for jelly roll, which literally means "gypsy's arm."

Note that the meat must marinate for at least 6 hours before roasting.

3 garlic cloves, peeled
⅛ teaspoon dry leaf oregano
⅛ teaspoon ground cumin
½ cup sour orange juice (or a 50-50 mixture of sweet orange juice and lime juice)
1 tablespoon red wine vinegar
1 cup dry white wine
1 large onion, peeled and finely chopped

1 bay leaf
1 flank steak, about 1 pound (see Note)
¼ cup vegetable oil
½ pound jamón de cocinar (cooking ham) or prosciutto, chopped
5 eggs
½ teaspoon salt
½ teaspoon freshly ground pepper

1. Mash the garlic, oregano, and cumin together into a paste. (A mortar and pestle works best, but you may mince the garlic finely with a knife or put it through a garlic press and mash the seasonings in with a fork.) Combine the garlic paste with the orange juice, vinegar, wine, onion, and bay leaf in a container suitable for marinating the meat.

2. Pound the flank steak with a meat hammer until it is about ¼ inch thick. Place the meat in the marinade, cover it, and refrigerate for at least 6 hours. Remove the meat, blot it with paper towels, and place it flat on a work surface. Reserve the marinade.

3. Heat 2 tablespoons of the oil in a heavy skillet over medium heat and sauté the ham for a few minutes. Beat the eggs with the salt

and pepper and stir them into the ham. Scramble the eggs quickly, being careful not to let them get dry.

4. Spread the egg mixture evenly over the steak within about ½ inch of the edges. Starting at one long end, roll the meat up jelly-roll fashion and tie it securely with kitchen string at 3-inch intervals along the length of the roll.

5. Heat the remaining 2 tablespoons of oil in a large dutch oven over medium-high heat and brown the meat on all sides, about 5 minutes total. Add the reserved marinade and bring to a boil. Reduce the heat, cover, and simmer for at least 2 hours, until the meat is tender.

6. Transfer the meat to a platter and let it rest for 5 or 10 minutes. Remove the string and cut into ½-inch slices. Remove the bay leaf and serve the pan juices on the side.

NOTE: Ask your butcher to cut the steak into a single piece that is about 12 inches long, 8 inches wide, and ½ inch thick.

BOLICHE MECHADO
(STUFFED EYE-OF-ROUND ROAST)

10 to 12 servings

This traditional recipe produces succulent slices of meat, each with an enticing pink dot of ham in the center. Although it is simple to make, boliche mechado requires planning because the meat should marinate for 48 hours. It is most often served with white rice and fried plantains.

¼ pound jamón de cocinar (cooking ham) or prosciutto
2 strips bacon
1 eye-of-round roast, about 5 pounds
2 large onions, peeled and thinly sliced
3 garlic cloves, peeled
1 teaspoon salt
½ teaspoon freshly ground pepper

½ teaspoon dry leaf oregano
2 cups sour orange juice (or a 50-50 mixture of sweet orange juice and lime juice)
½ cup dry white wine (or more if needed)
6 bay leaves
2 tablespoons vegetable oil
2 cups cooked black beans, puréed

1. Coarsely chop the ham and the bacon together.

2. With a thin, sharp knife or a skewer, make a tunnel 1 inch in diameter lengthwise through the center of the roast. Push the ham mixture into this cavity.

3. Layer half the onion slices on the bottom of a large container suitable for marinating the meat and place the roast on top of them.

4. Mash the garlic, salt, pepper, and oregano into a paste. (A mortar and pestle works best, but you may mince the garlic finely with a knife or put it through a garlic press and mash the seasonings in with a fork.) Combine the garlic paste with the orange juice, wine, and bay leaves. Pour this marinade over the roast and arrange the remaining onion slices on top.

5. Cover the meat and refrigerate it for 48 hours, basting the top three or four times with the marinade. Remove the roast and blot it dry with paper towels. Reserve the marinade.

6. Heat the oil in a large dutch oven over medium-high heat and brown the roast on all sides. Remove the onions from the marinade and sauté them with the meat just until they are transparent.

7. Pour the marinade over the roast and bring just to a boil. Reduce the heat, cover, and simmer for 4 hours, basting every half hour. (Add more wine if necessary to keep the liquid at least ¼ the depth of the roast.) Transfer the meat to a serving platter and let it rest for 10 minutes.

8. Stir the bean purée into the pan juices and heat through. Carve the meat into ½-inch slices and serve the black bean gravy on the side.

Picadillo (Savory Ground Beef)

Every Cuban cook has a special way of making picadillo. Some omit the capers or add ground pork to the beef. Others add cubed, fried potatoes or top each serving with a fried egg. There are those who claim the picadillo must simmer for an hour for optimal taste and still others who say one need only make a quick sofrito, toss in the rest of the ingredients, and cook it for a few minutes.

Here is a basic recipe with two variations. Whichever you choose, serve the picadillo with plenty of fluffy white rice. For a real Cuban feast, add a large pot of black beans, platters of fried ripe plantains and tostones, and Guacamole Cubano (page 209).

PICADILLO CLÁSICO
(CLASSIC PICADILLO)

6 servings

1 tablespoon vegetable oil
1 medium onion, peeled and chopped
1 large green bell pepper, cored, seeded, and chopped
3 garlic cloves, peeled and minced
1 pound extra-lean ground beef
¼ cup tomato sauce
¼ cup sliced, stuffed green olives
¼ cup raisins
1 tablespoon capers
2 tablespoons white vinegar
¼ teaspoon sugar
1 teaspoon salt
½ teaspoon freshly ground pepper
One 6-ounce jar of pimientos, drained and sliced
6 slices of French bread, fried in oil

1. Heat the oil in a large skillet over medium heat. Sauté the onion and green pepper until the onion is translucent, about 3 minutes. Add the garlic and cook 2 minutes more.

2. Add the beef and break it up well; there should be no lumps. Stir in the tomato sauce, olives, raisins, capers, vinegar, sugar, salt, and pepper. Reduce the heat to low, cover, and simmer for 20 minutes, or until the consistency is like that of sloppy joes.

3. Transfer the picadillo to a serving dish and garnish it with pimientos and rounds of fried bread.

VARIATIONS

Picadillo a la Criolla (Picadillo Creole Style): Omit the tomato sauce. After the picadillo has simmered for 20 minutes, stir in 4 or 5 beaten eggs and cook them until scrambled.

Picadillo con Papitas Fritas (Picadillo with Fried Potatoes): While the picadillo is simmering, fry 1 pound of peeled, cubed potatoes in ¼ cup of vegetable oil over medium-high heat until golden, about 10 minutes.

When the picadillo is done, add the potatoes and toss lightly to mix. (To reduce the fat content, my sister-in-law Isabelita La Rosa de Lluriá adds the raw, cubed potatoes to the meat instead.)

FRITAS
(CUBAN-STYLE HAMBURGERS)

6 servings

Fritas were eaten "on the go" in Cuba, much as one eats fast food in this country. I remember them being sold on the sidewalks in Havana and in the crowds at sporting events the way hot dogs are sold at Yankee Stadium. As a youngster I enjoyed what to me was the great luxury of buying fritas during the national regattas in Varadero from vendors who would set up little make-shift shops across the street from our elegant Club Náutico.

½ cup milk
I cup cubed stale bread
I small onion, peeled
I½ pounds lean ground beef
I egg
I teaspoon paprika

½ teaspoon freshly ground pepper
I teaspoon soy sauce
Vegetable oil
I dozen hamburger buns
4 cups canned shoestring potatoes

I. Pour the milk over the bread and set it aside to soak.

2. Place the onion in a food processor and pulse it until finely chopped. Add the bread mixture, the meat, egg, paprika, pepper, and soy sauce. Pulse it until well mixed.

3. Form the meat mixture into 12 balls and flatten them into patties.

4. Oil a grill or large skillet lightly and heat it over medium-high heat. Fry the patties until they are nicely brown on both sides.

5. Transfer the fritas to the buns, tucking a handful of shoestring potatoes on top of each meat patty.

Ropa vieja literally means "old clothes." The name is apt because the meat, having been used first to make broth is, as it were, "second-hand." I have begun this recipe with the broth-making, although in Cuban households of old this step was taken for granted. Serve this savory dish with white rice, fried plantains, and a Cuban salad.

FOR THE BROTH:

2 pounds beef brisket
1 sprig parsley
1 bay leaf
3 large onions, peeled and quartered

1 garlic clove, peeled
1 carrot, peeled and cut into chunks
1 teaspoon salt
1 teaspoon peppercorns

FOR THE SAUCE:

1 large green bell pepper
3 garlic cloves, peeled and minced
1 teaspoon salt
½ teaspoon freshly ground pepper
¼ teaspoon dry leaf oregano
⅓ cup vegetable oil
1 large onion, peeled and chopped

1 bay leaf
1 cup tomato sauce
½ cup reserved beef broth
½ cup dry white wine
1 tablespoon white wine vinegar
One 6-ounce jar pimientos, drained and sliced

PREPARE THE BROTH:

1. Place the meat in a large, heavy pot and cover it with water. Add the parsley, bay leaf, onions, garlic, carrot, salt, and peppercorns.

2. Bring the water to a boil over high heat. Reduce the heat to low and simmer, covered, for 2 hours.

3. Remove the meat from the pot and set it aside to cool. Reserve ½ cup of broth for the sauce and save the rest for another use.

PREPARE THE SAUCE:

1. Cut the green pepper in half, remove the seeds and stem, and place it, cut side down, on a greased cookie sheet. Put it under a hot broiler until it blisters. When it is cool enough to handle, remove the skin, cut the pepper into thin strips, and set it aside.

2. Mash the garlic, salt, pepper, and oregano into a paste. (A mortar and pestle works best, but you may mince the garlic finely with a knife or put it through a garlic press and mash the seasonings in with a fork.) Set it aside.

3. Heat the oil in a large skillet over medium heat. Sauté the chopped onion until it is translucent, about 3 minutes. Reduce the heat to medium-low, stir in the garlic mixture and bay leaf, and cook for 2 minutes. Stir in the tomato sauce, broth, wine, and vinegar, and simmer for 5 minutes more.

4. While the sauce is cooking, shred the meat with your fingers into 3- to 4-inch strands. Stir the meat and the green pepper strips into the sauce, cover, and simmer for about 20 minutes, to blend the flavors.

5. Remove the bay leaf, transfer the ropa vieja to a serving dish, and garnish it with pimientos.

VACA FRITA
(FRIED BEEF)

8 servings

This is another economical dish that we ate often when I was young. Only a step up from leftovers because it is made with meat that is first used for cooking broth, vaca frita was never considered elegant enough for company. Even its name is inelegant, literally meaning "fried cow." Nevertheless, I have fond memories of cozy family meals of vaca frita served with a purée of boniatos (see Steps 1 and 2, pages 232-33) and Guacamole Cubano (page 209).

FOR THE BROTH:

2 pounds beef brisket
1 sprig parsley
1 bay leaf
3 large onions, peeled and quartered

1 garlic clove, peeled
1 carrot, peeled and cut into chunks
1 teaspoon salt
1 teaspoon peppercorns

To Complete the Dish:

⅓ cup vegetable oil

2 large onions, peeled and chopped

3 garlic cloves, peeled and minced

½ teaspoon salt

1. Prepare the broth as directed in the recipe for Ropa Vieja (page 73).

2. Let the meat cool for an hour, then cut into thin, 3-inch-long strips.

3. Heat the oil in a large skillet over medium heat and sauté the onions until they are translucent, about 3 minutes. Add the garlic and sauté 2 minutes more. Stir in the salt.

4. Stir in the meat and fry until crisp.

I grew up thinking that this dish, so very popular in Cuba, was Italian. But as an adult I learned that, like the English muffin in England and vichyssoise in France, hígado a la Italiana is unknown in Italy. The closest thing to it that I have found in Italy is fegato alla Veneziana, which has no green pepper and is always served with polenta. Its Cuban cousin is, of course, served with white rice.

HÍGADO A LA ITALIANA
(LIVER "ITALIAN STYLE")

4 servings

2 garlic cloves, peeled and minced

½ teaspoon salt

¼ teaspoon freshly ground pepper

¼ cup white wine vinegar

¾ cup dry white wine

1 pound calves' liver, cleaned of any gristle and cut into 1-inch cubes, or if you prefer your liver well done, cut into ½-inch slices

1 large onion, peeled and thinly sliced

1 large green bell pepper, cored, seeded, and cut into thin strips

1 bay leaf, crushed

3 tablespoons vegetable oil

1. In a container suitable for marinating the meat, whisk together the garlic, salt, pepper, vinegar, and wine.

2. Add the liver, onion, green pepper, and bay leaf to the marinade, cover, and refrigerate it for at least 1 hour.

3. In a large skillet, warm the oil over medium heat. Add the liver and marinade and cook, stirring constantly, for about 10 minutes, or just until the liver is cooked on all sides.

RABO ALCAPARRADO

(OXTAILS WITH CAPER SAUCE)

8 servings

This dish was a specialty of Genoveva, the last cook Mamá had before she left Cuba. My father had died by then, and my mother had rented out her Varadero house and moved to an apartment in Havana. It was in 1959. I was home from Venezuela where Jack and I had lived for fourteen years. Fidel Castro had just taken over Cuba and there were already suspicions that he was a Communist. Genoveva was clearing the table and Mamá and I were doing *sobremesa*, "table talk," discussing the situation. Holding a knife in her hand, Genoveva piped in, "If there is going to be communism, I am going out in the street with this knife to fight against it!" Like so many others, she eventually fled Cuba for Miami.

Serve this old-fashioned dish with white rice, fried plantains, and an avocado salad.

4 large green bell peppers
2 oxtails, about 5 pounds total
½ cup vegetable oil
3 medium onions, peeled and
    chopped
8 cloves garlic, peeled and minced
1 cup tomato sauce
1 teaspoon dry leaf oregano

¼ teaspoon ground cumin
1 teaspoon salt
½ teaspoon freshly ground pepper
¼ cup chopped parsley
1 tablespoon white wine vinegar
1 cup capers
1 cup red wine

1. Cut each green pepper in half, remove the core and seeds, and place, cut side down, on a greased cookie sheet. Put under a hot broiler until the skin blisters. When the peppers are cool enough to handle, remove the skin, cut the peppers into thin strips, and set aside.

2. Remove the visible fat from the oxtails and cut them at the joints into 2- to 3-inch pieces. Wash them under cold running water and dry them with paper towels.

3. Heat the oil in a large dutch oven over medium heat and brown the oxtails. Remove them from the pan.

4. Add the onions and sauté until they are translucent, about 3 minutes. Add the garlic and cook 2 minutes more. Stir in the green pepper strips, tomato sauce, oregano, cumin, salt, and pepper and cook for 2 minutes.

5. Return the oxtails to the pan. Add the parsley, vinegar, capers, and wine. Stir well, reduce the heat to low, and simmer, covered, for about 2 hours, or until the meat is tender.

APORREADO DE TASAJO
(HASH OF JERKED BEEF)

8 servings

Although refrigeration has long since replaced salting as a means of preserving beef, the tasajo that was a mainstay of sailors passing through Cuba in the sixteenth century is still loved by Cubans. In Castro's Cuba, where food is so scarce, there is no tasajo, but in the United States it can be bought in Latin supermarkets.

As with bacalao, you need to plan ahead to allow soaking time. This classic Cuban dish is something like ropa vieja in that you shred the meat. Serve it with fluffy white rice.

1½ pounds jerked beef
4 garlic cloves, peeled and minced
¼ teaspoon freshly ground pepper
½ teaspoon dry leaf oregano
⅛ teaspoon ground cumin
½ cup vegetable oil
2 medium onions, peeled and chopped

2 large green bell peppers, cored, seeded, and chopped
¼ teaspoon sugar
1 teaspoon vinegar
1 cup tomato sauce
½ cup dry white wine
½ cup Beef Broth (page 13)
1 bay leaf

1. Cover the jerked beef with cold water and soak it for at least 8 hours. (There is no need to refrigerate it.)

2. Change the water and continue soaking for another hour. Drain again and rinse the beef under cold running water. Remove any fatty tissue from the surface of the meat and cut it into 2- to 3-inch pieces.

3. Place the meat in a large dutch oven, cover it with fresh water, and bring just to a boil. Reduce the heat, cover, and simmer for about an hour, until the meat is very tender.

4. Drain the meat. When it is cool enough to handle, flatten it with a meat hammer and shred it with your fingers into strips.

5. Mash the garlic, pepper, oregano, and cumin into a paste. (A mortar and pestle works best, but you may mince the garlic finely with a knife or put it through a garlic press and mash the seasonings in with a fork.)

6. In a large skillet, heat the oil over medium heat and sauté the onions and green peppers until the onions are translucent, about 3 minutes.

7. Add the garlic paste, sugar, vinegar, tomato sauce, wine, beef broth, bay leaf, and meat and simmer the mixture, covered, for 1 hour. Remove the bay leaf before serving.

My brothers, Pili and Lelén, with me. Cárdenas, 1926. *Author's collection*

The name of this drink derives from the English words "beef tea." It was given to children as a tonic, especially when they were convalescing. It was so delicious that it was almost worth getting the measles, mumps, or whooping cough to be rewarded with a small cup before each meal! Liver biftí was considered even more nourishing. Sometimes a bit of biftí de hígado was mixed into a bowl of soup or black beans to sneak extra iron into the diet of a liver-hating child.

This recipe for 8 ounces of very strong extract yields enough for about 6 liqueur-glass servings. Serve it as an aperitif, or instead of a soup course.

BIFTÍ
(BEEF EXTRACT)

6 servings

I pound of beef chuck or neck meat (what in Spanish we call *cogote*)

I medium onion, peeled and finely chopped

2 garlic cloves, peeled and minced

⅛ teaspoon salt

6 peppercorns (optional)

I. Have your butcher grind the meat twice—the finer the better.

2. Place the meat, onion, garlic, salt, and peppercorns in a heat-resistant 16-ounce glass jar with a glass lid. Close the lid tightly.

3. Place the jar in a saucepan and fill it with enough water so that it comes up to the same level as the jar contents. Simmer over medium heat for 1 hour, or until you see through the glass that the meat has released its blood-juice.

4. Strain the meat and pour the juice, or beef extract, into a glass measuring cup with a spout. Serve it warm.

NOTE: Save the ground beef. Mixed with a bowl of broth it makes a tasty jigote (see page 20).

VARIATION
Biftí de Hígado (Liver Extract): Replace the beef chuck with 12 ounces of chopped liver steak and add 1 small chopped green bell pepper. Proceed as directed above. (The leftover liver pieces are delicious served with rice.)

PUERCO (PORK)

Lechón Asado (Roast Suckling Pig) 85

Pierna de Puerco Asada (Roasted Fresh Ham) 86

Pierna de Puerco Rellena (Stuffed Rolled Boneless Pork
    Roast) 87

Puerco Asado Guajiro (Peasant-style Roast Pork) 88

Costillas de Puerco con Machuquillo (Pork Chops with Mashed
    Plantains) 90

Chicharrones de Pellejo (Crispy Fried Pork Rind) 91

Masitas de Puerco Fritas (Fried Little Pork Chunks) 92

Sandwich Cubano (Cuban Sandwich) 93

Patas con Garbanzos (Pig's Feet with Chick-Peas) 94

Butifarras de Don Faustino Dalmau (Don Faustino Dalmau's
    Pork Sausages) 95

Queso de Cabeza de Puerco (Pig's Head Cheese) 97

PUERCO (Pork)

*C*ubans developed an appetite for pork early: There were live pigs aboard Columbus's ships when he landed on the island in 1492. That preference was nurtured in the nineteenth century by the more than 120,000 Chinese who came to Cuba as contract laborers and who loved pork as much as the Spaniards did. So, you see, we have inherited our taste for pork from East and West alike.

Though pork was neither rare nor expensive in my time, it was precious. Every part of the animal was used in the form of stews, *chicharrones* (cracklings), and fried *masitas* (meat chunks), to name a few. On special occasions such as *noche buena* (Christmas Eve), *lechón asado* (roast suckling pig) was—and still is—an essential part of a Cuban feast.

Lechón asado was enjoyed under humbler circumstances as well. It was not uncommon on the road between Havana and Varadero to find *guajiros* (peasants) roasting a whole suckling pig in a pit. Travelers would stop to buy a hefty portion of meat served on fresh bread, sandwich style, with a cold Hatuey beer.

At home, the day before a feast, the suckling pig was unceremoniously slaughtered in the backyard. The gardener held the animal, folding its right front leg so that the elbow pointed to its heart. Then the cook stabbed the pig with a butcher knife in exactly that spot in order to put it out of its suffering as quickly as possible. Using very hot water, the cook cleaned and scraped the carcass with a razorlike instrument to remove all the hair. Once it was all shiny and clean-shaven, the pig was placed, belly up, on a rustic table and slit open. It was then disemboweled, decapitated, and amputated, except when the pig was to be roasted whole. All the organs plus the head and feet were refrigerated or salted for later use. When the surgery was complete, the pig was rubbed inside and out with coarse salt and hung from a tree by its hind legs for several hours. Then it was rubbed with marinade and roasted, either on a spit over an open fire or in a pit especially dug for that purpose.

The pig was carved in the kitchen before serving rather than displayed whole at the table as is sometimes done in this country.

Most people today have neither the time nor the inclination to go through the old-fashioned steps to prepare a pig. One can simply order an oven-ready pig from the butcher and start the preparations with the marinating step.

When ordering a pig, be sure to ask that the head and feet be removed but included so that you can make pig's head cheese and pig's feet as described in this chapter.

LECHÓN ASADO
(ROAST SUCKLING PIG)

20 servings

1 young pig (maximum 20 pounds)
5 cups sour orange juice (or a 50-50 mixture of sweet orange juice and lime juice)
2 tablespoons salt
2 tablespoons freshly ground pepper
3 tablespoons dry leaf oregano
3 large heads of garlic, cloves peeled
½ cup vegetable oil

1. Place the pig in a large roasting pan, belly up, and pour the orange juice over it, being sure to douse the cavity liberally.

2. Put the salt, pepper, oregano, garlic, and oil in a food processor and pulse until the garlic is well minced.

3. Rub the entire pig with this marinade and if you have a meat thermometer, place it in the thickest part of the pig's belly without touching the bone.

4. Roast the pig, uncovered, in a 200-degree oven for 9½ hours, basting every ½ hour.

5. Check to see if the skin is crispy and golden. If not, raise the oven temperature to 350 degrees. Roast for 30 minutes more. The pig will be done when a meat thermometer registers 170 degrees. You can also test for doneness by pricking the thigh with the point of a knife after 9 ½ hours; when the liquid runs clear, the meat is done.

6. Remove the pig from the oven and allow it to rest for 10 minutes before carving.

VARIATION

Stuffed Suckling Pig: You may stuff the pig with Moros y Cristianos (Rice with Black Beans, page 154) before roasting it as you would stuff a turkey with wild rice, sewing the cavity shut to insure that its contents do not spill. Proceed as directed above.

PIERNA DE PUERCO ASADA
(ROASTED FRESH HAM)

8 to 10 servings

Since whole suckling pig is cumbersome to prepare, many Cubans in Miami have adopted this recipe for small-scale festivities. It is usually served with rice, black beans, *yuca con mojo* (a sauce made with garlic, sour orange juice, and vegetable oil), and a green salad.

I fresh ham, about 6 pounds
I tablespoon salt
6 garlic cloves, peeled
I teaspoon pepper

I tablespoon dry leaf oregano
I cup sour orange juice (or a 50-50 mixture of sweet orange juice and lime juice)

1. Place the ham in a large roasting pan, sprinkle it on all sides with salt, and insert a meat thermometer if you are using one. Set it aside.

2. Mash the garlic, pepper, and oregano into a paste. (A mortar

and pestle works best, but you may mince the garlic finely with a knife or put it through a garlic press and mash the seasonings in with a fork.)

3. Mix the garlic paste with the orange juice and rub this marinade over the ham. Cover and refrigerate for at least 4 hours (overnight is best).

4. Preheat the oven to 350 degrees. Uncover the ham and roast it for about 3 hours, until the juices run clear when it is pricked with a sharp knife, or until a meat thermometer registers 170 degrees.

5. Remove the ham from the oven and allow it to rest for 10 minutes before carving.

PIERNA DE PUERCO RELLENA
(STUFFED ROLLED BONELESS PORK ROAST)

20 servings

This roast is sometimes called *a lo Cuba libre*, free Cuba style, but until the happy day when Cuba is free of communism, I prefer the simpler, more descriptive name. Delicious cold or hot, pierna de puerco rellena can be served as an elegant main course or a casual buffet dish. Note that you must stuff and marinate the roast the day before and that it cooks for 6 hours.

6 garlic cloves, peeled
1 teaspoon dry leaf oregano
1 tablespoon salt
1 bay leaf, crushed
1 tablespoon paprika
1½ cups sour orange juice (or a 50-50 mixture of sweet orange juice and lime juice)
1 boneless pork loin, about 10 pounds

2 carrots, peeled and grated
½ pound bacon, fried crisp and crushed
½ pound minced, cured ham
10 pitted prunes, minced
3 hard-boiled eggs, peeled
2 cups brown sugar
One 7-ounce bottle malta (see Note)

1. Mash the garlic, oregano, salt, bay leaf, and paprika into a paste. (A mortar and pestle works best, but you may mince the garlic finely with a knife or put it through a garlic press and mash the seasonings in with a fork.). Mix the garlic paste with the orange juice and set it aside.

2. Unroll the pork loin, trim off as much fat as possible, and lay it open in a large roasting pan. Thoroughly douse the inside of the pork loin with the marinade.

3. Spread the grated carrots over the marinade in an even layer, followed by the bacon, ham, and prunes. Place the eggs end to end on one side of the meat. Starting from that side, roll the meat up tightly and tie it securely with kitchen string.

4. Combine the brown sugar with half of the bottle of malta and pour this mixture over the pork loin to cover it. Wrap the pan tightly with plastic wrap and refrigerate the meat for at least 8 hours (overnight is best).

5. Preheat the oven to 200 degrees. Remove the plastic wrap, insert a meat thermometer into the pork loin, roast it for at least 6 hours, basting every ½ hour with the remaining malta.

6. When the thermometer registers 170 degrees, or the juices run clear, remove the meat from the oven. Let it rest for 10 minutes before slicing.

NOTE: Malta is a sweet, black malt beer with a low alcohol content that is sold in Latin markets. If you cannot find it you may substitute sweet orange juice or cola. Though the result will be very different, it will still be delicious.

PUERCO ASADO GUAJIRO

(PEASANT-STYLE ROAST PORK)

10 to 12 servings

There is an interesting story behind this unusual recipe. My cousin Juan Diez Argüelles spent twelve years in prison on the Isle of Pines for counterrevolutionary activities. While awaiting permission to leave Cuba after his release in 1971, he returned to our hometown. He walked every street of Cárdenas, hoping to strengthen his weakened muscles and to find old friends.

Failing to find anyone who had not sold his birthright to Castro, he decided to explore the surrounding rural areas. There, the peasants, or guajiros, still lived quietly in their *bohíos* (hovels) and enjoyed the luxury of existing in the gorgeous green countryside. They befriended Juan and one day invited him to eat with them.

The guajiros were roasting a homegrown suckling pig in a manner unlike any he had seen before: They quartered the pig, put it in a huge iron pot, covered it with lard, and cooked it over an open fire. Juan said it was lusciously tender and utterly greaseless.

This is how he reproduced the guajiros' recipe in my kitchen. Serve it with plenty of fluffy white rice, black beans, and fufú of Mashed Semiripe Plantains (page 188).

I tablespoon salt
5 pounds boneless pork loin
5 pounds pork lard, or enough to cover the meat

I teaspoon dry leaf oregano
4 bay leaves, crushed
½ cup Mojo Criollo (page 253)

1. Rub the salt into the pork and place the meat in a large dutch oven. Cover the pork completely with lard. Bring the lard to a boil over high heat.

2. Reduce the heat to medium, cover the pan, and cook at a slow boil for 2 hours. Make sure the meat is always well covered with lard so that no air reaches it; this prevents the meat from absorbing the lard.

3. Preheat the oven to 300 degrees.

4. Place a large colander over another large container and drain the pork, saving the lard for future use. Place the meat in a roasting pan. Sprinkle it with oregano and bay leaves, douse it with mojo, and roast it for 30 minutes.

5. Let the pork rest for 10 minutes before slicing.

COSTILLAS DE PUERCO CON MACHUQUILLO

(PORK CHOPS WITH MASHED PLANTAINS)

ॐ

6 servings

This Afro-Cuban dish was a favorite of Tía Catalina, one of my *tías políticas* (aunts-in-law, or by marriage). She was from a very refined family, and she turned up her nose at most hearty Cuban fare—black beans, garlicky vegetables, anything with plantains and the like—saying it was *comida ignoble*, ignoble food. As was the case with many wealthy Havana families, the kitchen in Tía Catalina's home had been run by a French chef since she was a child. But for some reason, when she was in our house she loved to eat the humble dish of fried pork chops served on a bed of machuquillo (mashed green plantains with cracklings). So I pass this recipe on to my readers with the assurance that it has met the snootiest standards!

6 pork chops, about 1 inch thick each
4 garlic cloves, peeled
1 teaspoon salt
¼ teaspoon ground black pepper
½ teaspoon dry leaf oregano

⅓ cup sour orange juice (or a 50-50 mixture of sweet orange juice and lime juice)
½ cup dry white wine
¼ cup vegetable oil
4 cups Machuquillo (page 188)

1. Trim the pork chops of any excess fat and place them in a container suitable for marinating.

2. Mash the garlic, salt, pepper, and oregano into a paste. (A mortar and pestle works best, but you may mince the garlic finely with a knife or put it through a garlic press and mash the seasonings in with a fork.) Mix the garlic paste with the orange juice and wine. Pour this marinade over the pork chops, cover them, and refrigerate for at least 1 hour and up to 4 hours. Blot the pork chops on paper towels. Reserve the marinade.

3. In a large skillet, warm the oil over medium heat and brown the pork chops on both sides.

4. Add the marinade, reduce the heat to low, and simmer, uncovered, for about an hour, or until all the liquid has evaporated. The pork chops should be thoroughly cooked and golden.

5. Serve on a bed of machuquillo.

This traditional Cuban snack is sold today in most Latin markets alongside plantain chips and other nibble foods. It was developed in the olden days as a way to make the fattiest, seemingly unusable parts of the pig into a crispy treat. I offer this old-fashioned recipe for nostalgic readers who wish to experiment, and for those who don't live where Latin foods are readily available. When purchasing a fresh ham (or any other part of the pig, for that matter), ask your butcher for the pig's skin.

CHICHARRONES DE PELLEJO

(CRISPY FRIED PORK RIND)

Boiling water   Lard for frying
Pig's skin   Salt

1. Bring a large pot of water to boil and immerse the pig's skin in it. Boil until the skin is swollen, about 15 minutes.

2. Drain the swollen rind on paper towels and when it is cool enough to handle, cut it into strips 1 inch wide and 3 to 4 inches long.

3. Place the strips of skin in a large, heavy skillet and cover them with cold lard. Warm the pan over medium heat, and once the lard begins to bubble, cook the skin for about 8 minutes. Raise the heat to medium-high for another minute or two and then to high for a minute or so, until the strips of skin are crispy and golden. Watch them carefully lest they burn.

4. Drain the chicharrones on paper towels and sprinkle them with salt if desired. Serve them warm or at room temperature.

My paternal grandfather, Miguel Lluriá y Rosell. He was one of the four founders of the Club Náutico. Varadero, 1916. *Author's collection*

MASITAS DE PUERCO FRITAS

(FRIED LITTLE PORK CHUNKS)

6 to 8 servings

In our house, my great-grandmother, Chicha, was the one who made masitas and its variation, carne de puerco frita con chicharrones. She was the one who supervised preparation of the suckling pig for festive occasions, and she also nurtured our love for traditional dishes such as this one.

2 pounds pork (flank or shoulder)
4 garlic cloves, peeled
1 teaspoon salt
½ teaspoon freshly ground pepper
1 teaspoon dry leaf oregano

½ cup sour orange juice (or a 50-50 mixture of sweet orange juice and lime juice)
¼ cup vegetable oil
½ cup water

1. Trim the meat of any excess fat and cut it into 2-inch chunks. Place it in a container suitable for marinating.

2. Mash the garlic, salt, pepper, and oregano into a paste. (A mortar and pestle works best, but you may mince the garlic finely with a knife or put it through a garlic press and mash the seasonings in with a fork.)

3. Combine the garlic paste with the orange juice. Pour the marinade over the pork, cover it, and refrigerate for about 1 hour.

4. Place the pork chunks in a large skillet with the oil and water. Discard the marinade. Fry the chops slowly over medium-low heat until the water has evaporated and the pork is tender and golden brown, about 2 hours.

VARIATION

Carne de Puerco Frita con Chicarrones: Cut 1 pound of pork fatback into 1-inch cubes and marinate along with the pork. Proceed as directed above. When the water has evaporated, the liquid lard will remain. (Once treasured by Cuban cooks, the lard can be reused if one is not worried about cholesterol.) The masitas will be tender and juicy and the chicharrones delightfully crisp. Remove them with a slotted spoon and drain on paper towels.

At *merienda* or tea time in Cuba, we sometimes had sandwiches as a snack. (We children especially loved *pan con timba*, which consisted simply of sliced guava paste between two pieces of bread.) Then, when Woolworth's opened its five and ten cent stores in Havana and other cities in the 1930s, it became fashionable to stop at *El Ten Cen* for a sandwich or other snack in the morning or afternoon, just *porque si*, for no special reason. But sandwiches never took the place of almuerzo, our full-course midday meal. Times change, of course, and today in Miami, sandwiches cubanos are a popular lunch on the go for cubanos and americanos alike.

Popular sandwiches are made from roast pork and beef steak, but perhaps the most popular is the *media noche*, the "midnight," which is made on a soft, sweet egg roll of the same name. If you are lucky enough to have access to a Cuban bakery, substitute that special roll for the bread in this recipe and you will have a media noche. If not, simply use French or Italian bread for a delicious facsimile of a Cuban sandwich.

SANDWICH CUBANO
(CUBAN SANDWICH)

I serving

One 8-inch piece of Cuban, French, or Italian bread, sliced lengthwise
Prepared mustard
1 or 2 thin slices roast pork
1 or 2 thin slices jamón en dulce (Cuban sweet ham) or plain baked or boiled ham

1 or 2 thin slices Gruyère or Swiss cheese
1 dill pickle, cut into long, thin slices
1 thin slice mortadella
Butter or margarine

1. If you have a sandwich press (a waffle iron with a griddle plate works well), preheat it. If not, warm a large, heavy skillet over medium heat.

2. Spread the inside of the bread lightly with mustard. Arrange the pork, ham, cheese, pickle, and mortadella, if desired, on the bread and close the sandwich. Spread the outside of the bread lightly with butter or margarine.

3. *Sandwich Press Method:* Close the press around the sandwich, compressing it somewhat, and let it toast until it is heated through and is lightly crispy on the outside.

4. *Skillet Method:* Place the sandwich in the skillet, and press it down with a flat, heavy object (I use a second, smaller cast-iron skillet). When the sandwich is lightly toasted on one side, turn it over and repeat.

PATAS CON GARBANZOS

(PIG'S FEET WITH CHICK-PEAS)

6 to 8 servings

This dish came to Cuba from Andalusia in the south of Spain, where many Cubans originated. In Spain it is served with bread, but in Cuba fluffy white rice is the starch of choice. Note that both the pig's feet and chick-peas must soak for 8 to 10 hours.

4 or 5 fresh pig's feet (about 3 pounds; ask the butcher to cut each into 4 pieces)
1 pound dried chick-peas
¼ pound salt pork, cubed
⅓ pound jamón de cocinar (raw ham), cubed, or prosciutto
2 small chorizos, sliced
4 strands saffron, toasted (see Note)
¼ cup hot Beef Broth (page 13)
4 medium potatoes, peeled and cubed

½ cup Spanish olive oil
1 large onion, peeled and chopped
1 medium green bell pepper, cored, seeded, and chopped
3 garlic cloves, peeled and minced
½ cup tomato sauce
1 teaspoon salt
½ teaspoon pepper
1 bay leaf
¾ cup raisins
¾ cup pitted green olives

1. Scrub the pig's feet well under cold running water. Place them in a large, heavy pot, cover them with water, and bring to a boil.

2. Remove the pot from the heat and let it cool to room temperature. Refrigerate the pig's feet—pot, water, and all—for 8 to 10 hours or overnight.

3. Place the chick-peas in a large container, cover them with

water, and soak them at room temperature for 8 to 10 hours or overnight. Drain the chick-peas and discard the water.

4. Place the pot containing the pig's feet on the stove over high heat. Add the chick-peas, salt pork, ham, and chorizos and bring to a boil. Continue boiling, stirring occasionally, for about 20 minutes, until the chick-peas are almost tender.

5. Mix the saffron with the hot beef broth and set it aside.

6. Add the potatoes to the pot and continue cooking until the potatoes and chick-peas are quite tender, about 20 minutes.

7. Meanwhile, heat the oil in a large skillet over medium heat. Sauté the onion and green pepper until the onion is translucent, about 3 minutes. Add the garlic and cook 2 minutes more. Stir in the tomato sauce, salt, pepper, bay leaf, and saffron beef broth. Simmer for a few minutes longer.

8. Add this sofrito to the pig's feet and chick-peas. Continue cooking over medium heat for about 15 minutes. Add the raisins and olives and simmer until the liquid thickens, about 5 minutes more.

9. Remove the bay leaf and serve.

NOTE: To toast saffron, place the strands in a dry skillet over medium heat for about 30 seconds, until they lose their moisture and can be crumbled into a powder.

BUTIFARRAS DE DON FAUSTINO DALMAU

(DON FAUSTINO DALMAU'S PORK SAUSAGES)

12 to 15 sausages

The best butifarras in my hometown—in fact, the best pork sausages I have eaten anywhere—were served at the Hotel La Dominica on the Parque de Colón, the central plaza of Cárdenas. On Sundays people gathered in the plaza to visit after morning Mass at the church of La Immaculada Concepción next door to the hotel. Many returned in the afternoon to hear the municipal band play from the *glorieta* or gazebo beside the statue of Christopher Columbus.

Even on weekdays, people congregated in the plaza to pass the time. The bar of La Dominica, which faced the main street, was a favorite spot for men to enjoy *tragos* (drinks) and ogle the passing ladies. They sometimes sampled the prized butifarras served as saladitos, or hors d'oeuvres, and many bought packages to take home.

Don Faustino Dalmau, the owner of the Hotel La Dominica, brought this recipe from his native Calaluña in the northeast of Spain and guarded it jealously all his life. His daughter-in-law, Nora Fernández Dalmau, is my friend and neighbor. After receiving permission from Don Faustino's sole surviving son, Rafael Dalmau, she shared this treasured family secret with me.

Don Faustino Dalmau and his wife Doña Matilde Treserra, proprietors of the restaurant in the Hotel La Dominica, which was renowned for its sausages. Cárdenas, circa 1935.
Nora Fernández Dalmau

3 yards pork tripe for sausage casing
2 sour oranges (or substitute one sweet orange and two limes)
3 limes
3 pounds ground pork (about 15 percent fat)

1 teaspoon salt
1 teaspoon freshly ground pepper
½ teaspoon nutmeg
½ cup vegetable oil

1. Using the handle of a wooden spoon or some other blunt instrument, turn the tripe inside out as you would a belt when sewing.

2. Squeeze the juice of the oranges and limes into a large pot. Then coarsely chop the fruit and add it, too. Add the tripe, cover it with water, and soak if for 12 to 18 hours. (There is no need to refrigerate it.)

3. Place the ground pork, salt, pepper, and nutmeg in a large mixing bowl and blend well.

4. Drain the tripe and stuff the meat mixture into it, twisting it every 6 inches and tying it with kitchen string. Discard the soaking liquid.

5. Bring a large pot of water to a boil. Place the sausages in it, lower the heat, and cook gently for 20 minutes. Drain the sausages and let them cool. Refrigerate or freeze them if you do not plan to cook them right away.

6. To cook the sausages, heat the oil in a large skillet over medium-low heat. Prick each sausage once or twice with a fine needle to let out any air, and fry them until nicely browned and cooked through.

QUESO DE CABEZA DE PUERCO
(PIG'S HEAD CHEESE)

10 servings

Head cheese resembles paté and is just as delicious as the most elegant paté de fois gras. It makes a lovely appetizer when served on a bed of lettuce with crackers or thinly sliced fresh bread. Nowadays many people avoid pork for health reasons, but my great-grandmother, Chicha, who lived to celebrate her 103rd birthday, loved this dish and ate it with abandon. This recipe requires some rather involved butchering that a good butcher will do for you.

1 pig's head
3 slices of dry Cuban or French bread
1 cup dry white wine
1½ pounds lean pork cut into large chunks
½ teaspoon nutmeg
4 teaspoons salt

½ teaspoon freshly ground pepper
2 carrots, peeled
2 sprigs parsley
1 bay leaf
3 medium onions, peeled
2 garlic cloves, peeled
6 peppercorns

1. Entering through the neck with a small, sharp knife, carefully clean and debone the pig's head without tearing the skin. Remove and discard all excess fat. Cut off and discard the ears and snout. Remove the tongue and set it aside.

2. Wash the head and tongue under cold running water to remove any blood. Cut the tongue into large chunks.

3. Put the bread to soak in the wine.

4. In a food processor, finely grind the chunks of pork and tongue with the nutmeg, 3 teaspoons of the salt, and the pepper. Add the bread and wine, and process until well mixed.

5. With a heavy needle and thread, sew the ear and snout openings shut. Stuff the head with the meat mixture and sew the neck opening shut. Wrap the head in cheesecloth and tie it securely with kitchen string.

6. Place the head in a large, heavy pot. Cover it with water and add the carrots, parsley, bay leaf, onions, garlic, peppercorns, and the remaining teaspoon of salt. Bring to a boil. Lower the heat, cover, and simmer for 3 hours.

7. Remove the pork head from the poaching broth and place it, still wrapped, in a large mixing bowl. Discard the broth. Place a heavy weight on top of the head (I use a large can of tomatoes placed inside another bowl) in order to flatten it. Cover it with plastic wrap and refrigerate overnight.

8. Remove the cloth.

9. Cut into slices to serve. (Each slice of head cheese will be surrounded by a sort of tender rind created by the skin.)

Pollo y Otras Aves (Chicken and Other Fowl)

POLLO Y OTRAS AVES (Chicken and Other Fowl)

*W*hen I was growing up there was no such thing as a chicken bought at a store already dressed and ready to cook. At home, chickens were always killed on the premises. I can still see the cook with her strong arm, twisting the neck of a chicken in our backyard, taking it to the kitchen, dipping it in boiling water, and taking it out again to pluck its feathers and disembowel it. Every part of the fowl was used. When a whole chicken was roasted, the giblets, the neck (all the way up to the head), and even the feet were made into broth.

"Free range" chickens are all the rage these days, but I learned years ago that chickens allowed to run about freely produced the best-tasting meat. And since our chickens were not restricted to the chicken coop, neither were they restricted to a specific diet. They were fed dry yellow corn, but in their wanderings about the yard they found bits of vegetation and little insects to supplement their diet. I am convinced that this further enriched the flavor of their meat and eggs. The only time I have ever found myself in agreement with Fidel Castro was in 1960 when he brought live chickens from Cuba to eat in New York while he visited the United Nations!

As for game birds, they were my father's province exclusively. After fishing, hunting was his favorite sport. When he came home carrying on his shoulders the *ahorcadera* (leather hunting strap) hung with pigeons and quails in bananalike bunches, he was a terror to the cook.

He would demand that the tiny fowl be plucked and cleaned immediately, and in what seemed an instant, feathers were flying all over the backyard. When they cleared, we knew we could look forward to a truly magnificent feast.

My cousins, friends, and I (far right) on the beach in front of the Club Náutico. Varadero, 1936. *Author's collection*

My sister Sofi gave me this recipe. Like my sister Ina, Sofi lives in Mexico now. Both of my sisters still cook old Cuba classic food no matter where they are. This recipe is simple, but delicious. Serve it with white rice to soak up the savory sauce.

¼ cup vegetable oil

One 6-pound roasting chicken, rinsed and patted dry

1 large onion, peeled and sliced in thin rings

2 bay leaves

1 cinnamon stick

15 garlic cloves, peeled and finely chopped

½ teaspoon salt

¼ teaspoon pepper

1 cup dry white wine

½ cup Cognac

POLLO ASADO EN CAZUELA
(PAN-ROASTED CHICKEN)

4 to 6 servings

1. In a large dutch oven, warm the oil over medium heat and brown the chicken well on all sides.

2. Add the onion and sauté until it is translucent, about 3 minutes. Stir in the bay leaves, cinnamon, garlic, salt, and pepper, and cook gently for 2 minutes more.

3. Pour in the wine and Cognac, reduce the heat to medium-low, and pan-roast the chicken, partially covered, for 1½ hours, basting every ½ hour.

4. Remove the bay leaves, transfer the chicken to a serving dish, and serve the cooking liquid on the side.

POLLO FRITO A LA CRIOLLA

(CUBAN CREOLE FRIED CHICKEN)

8 servings

In Cuba, chicken was never fried in a batter as is so popular in this country; it was marinated in sour orange juice and fried crispy and golden. These days in Miami there are chains of fast-food restaurants where Cuban entrepreneurs serve chicken fried in this traditional manner with rice, beans, plantains, yuca, and other Cuban side dishes.

5 garlic cloves, peeled
I teaspoon salt
½ teaspoon freshly ground pepper
I teaspoon dry leaf oregano
½ teaspoon ground cumin
½ cup sour orange juice (or a 50-50 mixture of sweet orange juice and lime juice)

2 chickens, about 2 pounds each, cut into serving pieces
½ large onion, peeled and sliced
½ cup vegetable oil

I. Mash the garlic with the salt, pepper, oregano, and cumin. (A mortar and pestle works best, but you may mince the garlic finely with a knife or put it through a garlic press and mash the seasonings in with a fork.) Stir in the orange juice and set aside.

2. Place the chicken pieces in a single layer in a glass or ceramic baking dish. Arrange the onion slices over them and pour on the marinade. Cover with plastic wrap and refrigerate I to 2 hours. Drain the chicken and blot it on paper towels. Discard the marinade.

3. Warm the oil over medium heat in a large skillet and fry the chicken pieces for 15 to 20 minutes on each side, until golden and cooked through.

4. Serve hot.

My niece María Verónica Lluriá Zúñiga, whom we call Ronnie, is the creator of this delectable dish. She may have been inspired by boliche mechado, roasted eye-of-round roast with black bean purée, but her chicken version is even more enticing. Serve it with fluffy white rice.

½ cup sour orange juice (or a 50-50 mixture of sweet orange juice and lime juice or vinegar)
2 garlic cloves, peeled and minced
I teaspoon salt
½ teaspoon freshly ground pepper
¼ teaspoon dry leaf oregano
One 4-pound chicken, cut into serving pieces
3 tablespoons vegetable oil

I small onion, peeled and chopped
I medium green bell pepper, cored, seeded, and chopped
I cup tomato sauce
I bay leaf
¼ cup dry white wine
I cup black bean purée (canned or homemade, see Frijoles Negros, page 150)

POLLO CON PURÉ DE FRIJOLES NEGROS

(CHICKEN WITH BLACK BEAN PURÉE)

❧

4 to 6 servings

I. Combine the orange juice, garlic, salt, pepper, and oregano in a container suitable for marinating. Add the chicken pieces to the marinade, cover, and refrigerate at least 8 hours or overnight. Blot the chicken on paper towels. Reserve the marinade.

2. In a large, heavy skillet, heat the oil over medium-high heat and brown the chicken on both sides. Blot the pieces on paper towels again.

3. Reduce the heat to medium, add the onion and green pepper, and sauté until the onion is translucent, about 3 minutes.

4. Return the chicken pieces to the skillet. Add the reserved marinade, tomato sauce, bay leaf, and wine. Bring the sauce to a boil, then lower the heat, cover, and simmer for about I hour, until the chicken is tender.

5. About 5 minutes before serving, remove the bay leaf, stir in the black bean purée, and allow the sauce to simmer briefly.

6. Transfer the chicken to a serving dish and spoon the sauce over it.

FRICASÉ DE POLLO

(CUBAN-STYLE CHICKEN FRICASSEE)

8 servings

This is one of many Andalusian dishes introduced to our home by my father's mother, Abuela Carmela. My mother served it often. Though she had been raised in the traditions of her Basque and Catalonian ancestors, she enthusiastically adopted her mother-in-law's ways.

½ cup sour orange juice (or a 50-50 mixture of sweet orange juice and lime juice)
4 garlic cloves, peeled and minced
1½ teaspoons salt
½ teaspoon freshly ground pepper
4 pounds chicken thighs, legs, and breasts, skinned
⅓ cup vegetable oil
2 large onions, peeled and chopped

1 large green bell pepper, cored, seeded, and chopped
1 cup tomato sauce
1 cup dry white wine
¼ cup capers
½ cup stuffed green olives
½ cup raisins
1 pound potatoes, peeled and cubed

1. Combine the orange juice, garlic, salt, and pepper in a container suitable for marinating the chicken. Add the chicken pieces to the marinade, cover, and refrigerate 1 to 2 hours. Remove the chicken and blot it on paper towels. Reserve the marinade.

2. Warm the oil in a large dutch oven over medium heat and brown the chicken.

3. Add the onions and green pepper and sauté them with the chicken until the onions are translucent, about 3 minutes. Add the tomato sauce, wine, reserved marinade, capers, olives, raisins, and potatoes. Reduce the heat to low, cover the pan, and simmer for 30 minutes.

4. Transfer the chicken to a serving dish and spoon the sauce over it.

My mother had a sweet tooth. She used to heap sugar into her coffee with abandon and she adored desserts of all sorts. Even in main courses, she relished a touch of sweetness. After Mamá was no longer with us, I found among her rosaries and other precious belongings this recipe, written in her mother-in-law's hand. No wonder she treasured it; the prunes, brown sugar, and sherry impart a delightful sweetness to the chicken that is offset by the saltiness of the capers and olives.

This is an ideal party dish because it can easily be made ahead of time in large quantities. I have often prepared it the night before, leaving only the cooking to an hour and a half before dinner.

PECHUGAS DE POLLA A LA ANDALUZA
(ANDALUSIAN CHICKEN BREASTS)

I head of garlic, cloves peeled and minced

¼ cup dry leaf oregano

I teaspoon salt

2 teaspoons freshly ground pepper

¾ cup vegetable oil

½ cup red wine vinegar

I cup pitted prunes left whole

½ cup stuffed green olives left whole

2 red bell peppers, cored, seeded, and sliced lengthwise

5 bay leaves

½ cup capers

2 tablespoons lime juice

10 chicken breasts, boned, skinned, and split

I cup dry sherry

I cup packed brown sugar

¼ cup finely chopped parsley

½ cup slivered almonds, lightly toasted

I. In a container suitable for marinating the chicken, combine the garlic, oregano, salt, pepper, oil, vinegar, prunes, olives, red bell peppers, bay leaves, capers, and lime juice. Immerse the chicken breasts in this marinade, cover, and refrigerate 8 to 12 hours.

2. An hour and a half before serving time, preheat the oven to 325 degrees.

3. Place the chicken in a single layer in a large baking dish (I use a paella pan). Remove the bay leaves and pour the marinade over the chicken. Place the peppers on top. Cover the pan tightly with foil and bake for I hour.

4. Remove the pan from the oven and uncover it. Pour the sherry over the chicken and sprinkle on the brown sugar. Return the pan, uncovered, to the oven for 15 minutes, or until the brown sugar is crispy. (Be careful not to burn it.)

5. Garnish the chicken with parsley and almonds, and serve with fluffy white rice.

BISTEQUITOS DE POLLO
(CHICKEN STEAKS)

4 servings

My neighborhood Cuban diner in Miami, El 20 de Mayo (named for Cuba's Independence Day), makes an especially good chicken-breast steak that takes only minutes to prepare. The hospitable cook not only wrote down the recipe for me but invited me into the tiny, spotless kitchen to watch her make it.

4 teaspoons Mojo Criollo (page 253)
4 teaspoons freshly squeezed lime juice
½ teaspoon salt
¼ teaspoon freshly ground pepper
4 garlic cloves, peeled and minced

4 boneless chicken breasts, skinned and flattened with a meat mallet
1 tablespoon vegetable oil
1 large onion, peeled and sliced in thin rings
2 tablespoons butter

1. In a container suitable for marinating, combine the mojo criollo, lime juice, salt, pepper, and garlic. Add the chicken to this marinade, cover it, and refrigerate 25 minutes to 1 hour.

2. Heat the oil in a small skillet over medium heat and sauté the onion until wilted.

3. Heat the butter over medium-high heat on a griddle or in a large skillet.

4. Remove the chicken from the marinade and blot it on paper towels. Discard the marinade. Sauté the chicken in the hot butter for 3 to 4 minutes per side, or until it is nicely golden and cooked through.

5. Transfer the chicken to individual plates, and garnish it with the onion rings.

Most Americans are more familiar with Italian cannelloni than Spanish canelones, but Spaniards have been eating these stuffed pasta tubes for centuries, and Cubans have been enjoying them since colonial times.

This recipe is from La Reguladora, a Havana restaurant that was a favorite of tobacco magnates. La Reguladora was as well known for its delicious canelones as for its distinguished clientele. This recipe was given to me by my sister-in-law, Carmita Diaz, whose family dined there on special occasions. Carmita has modernized it by using a blender, a food processor, frozen spinach, and packaged pasta (she uses manicotti when she cannot find cannelloni). You may, of course, use homemade cannelloni, as we did in Cuba, or fresh ones from a specialty store.

¼ cup plus 2 tablespoons vegetable oil

1 large onion, peeled and chopped

½ teaspoon dry leaf oregano

1 bay leaf

1 cup tomato sauce

2 cups coarsely chopped roasted chicken meat

½ calf brain (optional)

One 10-ounce package frozen chopped spinach, thawed and drained (or 1 pound fresh spinach)

1½ cups Heavy Béchamel (page 254), onion omitted

1 tablespoon salt

One 12-ounce package cannelloni or manicotti shells

1½ cups Light Béchamel (page 254), onion omitted

½ cup freshly grated Parmesan cheese

1. Warm ¼ cup of the oil in a saucepan over medium heat and sauté the onion until translucent, about 5 minutes. Add the oregano, bay leaf, and tomato sauce and simmer for about 15 minutes. Remove the bay leaf and set the sauce aside.

2. In a food processor, grind the chicken, brain, and spinach into a paste. Stir it together with the heavy béchamel sauce and set it aside.

3. Fill a large stock pot with water, add the salt and 1 tablespoon of the oil, and bring it to a rapid boil over high heat. Drop in the cannelloni, one by one, and boil until barely tender, about 5 minutes. Drain them and set them aside on a damp towel to cool.

4. Preheat the oven to 400 degrees. Spread the remaining 1 tablespoon of oil in the bottom of a 9-by-13-inch baking dish.

5. Spoon the chicken filling into the cannelloni, and arrange them in a single layer in the baking dish. (If any break, patch them together and place them patched sides down.)

6. Cover the cannelloni with the reserved tomato sauce and then the light béchamel sauce. Sprinkle on the Parmesan cheese.

7. Bake for about 10 minutes, until barely golden.

PASTEL DE POLLO Y MAÍZ
(CHICKEN PIE WITH CORN)

6 to 8 servings

This spectacular dish is one of my sister Ina's favorites. Although she now lives in Mexico and has learned many recipes from that country's extensive cuisine, she still clings to her preference for our old Cuban classics.

16 ears fresh sweet corn (or 4 cups well-drained canned or frozen corn kernels)

8 tablespoons (1 stick) plus 1 teaspoon unsalted butter

1 tablespoon sugar

1 tablespoon salt

½ cup hot Chicken Broth (page 13)

12 pitted prunes, left whole or sliced

3 tablespoons vegetable oil

1 large onion, peeled and finely chopped

3 cups crushed tomatoes

1 teaspoon freshly ground pepper

3 cups cubed, cooked chicken breast meat

½ cup pimiento-stuffed olives, left whole or sliced

1 tablespoon capers

4 egg yolks

2 hard-boiled eggs, sliced

⅓ cup slivered almonds

1. Husk the corn, and cut the kernels from the cobs with a sharp knife.

2. Purée the corn kernels in a blender or food processor.

3. In a large skillet over medium heat, melt the stick of butter. Stir in the corn purée, sugar, and 1 teaspoon of the salt. Turn the heat to low and simmer, stirring constantly, for about 20 minutes, until

the purée is very thick and pulls away easily from the sides of the pan. Set it aside to cool.

4. Pour the hot broth over the prunes and set them aside to soak.

5. In another large skillet, heat the oil over medium heat and sauté the onion until limp, about 2 minutes. Stir in the tomatoes, pepper, and the remaining 2 teaspoons of salt. Lower the heat and simmer for about 3 minutes. Stir in the prunes and broth, the chicken, olives, and capers. Remove from the heat.

6. Grease a 2-quart baking dish with the remaining teaspoon of butter. Preheat the oven to 350 degrees.

7. Beat the egg yolks until lemon-colored and stir them into the corn purée until well blended.

8. Pour half the purée into the baking dish and spread it evenly over the bottom and sides. Pour in the chicken mixture and smooth it with a spatula. Layer on the egg slices and spread on the remaining corn purée.

9. Bake for 45 minutes. Remove the pie from the oven, top it with the almonds, and bake it for about 10 minutes more, just until the almonds are toasted. Serve immediately.

PASTEL DE POLLO CON MASA REAL
(CHICKEN PIE WITH ROYAL CRUST)

8 servings

This dish has become so standard for festive occasions in Cuban communities that there are enterprising caterers in Miami who specialize in it. It is especially popular on feast days—the day in the church calendar on which a person's namesake saint ascended to heaven. In Cuba years ago, it was customary on certain feast days to serenade the celebrants—all the Juans or Johns on June 24, for instance.

Pastel de pollo is too rich to eat often but, as they say, "*Un día es un día, como el día de tu Santo*"—"There is only one day like your feast day." And one needn't trouble one's conscience over a rare indulgence.

Though pastel de pollo takes several hours to make, the filling and crust can be made a day ahead of time and refrigerated to ease preparation.

FOR THE FILLING:

4 garlic cloves, peeled
1½ teaspoons salt
½ teaspoon freshly ground pepper
½ cup sour orange juice (or a
    50-50 mixture of sweet orange
    juice and lime juice)
2 pounds boneless, skinless chicken
    breast, cut in 1-inch cubes
⅓ cup vegetable oil
1 large onion, peeled and chopped
1 large green pepper, cored, seeded,
    and chopped
½ cup tomato sauce
1 cup dry white wine
2 tablespoons capers
⅓ cup stuffed green olives, left
    whole or sliced
⅓ cup raisins
⅓ cup blanched toasted almonds

FOR THE CRUST:

4 cups flour
½ cup sugar
2 teaspoons baking powder
1 teaspoon salt
8 tablespoons (1 stick) butter
½ cup lard (or substitute solid
    vegetable shortening)
4 egg yolks
¼ cup dry white wine
1 teaspoon grated lemon zest
⅛ teaspoon grated nutmeg
1 beaten egg (optional)

MAKE THE FILLING:

1. Mash the garlic, salt, and pepper into a paste. (A mortar and pestle works best, but you may mince the garlic finely with a knife or put it through a garlic press and mash the seasonings in with a fork.) Stir the garlic paste into the orange juice.

2. Place the chicken pieces in a large glass mixing bowl and pour the marinade over them. Cover and refrigerate for at least 1 hour. Remove the chicken and blot it dry on paper towels. Reserve the marinade.

3. Heat the oil in a large, heavy skillet over medium heat and brown the chicken.

4. Stir in the onion and green pepper and sauté until the onion is translucent, about 3 minutes. Stir in the tomato sauce, wine, capers, olives, raisins, almonds, and the reserved marinade. Cover the pan, reduce the heat, and simmer for 30 minutes.

5. Remove the filling from the heat and allow to cool while you make the crust.

MAKE THE CRUST:

1. Sift the flour, sugar, baking powder, and salt together into a mixing bowl.

2. Work the butter and lard into the flour mixture with two knives or a pastry blender until it looks like crumbs.

3. Make a well in the center and pour in the egg yolks, wine, lemon zest, and nutmeg. Continue working with the knives and then your hands, just until blended.

4. Divide the dough into two equal balls. Place each on a floured square of waxed paper and roll into a circle about ½ inch thick and 12 inches in diameter.

COMPLETE THE DISH:

1. Preheat the oven to 425 degrees.

2. Place one circle of dough in a 9-inch pie pan so that ½ inch of the dough hangs over the sides, and spoon in the filling.

3. Top the filling with the second circle of dough. Trim the edges and seal them by scoring with the tines of a fork. Make a few slashes in the top to let out the steam. If you like a shiny crust, brush the top with beaten egg.

4. Bake for 10 minutes. Reduce the temperature to 350 degrees and continue baking for about 35 minutes more, until the crust is golden.

PAVO RELLENO DE MAMÁ

(MAMÁ'S STUFFED TURKEY)

❧

25 to 30 servings

Lechón asado or roast suckling pig takes center stage at a Cuban Christmas feast, but in our home guinea hens or turkey sometimes accompanied the pork. This turkey was my mother's favorite; although classically Cuban, its delicious filling is much more delicate than the pork liver and sausage stuffing served in other homes.

Mamá favored the delicate, even dainty things of life. She was cultured and refined and her food was similarly discreet. While Papá's dishes were abundantly flavorful and pungent, hers tended to be subtly seasoned with aromatic spices and fruits.

This stuffing is typical of her recipes, its delicacy reminiscent of her quiet dignity.

One 20-pound turkey
7 garlic cloves, peeled
1¼ teaspoons salt
1 teaspoon freshly ground
  pepper
1 cup sour orange juice (or a 50-50
  mixture of sweet orange juice
  and lime juice)
1 bay leaf
1 carrot, peeled
2 cups water
2 tablespoons butter

2 large onions, peeled and chopped
4 cups coarse bread crumbs, pulled
  by hand from a fresh loaf
1 cup milk
1 cup dry white wine
1 cup peeled, roasted chestnuts
1 cup coarsely chopped jamón de
  cocinar (raw ham) or prosciutto
¼ teaspoon nutmeg
1 cup blanched and peeled
  almonds
2 cups raisins

1. Remove the giblets and refrigerate. Rinse the turkey under cold running water, pat it dry, and place it, breast up, in a large roasting pan.

2. Mash 6 of the garlic cloves into a paste with 1 teaspoon each of the salt and pepper. (A mortar and pestle works best, but you may mince the garlic finely with a knife or put it through a garlic press and mash the seasonings in with a fork.)

3. Mix the orange juice with the garlic paste and pour it over the turkey, inside and out. Cover the turkey with plastic wrap and refrigerate it for at least 3 hours.

4. While the turkey is marinating, rinse the giblets and place them in a small saucepan with the remaining garlic clove, the bay leaf, carrot, water, and ¼ teaspoon salt. Bring to a boil, reduce the heat to medium, and cook about 1 hour, until the gizzard, the toughest of the giblets, is tender. Strain the giblets and set aside; refrigerate the broth.

5. In a large skillet, melt the butter over medium heat and sauté the onions until translucent, about 3 minutes. Remove them from the heat.

6. Put the bread crumbs to soak with the milk and wine in a large mixing bowl.

7. In a food processor, grind the cooked giblets, chestnuts, and ham into a paste.

8. Stir the onions, the giblet mixture, nutmeg, almonds, and raisins into the soaked bread, mixing well.

9. Preheat the oven to 350 degrees.

10. Remove the plastic wrap from the turkey and fill the body cavity with the stuffing. Close it securely by sewing it with a needle and thick thread or by using skewers and crisscrossed string.

11. Roast the turkey, basting it often, for about 6½ hours, or until the juices run clear when you pierce a thigh with a knife.

12. Remove the turkey from the oven and let it stand for about 20 minutes before carving.

PICHONES DE MI PAPÁ

(MY FATHER'S PIGEONS)

❧

8 servings

This is another of the typical Andalusian recipes my father learned from his mother, the ever joyful Abuela Carmela. Like the other recipes for game birds in this chapter, it calls for a substantial amount of fat; the meat is dry and needs the added moisture. Today, I use canola oil instead of lard. You can prepare quail, partridge, pheasant, or Cornish hens in this manner, too.

½ cup sour orange juice (or a 50-50 mixture of sweet orange juice and lime juice)
1 teaspoon salt
1 teaspoon freshly ground pepper
8 pigeons, plucked and cleaned
½ cup lard or vegetable oil

8 slices Cuban or French bread
40 blanched and peeled almonds
8 large onions, peeled and chopped
3 garlic cloves, peeled and minced
¼ cup tomato sauce
2 cups Chicken Broth (page 13)
1 cup dry red wine

1. Combine the orange juice, salt, and pepper in a container suitable for marinating. Place the pigeons in the marinade, cover, and refrigerate 1 to 2 hours.

2. In a large dutch oven, melt the lard over medium heat.

3. Remove the pigeons from the marinade and pat them dry with paper towels. Discard the marinade. Brown the birds one by one in the hot lard and set them aside.

4. In the same pan, fry the bread slices until browned on both sides and set them aside on paper towels to drain. Sauté the almonds until golden and transfer them to paper towels. Using a mortar and pestle or a food processor, mash the bread and almonds into a paste and set it aside.

5. Sauté the onions until translucent, about 3 minutes. Return the birds to the pan. Add the garlic and cook 2 minutes more. Stir in the tomato sauce, broth, and wine. Cover the pan, reduce the heat to low, and simmer for about 2 hours, until the birds are tender.

6. Transfer the cooked pigeons to a serving dish and cover with foil to keep warm.

7. Stir the bread mixture into the pan juices and cook over low

heat. When the sauce has thickened, spoon it over and around the pigeons.

8. Serve immediately with fluffy white rice.

This was another of my father's favorite recipes. Serve it with fluffy white rice.

PERDICES CON ACEITUNAS

(PARTRIDGES WITH OLIVES)

6 servings

4 garlic cloves, peeled
I teaspoon salt
¼ teaspoon freshly ground pepper
I teaspoon dry leaf oregano
I teaspoon dry leaf thyme
¼ cup sour orange juice (or a 50-50 mixture of sweet orange juice and lime juice)

I cup dry white wine
2 tablespoons white wine vinegar
6 partridges, plucked and cleaned
I cup lard or vegetable oil
I bay leaf
2 cups Chicken Broth (page 13)
20 pitted green olives, sliced

1. Mash the garlic, salt, pepper, oregano, and thyme into a paste. (A mortar and pestle works best, but you may mince the garlic finely with a knife or put it through a garlic press and mash the seasonings in with a fork.)

2. Combine the garlic paste with the orange juice, wine, and vinegar in a container suitable for marinating. Place the birds in the marinade, cover, and refrigerate 1 to 2 hours.

3. Melt the lard over medium-high heat in a large dutch oven.

4. Remove the birds from the marinade and pat them dry with paper towels. Reserve the marinade. Brown the partridges one by one.

5. When the last bird is browned, return them all to the pan and add the bay leaf, broth, reserved marinade, and olives. Reduce the heat to low, cover the pan, and cook for about 1 hour or until the birds are tender.

6. Transfer the partridges to a serving dish. Remove the bay leaf and ladle the sauce over the birds.

AVES DE JUAN DIEZ ARGÜELLES

(JUAN DIEZ ARGÜELLES' FOWL)

4 servings

My cousin's husband, Juan Diez Argüelles, is a formidable hunter of game birds in this country, as he was in Cuba, but it is only in exile that he has developed his prodigious talents as a cook. His recipe for pheasants employs the same seasoning, with little variation, that was used in Cuba for game birds. Quail, pigeon, partridge, duck, and even Cornish hen are delicious prepared this way.

¼ cup minced onion
6 garlic cloves, peeled and minced
1 tablespoon freshly ground pepper
1 tablespoon salt
4 bay leaves
2 teaspoons dry leaf oregano
1 teaspoon ground cumin
¼ cup Worcestershire sauce
½ cup dry red wine
¼ cup dry white wine
¾ cup water

4 pheasant breasts, boned
3 cups lard or vegetable oil
1 bunch green onions, chopped
1 medium red onion, peeled and chopped
1 large green bell pepper, cored, seeded, and chopped
4 tablespoons (½ stick) unsalted butter
8 ounces fresh mushrooms, sliced

1. Combine the onion, 2 minced garlic cloves, pepper, salt, bay leaves, oregano, cumin, Worcestershire sauce, red and white wines, and water in a container suitable for marinating. Place the pheasant breasts in this marinade, cover them, and refrigerate for 24 hours, turning several times.

2. Melt the lard over medium-high heat in a large dutch oven.

3. Remove the breasts from the marinade and pat them dry with paper towels. Reserve the marinade. Brown the pheasant on both sides and set it aside.

4. Drain all but ½ cup of the hot lard from the pan. (Be careful not to burn yourself.) Sauté the green and red onions and green pepper until the onions are translucent, about 3 minutes. Add the remaining 4 minced garlic cloves, reduce the heat to low, and cook for 2 minutes more.

5. Return the breasts to the dutch oven. Strain the marinade over them and cook, uncovered, for 10 minutes.

6. Meanwhile, melt the butter in a skillet over medium heat and sauté the mushrooms until golden. Add the mushrooms and their sautéing juices to the dutch oven. Cover the pan and simmer the pheasant breasts until they are tender, about 2 hours.

7. Transfer the breasts to individual plates and ladle the sauce over them.

My mother and father on their honeymoon. New York City, 1917.
Author's collection

ARROCES (RICE ENTRÉES)

Arroces (Rice Entrées)

$\mathcal{C}$ubans inherited their love of rice from Eastern and Western influences alike. From the Chinese we acquired a taste for—I would even say a dependence on—white rice as an accompaniment at almost every meal. And from the Spanish we learned to make delectable entrées that combine yellow rice with a great variety of ingredients, from chorizo to seafood.

A transgression committed by Anglo- and Cuban-American cooks alike is to use long-grain rice to cook Spanish-style yellow rice dishes. In Spain, arroz de Valencia is used for all purposes and to substitute long-grain rice for short-grain Valencia rice is a culinary mortal sin!

A note about pans: It is not necessary to have a *paellera*—the wide, shallow, metal pan used in Spain—to make the rice dishes in this chapter. A shallow, flameproof casserole about 16 inches in diameter will do nicely. Cubans like to use an earthenware variety that cooks well and is attractive for serving. You may use a large skillet or sauté pan, though you will want to transfer your creation to a serving dish in that case.

As far as his family and many friends were concerned, my father made the best paella ever, and one of his grandsons has followed in his footsteps. My nephew Miguel Lluriá V, whom we call Mikie, is an accomplished cook who makes a really spectacular paella. This recipe is for his seafood version, but "when the mood strikes me," he says, "I also add pork and chicken." If the mood strikes you, sauté the meat in the oil before making the sofrito and return it to the pan before adding the seafood to allow it time to cook through.

PAELLA DE MIKIE LLURIÁ

(MIKIE LLURIÁ'S PAELLA)

6 servings

FOR THE BROTH:

2 live lobsters, about I pound each
12 jumbo shrimp
I fish head, quartered (optional)
I carrot, peeled
I small onion, peeled
½ medium green bell pepper, cored and seeded
2 garlic cloves, peeled
I bay leaf
I tablespoon salt
6 peppercorns

TO COMPLETE THE DISH:

½ cup Spanish olive oil
I medium onion, peeled and finely chopped
½ medium green bell pepper, cored, seeded, and finely chopped
3 garlic cloves, peeled and minced
I bay leaf
2 tomatoes, peeled and chopped (or ½ cup canned tomato sauce)
4 strands saffron, toasted in a dry skillet over medium heat for 30 seconds or until they lose their moisture
2 cups Valencia (short-grain) rice
6 fresh or frozen squid, cleaned and cut into thin rings (see Note)
18 or 20 small raw clams
4 to 6 raw stone crab claws
½ cup dry white wine
½ cup canned petit pois (tiny peas) or small frozen peas, thawed
One 6-ounce jar pimientos, drained

TO MAKE THE BROTH:

1. Remove the tails from the lobsters. Leaving the shells on, cut the tails into pieces at their natural sections. Refrigerate the tail pieces and put the lobster bodies in a large stock pot.

2. Shell and devein the shrimp and refrigerate them. Add the shells to the stock pot.

3. Add 4½ cups of water to the stock pot along with the fish head, carrot, onion, green pepper, garlic, bay leaf, salt, and peppercorns. Bring to a boil, lower the heat, and simmer, covered, for 1 hour. Strain the broth and set it aside; you should have about 4 cups. Discard the shells and other solids.

TO COMPLETE THE DISH:

1. In a paellera or other wide, shallow pan, heat the oil over medium heat until fragrant. Sauté the onion and green pepper until the onion is translucent, about 3 minutes. Add the garlic and cook 2 minutes more. Stir in the bay leaf, tomatoes, and saffron, and cook for a few minutes longer.

2. Stir in the rice, and pour in the reserved broth. Bring it to a boil and cook, uncovered, over medium-high heat for about 10 minutes, until the rice begins to "open up."

3. Add the reserved lobster tails, the squid, clams, crab claws, and reserved shrimp, burying them in the rice. Pour in the wine and continue to cook, uncovered, for about 20 minutes, until the rice has absorbed most of the liquid.

4. Remove the paella from the heat, cover it loosely with aluminum foil, and let it rest for about 15 minutes.

5. Just before serving, heat the peas and pimientos (it takes about 30 seconds in the microwave) and use them to garnish the paella.

NOTE: Directions for cleaning fresh squid are found on page 59. If you are able to find it, freeze the precious ink for use in Calamares en su Tinta (page 59).

What is essential for this dish, as for all seafood dishes, is absolute freshness. Buy your fish from a reliable fishmonger, and even then, look at the fish to make sure its gills are bright red and its eyes are not sunken. In Cuba, we always saw the fish jumping before it was cooked, and that is still the best way.

2 pounds snapper or grouper steaks
¼ cup freshly squeezed lime juice
¼ cup Spanish olive oil
1 large onion, peeled and chopped
1 large green bell pepper, cored, seeded, and chopped
4 garlic cloves, peeled and minced
½ cup flour
1 teaspoon salt
½ teaspoon freshly ground pepper
¼ cup chopped parsley
4 strands saffron, toasted in a dry skillet over medium heat for about 30 seconds or until they lose their moisture
¼ cup tomato purée
2 cups Valencia (short-grain) rice
2¾ cups Fish Broth (page 13)
One 6-ounce jar pimientos, drained and liquid reserved

1. Place the fish in a container suitable for marinating. Pour the lime juice over it, cover, and refrigerate for 1 hour.

2. Heat the oil over medium heat in a paellera or large skillet (I use an earthenware pan). Sauté the onion and green pepper until the onion is translucent, about 3 minutes. Stir in the garlic and cook for 2 minutes more.

3. Mix the flour with the salt, pepper, and parsley, and dredge the fish steaks in it. Place the fish in the simmering sofrito and gently cook it for about 2 minutes on each side. Remove the fish and set it aside.

4. Add the saffron, tomato purée, rice, and broth to the sofrito. Stir lightly and simmer on low heat, uncovered, until the rice begins to dry, about 25 minutes.

5. Return the fish steaks to the pan and pour in the liquid from the canned pimientos. Turn off the heat, cover the pan, and let the rice finish cooking on the warm burner, about 10 minutes. Add a little more broth if the mixture is too dry.

6. Cut the pimientos into strips and garnish the finished dish with them.

ARROZ CON ALMEJAS
(RICE WITH CLAMS)

≈

6 to 8 servings

In Varadero, we used to collect our beloved *almejitas* (little clams) on the sand right where the waves broke. These triangular mollusks were about an inch long at the largest part of the shell, and inside, the edible part was only about the size of a child's little fingernail. When each had his or her little bucket full, we children brought the clams home to the cook, who would make our favorite arroz con almejas. We felt so important, as though we were real food providers like Papá.

Rice with clams is not easy to eat gracefully. One must have patience and not worry about messy fingers, for although the clams open when cooked, they are covered with rice and hard to get at with a fork and knife. I suggest finger bowls at each place setting, and plenty of paper napkins.

3 pounds cherrystone clams (in my childhood, 3 toy buckets full) or 1 pound littleneck clams
3 garlic cloves, peeled
1 teaspoon salt
½ teaspoon freshly ground pepper
¼ cup olive oil
2 medium onions, peeled and chopped

1 large green bell pepper, cored, seeded, and chopped
2 tablespoons minced parsley
½ cup tomato sauce
12 ounces Valencia (short-grain) rice
2 cups Fish Broth (page 13; or 2 fish bouillon cubes dissolved in 2 cups water)
1 cup dry white wine

1. Wash the clams well under cold running water until no sand is left on them.

2. Mash the garlic, salt, and pepper into a paste. (A mortar and pestle works best, but you may mince the garlic finely with a knife or put it through a garlic press and mash the seasonings in with a fork.)

3. In a paellera or other wide, shallow pan, heat the oil over medium heat. Sauté the onions, green pepper, and parsley until the onions are translucent, about 3 minutes. Stir in the garlic paste and tomato sauce and cook for 2 minutes more.

4. Add the clams, and shake the pan gently to mix them in. Add the rice, broth, and wine. Bring to a boil, lower the heat, and cook gently, uncovered, until the liquid is almost all absorbed, about 30 minutes.

5. Serve immediately with a green salad and crusty bread.

NOTE: Bouillon cubes did not exist in the old days, but today I sometimes use them to enhance flavor. If you use them, reduce the salt to ½ teaspoon.

ARROZ CON CAMARONES
(RICE WITH SHRIMP)

6 servings

2 pounds fresh, medium-size shrimp
4¼ cups water
⅔ cup Spanish olive oil
I large onion, peeled and chopped
I large green bell pepper, cored, seeded, and chopped
3 garlic cloves, peeled and minced
½ cup tomato sauce
½ cup dry white wine

I teaspoon salt
½ teaspoon freshly ground pepper
4 strands saffron, toasted in a dry skillet over medium heat for about 30 seconds or until they lose their moisture
¼ teaspoon ground cumin
¼ teaspoon dry leaf oregano
I bay leaf
2 cups Valencia (short-grain) rice

1. Shell, devein, and refrigerate the shrimp.

2. Place the shrimp shells in a saucepan with the water and boil for about 15 minutes. Strain and reserve 3 cups of the water. Discard the shells.

3. In a paellera or other wide, shallow pan, heat the oil over medium heat until fragrant, and sauté the shrimp quickly, just until it turns pink. Refrigerate it again.

4. In the same oil, sauté the onion and green pepper until the onion is translucent, about 3 minutes. Stir in the garlic and cook 2 minutes more. Stir in the tomato sauce, wine, salt, pepper, saffron, cumin, oregano, and bay leaf, and cook for a few minutes longer.

5. Add the rice and the reserved 3 cups shrimp water. Bring just to a boil, reduce the heat to low, cover the pan, and cook gently for about 30 minutes, until the rice is tender and almost dry. Add the shrimp 5 minutes before the rice is done.

ARROZ CON CAMARONES EN OLLA DE PRESIÓN

(RICE WITH SHRIMP IN THE PRESSURE COOKER)

❧

6 to 8 servings

It has been said that "pressure cooking is pleasure cooking." I truly believe this.

2 pounds fresh, medium-size shrimp
2¼ cups water
1 bay leaf
1 teaspoon salt
¼ cup Spanish olive oil
1 large onion, peeled and chopped
1 small green bell pepper, cored, seeded, and chopped
3 garlic cloves, peeled and minced

¼ cup tomato sauce
2 cups Valencia (short-grain) rice
2 teaspoons freshly squeezed lime juice
¼ teaspoon freshly ground pepper
1 teaspoon paprika
One 12-ounce can or bottle of beer
One 6-ounce jar pimientos, drained and liquid reserved

1. Shell, devein, and refrigerate the shrimp.

2. Place the shrimp shells in a pan with the water, bay leaf, and salt. Boil, uncovered, for about 15 minutes. Drain and reserve the broth; you should have 2 cups. Discard the shells and bay leaf.

3. In the pressure cooker, heat the oil over medium heat until fragrant. Sauté the onion and green pepper until the onion is translucent, about 3 minutes. Stir in the garlic and cook 2 minutes more. Stir in the tomato sauce and cook for a few minutes longer.

4. Add the shrimp and rice and stir lightly. Add the reserved shrimp water, the lime juice, pepper, paprika, beer, and the liquid from the pimientos.

5. Lock the lid into place and put the pressure regulator on the vent pipe. Heat the cooker over high heat until the regulator starts to whistle and dance, indicating that high pressure has been reached. Reduce the heat to medium, maintaining high pressure, and cook for 5 minutes.

6. Cut the pimientos into strips.

7. Remove the cooker from the heat and place it under cold running water until no more steam escapes. Remove the regulator, open

the lid, and test the rice. If it seems too firm, simmer it for 2 or 3 more minutes, covered, but without pressure.

8. Fluff the rice with a fork. Transfer it to a serving dish and garnish it with the pimientos.

Like salted codfish and jerked beef, dried shrimp was very popular in old Cuba although the fresh equivalent was plentiful. Perhaps Cubans owe their taste for dried shrimp to the Chinese immigrants, who used it with great ingenuity. The inexpensive little Chinese restaurants in Cuba, called *fondas*, served not only Chinese specialties, but Cuban dishes prepared with a Chinese flair.

In any event, you can find dried shrimp in Asian markets as well as in the Latin section of some supermarkets. Like all other dried, salted food, camarones secos must be soaked before cooking.

ARROZ CON CAMARONES SECOS
(RICE WITH DRIED SHRIMP)

6 to 8 servings

8 ounces dried shrimp
½ cup Spanish olive oil
I large onion, peeled and chopped
I large green bell pepper, cored, seeded, and chopped
3 garlic cloves, peeled and minced
¼ cup tomato sauce
2 cups Valencia (short-grain) rice
3 cups Fish Broth or Chicken Broth (page 13)
½ cup dry white wine

4 strands saffron, toasted in a dry skillet over medium heat for about 30 seconds or until they lose their moisture
¼ teaspoon salt
½ teaspoon freshly ground pepper
¼ teaspoon dry leaf oregano
⅛ teaspoon cumin
I bay leaf
¼ cup canned petit pois (tiny peas) or small frozen peas, thawed
One 6-ounce jar of pimientos, drained and cut into strips

I. Cover the shrimp with water and soak them for about an hour. Drain them, discard the salty water, and set the shrimp aside.

2. In a paellera or other wide, shallow pan, warm the oil over medium heat. Sauté the onion and green pepper until the onion is

translucent, about 3 minutes. Stir in the garlic and cook 2 minutes more. Stir in the tomato sauce and cook for a few minutes longer.

3. Add the rice, broth, wine, saffron, salt, pepper, oregano, cumin, and bay leaf. Stir lightly and add the shrimp. Bring to a boil, lower the heat, cover, and cook gently for 30 minutes, or until the rice has absorbed most of the liquid.

4. Warm the peas and pimientos separately, and garnish the finished dish with them.

ARROZ CON CALAMARES

(RICE WITH SQUID)

4 to 6 servings

The first step for preparing this dish is to make the calamares en su tinta. It is quite common among Cubans to begin with canned squid in its own ink, which, while inferior to the homemade variety, is still good. A garnish of parsley sprigs is not traditional, but it adds a fresh and colorful touch to a dish that does not have much eye appeal despite its delicious flavor.

3 cloves garlic, peeled
2 fish bouillon cubes (optional)
½ teaspoon freshly ground pepper
2 tablespoons Spanish olive oil
1 medium green bell pepper, cored, seeded, and finely chopped
¼ cup finely chopped parsley, plus 2 whole sprigs
2 cups Valencia (short-grain) rice
2½ cups water
3 cups Calamares en su Tinta (page 59; see Note)

1. Mash the garlic, bouillon cubes, and pepper into a paste. (A mortar and pestle works best, but you may mince the garlic finely with a knife or put it through a garlic press and mash the seasonings in with a fork.)

2. In a paellera or other wide, shallow pan, warm the oil over medium heat and sauté the green pepper for 2 minutes. Stir in the garlic paste and cook another 2 minutes.

3. Stir in the chopped parsley, rice, water, and calamares en su tinta. Bring to a boil, lower the heat, cover, and cook gently for about 30 minutes, until the rice is tender but still moist.

4. Garnish the dish with the parsley sprigs.

NOTE: You may substitute two 12-ounce cans of calamares en su tinta. If you do so, use only 1 bouillon cube. For arroz con calamares from a can, add ½ cup chopped onions to the sofrito. When using homemade squid in its ink, the onions are abundantly present there.

ARROZ CON POLLO
(RICE WITH CHICKEN)

≋

6 to 8 servings

At my husband's home in Coatesville, Pennsylvania, when we were newlyweds, his Aunt Maggie asked me what my favorite dish was, and I replied that it was rice with chicken, meaning, of course, arroz con pollo. But Aunt Maggie, who served deliciously creamy mashed potatoes at every meal, did not have a clue what I meant. The main course at the next meal she served us was a dish of the mushiest, most unappetizing rice I had ever seen, accompanied by stewed chicken. What a pale and tasteless dish! Of course, I appreciated the gesture, and consumed the meal with feigned gusto.

Here, then, is the recipe for Cuban rice with chicken—a rather different affair from Aunt Maggie's version. Arroz con pollo is economical as well as easy—a reliable and relatively quick dish to prepare in an "emergency" for unexpected guests.

3 garlic cloves, peeled
1 tablespoon salt
1 teaspoon pepper
¼ cup sour orange juice (or a 50-50 mixture of sweet orange juice and lime juice)
4 pounds skinned chicken thighs, legs, and breasts
¼ cup vegetable oil
2 medium onions, peeled and finely chopped
1 large green pepper, cored, seeded, and finely chopped
3 cups Chicken Broth (page 13)

4 strands saffron, toasted in a dry skillet over medium heat for about 30 seconds or until they lose their moisture
2 tablespoons tomato sauce
2 cups Valencia (short-grain) rice
Beer, dry white wine, or additional chicken broth
Two 8-ounce cans petit pois (tiny peas), drained, or 1 cup tiny frozen peas, thawed
One 6-ounce jar pimientos, drained and cut into strips

1. Mash the garlic into a paste with the salt and pepper. (A mortar and pestle works best, but you may mince the garlic finely with a knife or put it through a garlic press and mash the seasonings in with a fork.)

2. Add the orange juice and pour this marinade over the chicken pieces. Refrigerate for about 1 hour.

3. Heat the oil over medium heat in a paellera or other wide, shallow pan.

4. Blot the chicken pieces on paper towels and brown them in the hot oil. Reserve the marinade. Set the browned chicken pieces aside.

5. In the same oil, sauté the onions and green pepper until the onions are translucent, about 3 minutes. Add the broth, saffron, tomato sauce, reserved marinade, and the chicken and simmer for about 5 minutes.

6. Add the rice and stir just enough to cover it with liquid. If the rice is not fully covered, add more broth, wine, or beer. Simmer, uncovered, until all the liquid has been absorbed and the rice is cooked, about 30 minutes. Add more broth, wine, or beer if needed.

7. Remove the pan from the heat while you warm the peas and pimientos separately. Garnish the arroz con pollo with them and serve.

ARROZ CON POLLO A LA CHORRERA

(RICE AND CHICKEN WITH FRILLS)

12 servings

This recipe goes back to colonial times in Cuba and is one that María Antonieta de los Reyes Gavilán included in her classic cookbook, *Delicias de la Mesa.* The *chorrera* in the title has three possible meanings. A chorrera was a lacy collar and bib ensemble that was part of a colonial gentleman's formal attire at gala occasions; this dish, with its artichoke and mushroom "frills," is definitely gala fare. Chorrera is also a place where a *chorro*, or stream of liquid, falls; in this case, half a liter of Bacardí rum is poured into the arroz con pollo in one long chorro. Then there is the fortress "La Chorrera," which, like the famous Morro Castle, is one of Havana's landmarks from colonial times.

3 chickens, about 2 pounds each,
cut into serving pieces
1 tablespoon salt
1½ cups freshly squeezed lime juice
½ liter white Bacardí rum (about 4
cups)
¾ cup Spanish olive oil
3 large onions, peeled and chopped
4 large green bell peppers, cored,
seeded, and chopped
6 garlic cloves, peeled and minced
8 plum tomatoes, seeded and
diced, with juice reserved (or
one 35-ounce can)
10 peppercorns
One 6-ounce jar pimientos, drained
and sliced, with liquid reserved

10 cups Chicken Broth (page 13)
10 strands saffron, toasted in a dry
skillet over medium heat for
about 30 seconds or until they
lose their moisture
7½ cups Valencia (short-grain) rice
2 tablespoons unsalted butter
2 cups sliced fresh mushrooms
(see Note)
One 8-ounce can Spanish
artichokes (not marinated),
drained
One 6-ounce can petit pois,
drained, or 1 cup tiny frozen
peas, thawed

1. Place the chicken pieces in a large bowl and sprinkle them with salt. Pour the lime juice and rum over the chicken and set it aside.

2. Warm the oil over medium heat in a large paellera or another wide, shallow pan, and sauté the onions and green peppers until the onions are translucent, about 3 minutes. Add the garlic and cook gently for 2 minutes more. Add the tomatoes and their juice and simmer for an additional 5 minutes.

3. Add the chicken and marinade, the peppercorns, and the liquid from the canned pimientos. Simmer for 5 minutes. Add the chicken broth and saffron, then increase the heat to medium-high and cook for 10 minutes.

4. Stir in the rice. Bring to a boil, then reduce the heat to low, cover with foil, and cook for 30 minutes, or until the rice has absorbed the liquid but is still moist.

5. While the rice is cooking, melt the butter in a medium-size skillet and sauté the mushrooms until they give up their liquid, about 5 minutes. Stir in the artichokes and heat through.

6. Remove the chicken from the heat, uncover it, fold in the mushrooms and artichokes, and cover again with foil. Let rest for a few minutes. (The rice will continue to cook.)

7. Warm the peas separately. Uncover the arroz con pollo, garnish with the peas and pimientos, and serve.

NOTE: In Cuba we used canned mushrooms, but it seems a shame not to use fresh when they are so readily available in this country.

ARROZ RELLENO
(STUFFED RICE)

6 to 8 servings

This attractive dish is especially suitable for a buffet. While the ingredients are similar to those of arroz con pollo, the method of preparation is quite different, as is the final appearance.

3 tablespoons vegetable oil
2 medium onions, peeled and finely chopped
I large green bell pepper, cored, seeded, and finely chopped
3 garlic cloves, peeled and minced
2 cups shredded, cooked chicken meat
I teaspoon salt
½ teaspoon freshly ground pepper
4 strands saffron, toasted in a dry skillet over medium heat for

about 30 seconds or until they lose their moisture
2 tablespoons tomato sauce
3 cups Chicken Broth (page 13)
½ cup dry white wine
2 cups Valencia (short-grain) rice
2 cups canned petit pois (tiny peas), drained, or 2 cups tiny frozen peas, thawed
One 6-ounce jar pimientos, drained and cut into strips
I teaspoon butter

I. Warm the oil over medium heat in a large skillet. Sauté the onions and green pepper until the onions are translucent, about 3 minutes. Stir in the garlic and cook 2 minutes more.

2. Stir in the chicken, salt, pepper, saffron, and tomato sauce, and simmer for 5 minutes. Remove the chicken with a slotted spoon and cover to keep it warm.

3. Add the broth and wine, and bring to a boil. Add the rice, and stir it lightly so that it doesn't stick. Cover the pan, lower the heat, and cook gently until the rice has absorbed the liquid, about 30 minutes.

4. Warm the peas and pimientos separately.

5. Butter a 10-inch ring mold and place half the rice in it. Place the reserved chicken in the mold and cover it with the rest of the rice.

6. Unmold the arroz relleno onto a serving platter and garnish it with the peas and pimientos.

When a whole chicken was cooked at home, the giblets were usually used to make broth. But sometimes the cook would save them in the icebox until there were enough to make this dish, which is quite similar to the "dirty rice" eaten in New Orleans.

ARROZ CON MENUDOS
(RICE WITH GIBLETS)

6 to 8 servings

¼ cup vegetable oil
3 garlic cloves, peeled
2 large onions, peeled and chopped
1 medium green pepper, peeled, seeded, and chopped
5 sets of chicken giblets (liver, heart, and gizzard), coarsely chopped
2 cups Valencia (short-grain) rice

2 cups Chicken Broth (page 13)
1 cup dry white wine
4 strands saffron, toasted in a dry skillet over medium heat for about 30 seconds or until they lose their moisture
1 teaspoon salt
½ teaspoon freshly ground pepper
2 sprigs parsley, chopped

1. Warm the oil over medium heat in a paellera or other wide, shallow pan. Sauté the garlic until golden brown. Remove it with a slotted spoon and discard it.

2. In the same oil, sauté the onions and green pepper for 2 minutes.

3. Stir in the giblets, reduce the heat, and cook gently for about 25 minutes, until the gizzard, which is the toughest, is tender.

4. Stir in the rice, broth, wine, saffron, salt, and pepper. Bring to a boil, then reduce the heat, cover the pan, and simmer until the rice has absorbed the liquid, about 30 minutes.

5. Garnish with parsley and serve hot with a green salad and crusty bread.

ARROZ CON TASAJO Y PLÁTANOS

(RICE WITH JERKED BEEF AND PLANTAINS)

6 to 8 servings

This dish is at least as old as the *trapiches,* the sugar mills, of Cuba, which were built in the 1520s. It goes back to colonial times, or, as our grandparents would refer to it, *El Tiempo de España.* It was given to me by Dulce Zúñiga.

As with ajiaco, another peasant dish, the plantain is cooked with its skin on, and each diner must peel it for himself. As always when cooking with tasajo, it is imperative to soak it a day ahead of time.

½ pound tasajo (jerked beef)
¼ cup lard or vegetable oil
1 large onion, peeled and chopped
1 large green pepper, cored, seeded, and chopped
3 garlic cloves, peeled and minced
1 cup tomato sauce
4 strands saffron, toasted in a dry skillet over medium heat for about 30 seconds or until they lose their moisture
¼ teaspoon freshly ground pepper
⅛ teaspoon ground cumin
2 cups Valencia (short-grain) rice
3 cups water
1 large, semiripe plantain

1. Cut the jerked beef into small chunks, place it in a deep pan, cover it with water, and soak it for at least 8 hours. Change the water and continue soaking for 1 more hour.

2. Discard the salty water and rinse the beef. Shred it with your fingers and set it aside.

3. In a paellera or other wide, shallow pan, heat the lard or oil over medium heat. Sauté the onion and green pepper until the onion is translucent, about 3 minutes. Stir in the garlic and cook for 2 minutes more. Stir in the tomato sauce, reduce the heat, and cook gently for a few minutes longer.

4. Add the saffron, pepper, cumin, tasajo, rice, and water. Bring to a boil.

5. Leaving the skin on, cut the plantain into 1-inch rounds. Add them to the rice and cover the pan.

6. Reduce the heat and simmer 30 minutes, or until the rice is tender and has absorbed most of the liquid.

Although Cubans usually cook beans in the same water in which they are soaked, I make an exception for chick-peas. I think they taste better when cooked in fresh water.

1⅓ cup dry chick-peas
3 garlic cloves, peeled
1 teaspoon salt
½ teaspoon freshly ground pepper
2 chorizos or ½ pound jamón de cocinar (raw ham) or prosciutto
¼ cup vegetable oil
1 large onion, peeled and chopped
1 large green bell pepper, cored, seeded, and chopped
½ cup tomato sauce
2 cups Valencia (short-grain) rice
½ cup dry white wine
4 strands saffron, toasted in a dry skillet over medium heat for about 30 seconds or until they lose their moisture

1. Place the chick-peas in a colander and rinse them well, removing any impurities.

2. Put the chick-peas in a large pot, cover them with water, and soak them for 8 to 10 hours. Drain them.

3. Measure 6 cups of fresh water into the pot and bring it to a boil. Add the chick-peas, cover, lower the heat, and simmer for about 45 minutes, until they are tender but not mushy. Drain the chick-peas, reserving 3 cups of the cooking water.

4. Mash the garlic, salt, and pepper into a paste. (A mortar and pestle works best, but you may mince the garlic finely with a knife or put it through a garlic press and mash the seasonings in with a fork.)

5. Skin the chorizos and slice them into ½-inch rounds. (If using ham, cut it into 1-inch cubes.)

6. Heat the oil over medium heat in a paellera or other wide, shallow pan, and lightly sauté the meat.

7. Add the onion and green pepper to the pan and sauté them until the onion is translucent, about 3 minutes. Stir in the garlic paste and cook for 2 minutes more. Stir in the tomato sauce and cook for a few minutes longer.

8. Add the rice, reserved chick-pea water, wine, and saffron, and stir lightly. Add the chick-peas, bring to a boil, reduce the heat, cover, and simmer for about 30 minutes, until the rice is tender and has absorbed most of the liquid.

9. Fluff the rice with a fork and serve.

ARROZ CON QUIMBOMBÓ

(RICE WITH OKRA)

❧

6 to 8 servings

This Afro-Cuban dish is like Afro-Cuban music: rich and sensuous.

In order to prevent okra from becoming sticky, it is imperative that you wash it whole and allow it to dry thoroughly before slicing and cooking it. This is my mother's method. It works perfectly. Some cooks soak the cut okra in water and lime juice.

½ pound fresh okra
½ cup vegetable oil
I large onion, peeled and chopped
I medium green bell pepper, cored, seeded, and chopped
3 cloves garlic, peeled and minced
I cup tomato sauce
I tablespoon white vinegar
¼ pound jamón de cocinar (raw

ham) or prosciutto, cut into I-inch cubes
I small chorizo, skinned and cut into ½-inch rounds
2½ cups Chicken Broth (page 13)
½ cup dry white wine
I teaspoon salt
½ teaspoon freshly ground pepper
2 cups Valencia (short-grain) rice

1. Wash the okra pods in cold water and drain them. Blot the pods with paper towels and set them aside on more paper towels to dry completely.

2. Heat the oil over medium heat in a paellera or other wide, shallow pan. Sauté the onion and green pepper until the onion is translucent, about 3 minutes. Add the garlic and cook 2 minutes more. Stir in the tomato sauce and vinegar and cook for a few minutes longer.

3. Begin slicing the okra into ½-inch rounds, dropping them into the simmering sofrito as you go. Stir in the ham and chorizo, and cook for about 5 minutes.

4. Add the broth, wine, salt, pepper, and rice, stirring lightly. Bring the mixture to a boil, lower the heat, cover, and simmer for about 30 minutes, until the rice is tender and has absorbed most of the liquid.

My brother, Pancho, Jack, and I dining at La Zaragozana, one of Cuba's most famous restaurants. Havana, 1947. *Author's collection*

$\mathcal{A}$RROZ Y $\mathcal{F}$RIJOLES (RICE AND BEANS)

Arroz y Frijoles (Rice and Beans)

Si cocinas como caminas, me como hasta la raspa! (If you cook the way you walk, I'll eat it all—even the crust!)

This is a fresh remark that Cuban men made to women who had sexy ways of walking. In this country today, they would be considered male chauvinist pigs!

When I was a child, preparing rice was a time-consuming process that began early in the day. Once the cook had put the day's broth on to simmer, she would sit down to *escoger* (choose) the rice, that is, separate the good grains from the bad. Rice in those days was not clean, nor did it come in neat packages, ready to cook. It was brought *al por mayor* (wholesale) and kept in large ceramic containers. The cook had to pick through it grain by grain, selecting only the perfect ones for cooking. Then she would wash it well but quickly, for soaked rice cooks into a mushy mess.

The rice was always made long before dinner and kept warm over the coals so that a thick crust, or *raspa*, formed at the bottom of the pot. The raspa had a nutty flavor, and though it was never served at the family dinner table, it was considered a great delicacy. We children loved it, but rarely were allowed to have any; it was considered the cook's property. One cook in particular, named Florencia, would make sure there was always a thick raspa on the bottom of the pan so that she could take it home to her family, ever loathe to squander this treasure on spoiled children.

Fluffy white rice is served at almost every Cuban meal, and the ability to make perfect white rice is perhaps the most indispensable skill of Cuban cooking. Cuban rice should neither be mushy nor, as the Italians say, al dente. It should be light and airy—never sticky. It is the foundation of such a large proportion of Cuba's distinctive dishes that woe to the cook who has not mastered its secrets.

From a great variety of other immigrants, Americans have learned the cuisines of many parts of the world, becoming, in many ways, sophisticated gourmets. But it seems to me that North Americans, as a rule, still know little about how to cook plain white rice. In too many households, abominations such as quick-cooking rice are regularly used because otherwise good cooks have not learned how to make this basic food.

Of the many easy ways to make good, fluffy, white rice I have included two most commonly used by Cubans, one using a pressure cooker and the other using a conventional pot. For those interested in old-fashioned ways, I have included the method used in my childhood. (Many Cubans in exile—though I am not among them—are partial to electric rice makers, especially the one produced by Hitachi; for that you need only follow the manufacturer's instructions.)

You will also find in this chapter recipes for beans, especially black beans, perhaps the most typical of Cuban dishes. Served with fluffy white rice, frijoles negros is a dish for the gods and a traditional staple of Cubans, who while not always rich with money, were once rich with beans. Alas, under Fidel Castro there are no more black beans in Cuba!

My children, who grew up in many countries but especially in Venezuela and Cuba, once listened to a priest in New Jersey deliver a homily intended to stimulate donations to the missions in Latin America. "Those poor people down there," he declared, "live on nothing but rice and beans." My world-traveled children, who to this day feel there is nothing better than rice and beans, were not moved to contribute to the cause. Had the priest said that the poor children were forced to subsist on hamburgers and hot dogs, he might have elicited a more generous response from them!

This is the way rice was cooked on the charcoal stove of our kitchen years ago. The quantities vary depending on the number of people there are to feed. I allow about ⅓ cup of uncooked rice per person.

Rice   Water
Salt   Pork lard

1. Place the rice and salt in a large, heavy pot with a tight lid. Add water to about 4 inches above the rice.

2. Bring the water to a boil, cover the pot, and lower the heat. (The cook would accomplish this by removing some of the burning coals from the charcoal stove.) Let the rice simmer until tender but firm.

3. Pour the rice into a large sieve and let all the starchy water run out.

4. Return the rice to the pan and fluff it with enough pork lard to separate the grains and make them shiny. Cover the pan again and let the rice rest over very low heat until serving time.

5. Serve the fluffy white rice, and save the raspa—the nutty, crunchy crust at the bottom of the pan—for a special treat.

ARROZ BLANCO CUBANO A LA ANTIGUA

(WHITE RICE THE OLD-FASHIONED CUBAN WAY)

This is my favorite way to make rice. It is quick and easy, and it never fails.

1 garlic clove, peeled   2 cups water
3 tablespoons vegetable oil   2 teaspoons salt (see Note)
2 cups long-grain rice

1. Press the garlic with the side of a knife to crush it slightly.

2. Heat 2 tablespoons of the oil in a 4-quart pressure cooker over medium heat. Sauté the garlic until brown but not burned, and discard it. Add the rice and stir it lightly. Add the water and salt.

3. Lock the lid into place and put the pressure regulator on the vent pipe. Heat the cooker over high heat until the regulator starts to whistle and dance, indicating that high pressure has been reached.

ARROZ BLANCO DESGRANADO EN OLLA DE PRESIÓN

(FLUFFY WHITE RICE IN THE PRESSURE COOKER)

6 servings

Reduce the heat to medium, maintaining high pressure, and cook for 5 minutes.

4. Remove the cooker from the heat and cool it under cold running water. When no more traces of steam escape from the vent pipe, open the pressure cooker. Pour in the remaining 1 tablespoon of oil, fluffing the rice lightly with a fork so that every grain is loose.

NOTE: If you prefer not to use salt, you may substitute 2 tablespoons of lime juice.

ARROZ BLANCO DESGRANADO A LA CUBANA MODERNA

(FLUFFY WHITE RICE THE MODERN CUBAN WAY)

8 to 10 servings

If you do not have a pressure cooker or dislike using one, try this method of cooking rice or the variation that follows. In the variation, the rice cooks freely in a large quantity of water, almost like pasta.

2 garlic cloves, peeled
3 tablespoons vegetable oil
3 cups long-grain rice

3½ cups water
1 tablespoon salt (see Note)

1. Press the garlic with the side of a knife to crush it slightly.

2. Heat 2 tablespoons of the oil over medium heat in a large saucepan. Sauté the garlic until brown but not burned, and discard it. (You may like to try leaving it in as I sometimes do, for additional flavor.)

3. Add the rice and stir lightly. Add the water and salt, and raise the heat. Bring to a boil, lower the heat, cover, and simmer for about 25 minutes, until the rice is well cooked but not mushy.

4. Pour in the remaining 1 tablespoon of oil, fluffing the rice as you do so with a fork so that every grain is loose.

NOTE: If you prefer not to use salt, you may substitute 3 tablespoons of lime juice.

VARIATION

Arroz Blanco Desgranado No. 2: Place the desired amount of rice—about ⅓ of a cup per serving—in a sieve and rinse it under cold running water. Place it in a large pot with at least 5 cups of water per cup of rice. Bring the water to a boil, reduce the heat to medium-low, and simmer the rice, uncovered, for 15 minutes. Strain it into a sieve and rinse it thoroughly with hot running water. Transfer it to a serving bowl and add about ½ teaspoon of salt and 1 tablespoon of vegetable oil per cup of rice, fluffing it with a fork as you do so.

Compadre denotes the relationship between you and the godfather of your child, as *comadre* denotes the godmother. In other words, compadres and comadres are your "coparents." The word *compadre* is also a slang way to address a friend. One might say to a friend, "*Oye, compadre, ven acá; dime la verdad.*" ("Hey, compadre, come, come; tell me the truth.")

Arroz sin compadre may be thus named because it stands alone, as it were, without meat or fish to keep it company. Something like an Italian risotto verde, this dish does just fine on its own, with only its vegetable ingredients for companionship, but it is also a worthy friend to just about any entrée.

3 garlic cloves, peeled
4 peppercorns
3 tablespoons vegetable oil
¼ cup freshly squeezed lime juice
2 cups long-grain rice
3 cups water or broth (see Note)

1 medium onion, peeled and chopped
1 large green bell pepper, peeled, seeded, and chopped
½ cup finely chopped parsley and 2 parsley sprigs

1. Mash the garlic and peppercorns into a paste with a mortar and pestle. (If you don't have a mortar and pestle, mince the garlic finely with a knife or put it through a garlic press; omit the peppercorns and mash ½ teaspoon freshly ground pepper into the garlic with a fork.)

2. Warm 1 tablespoon of the oil over medium heat in a large saucepan, and sauté the garlic paste for a minute or two, until it is soft.

3. Add the lime juice and the rice and stir lightly. Add the water or broth and stir again. Bring to a boil, lower the heat, cover, and simmer the rice until cooked, about 25 minutes.

4. While the rice is cooking, heat the remaining 2 tablespoons of oil over medium heat in a large skillet. Sauté the onion, green pepper, and chopped parsley until the onion is translucent, about 3 minutes.

5. Stir this sofrito into the simmering rice. If the grains are still a bit hard, continue simmering until the rice is tender but not mushy. Just before serving, fluff the rice with a fork and garnish it with the sprigs of parsley.

NOTE: I generally use chicken or vegetable broth I have on hand.

FRIJOLES NEGROS
(BLACK BEANS)

8 servings

Served with fluffy white rice, this heavenly dish is an indispensable accompaniment to many Cuban foods, or a nutritious entrée all by itself. It also can be puréed and served with croutons or avocado slices as black bean soup for a tasty first course.

The variation at the end of the recipe is from my cousin Juan Diez-Argüelles, whose black beans are the richest I have ever tasted, made without regard to calorie or cholesterol content. Juan cooks with all the passion and personal investment with which he once conducted counterrevolutionary activities in Cuba. Having served a hefty prison term for that bit of rule-breaking, he is fearlessly "incorrect" with regard to modern health conventions. Now in his late seventies, he is unconvinced that his eating habits are in need of change.

You will note that the beans are cooked in their soaking water. Some cookbooks say that one must drain the soaked beans and cook them in fresh water in order to avoid flatulence. However, doing so takes away some of the color and *gracia*, or "grace," of the beans. Cubans always cook their black beans in the soaking water, and no one I know has ever suffered gastric distress as a result.

For Cooking the Beans:

1 pound dry black beans

2½ quarts water

1 green bell pepper, cored, seeded, and cut into strips

2 garlic cloves, peeled and lightly crushed but left whole

1 large slice of onion (optional)

To Complete the Dish:

⅓ cup Spanish olive oil

2 medium onions, peeled and finely chopped

1 large green pepper, cored, seeded, and finely chopped

6 garlic cloves, peeled and minced

1 teaspoon salt

½ teaspoon freshly ground pepper

½ teaspoon ground cumin

½ teaspoon dry leaf oregano

1 bay leaf

1 tablespoon raw or brown sugar

2 tablespoons white wine vinegar

SOAK AND COOK THE BEANS:

1. Place the beans in a colander and rinse them under cold running water, removing any impurities.

2. Transfer the beans to a large pot, cover them with the water, and soak for at least 8 hours.

3. Add the green pepper, garlic, and onion to the pot and bring it to a boil.

4. Lower the heat to medium, cover, and cook the beans until they are tender, about 1 hour. (Check them after about 45 minutes, though, for some black beans require less cooking time.) Skim the *espuma* or foam from the top of the pot periodically with an *espumadera*, a fine-slotted spoon designed for this purpose.

COMPLETE THE DISH:

1. While the beans are cooking, warm the oil over medium heat in a large, heavy skillet. Sauté the onions and green pepper until the onions are translucent, about 3 minutes. Stir in the garlic, salt, pepper, cumin, and oregano, and cook for 2 minutes more.

2. Remove this sofrito from the heat and place half of it in the food processor. Add a large ladleful of cooked beans and pulse until puréed.

3. Stir the purée, the remaining sofrito, the bay leaf, and sugar into the beans. Bring the beans to a boil again, lower the heat, and simmer, uncovered, until the cooking liquid has the consistency of thick gravy. Stir frequently so that the beans do not stick to the bottom of the pot.

4. Just before serving, remove the bay leaf, stir in the vinegar, and, if desired, a little more olive oil to further enhance the flavor and texture.

VARIATION

Frijoles Negros Muy Ricos (Very Rich Black Beans): Complete the dish as directed, adding 2 cups cubed jamón de cocinar (raw ham) or prosciutto in Step 3 with the bay leaf and sugar. When ready to serve, top the beans with 2 cups Chicharrones de Pellajo (page 91).

FRIJOLES NEGROS FESTIVOS

(FESTIVE BLACK BEANS)

8 to 10 servings

My granddaughter Monica once announced that the family recipe for black beans gets better with every generation. Although I'm partial to my own traditional recipe, it seems only fair to include at least one "new and improved" version here.

While Monica's mother, Titi, was led by her good melting-pot instincts to serve frijoles with kielbasa on the side, my daughter Peggy cooks hers with Italian sausage and other spicy additions. Titi's recipe, Polish addition notwithstanding, is still very much in the classic tradition. Peggy's, however, is a radical departure. Easily made ahead of time, it is an ideal party food. Peggy often makes it in a triple batch to serve at parties for the writers who read their works at the New York State Summer Writers's Institute that she and her husband, Professor Robert Boyers, host in Saratoga, New York.

For Cooking the Beans:

I pound dry black beans
2½ quarts water
I green bell pepper, cored, seeded,
    and cut into strips

2 garlic cloves, peeled and lightly
    crushed but whole
I large peeled sliced onion
    (optional)

To Complete the Dish:

I jamón de cocinar (raw ham) end
    or prosciutto (see Note)
⅓ cup olive oil
2 medium onions, peeled and
    chopped
I green bell pepper, cored, seeded,
    and chopped
6 garlic cloves, peeled and minced
1½ teaspoons salt
2 teaspoons freshly ground pepper
I tablespoon dry leaf oregano
2 tablespoons ground cumin

2 bay leaves
I tablespoon brown sugar
½ teaspoon Tabasco
4 hot Italian sausages, sliced into
    bite-size rounds
2 sweet Italian sausages, sliced into
    bite-size rounds
¼ cup sherry
I sweet red pepper, cored, seeded,
    and sliced in strips
2 tablespoons red wine vinegar
3 tablespoons chopped parsley

SOAK AND COOK THE BEANS:

    1. Place the beans in a colander and rinse them under cold running water, removing any impurities.

    2. Transfer the beans to a large pot, cover them with the water, and soak for at least 8 hours.

    3. Add the green pepper, garlic, and onion to the pot and bring to a boil.

    4. Lower the heat and simmer the beans until they are tender, about I hour. (Check them after about 45 minutes, though, for some black beans require less cooking time.) Skim the foam from the top of the pot periodically.

COMPLETE THE DISH:

1. Add the ham end to the boiling beans.

2. In a large, heavy skillet, warm the oil over medium heat and sauté the onions and green pepper until the onions are translucent, about 3 minutes. Stir in the garlic and cook for 2 minutes more.

3. Stir in the salt, pepper, oregano, and cumin. Remove this sofrito from the heat and place half of it in the food processor. Add a large ladleful of cooked beans and pulse until puréed.

4. Stir the purée, the remaining sofrito, the bay leaves, sugar, and Tabasco.

5. Bring the beans to a boil again, lower the heat, and simmer, uncovered, until the cooking liquid has the consistency of thick gravy. Stir frequently so that the beans don't stick to the bottom of the pot.

6. While the mixture is thickening, sauté the Italian sausages in the skillet in which the sofrito was cooked. Drain them on paper towels and add them to the beans.

7. Remove the ham end from the beans, chop it, remove and discard any fat, skin, or bone, and return it to the pot. Stir in the sherry.

8. Lightly sauté the red pepper strips in the sausage grease left in the skillet.

9. Just before serving, remove the bay leaves and stir in the vinegar. Pour the beans into a large serving bowl or soup tureen and garnish with the red pepper strips and chopped parsley.

NOTE: Butchers are often glad to give ham ends to eager cooks.

MOROS Y CRISTIANOS
(RICE WITH BLACK BEANS)

8 servings

The Moors of the Islamic empire occupied the south of Spain from 711 to the year of America's "discovery," 1492. Tradition has it that after the Catholic monarchs drove the dark-skinned Moors from Spain, the Spaniards who colonized Cuba invented this delectable dish of black beans mixed with white rice and named it for the momentous events back home.

I always cook moros y cristianos in the pressure cooker because it is so quick, but you will find directions for making them in a conventional pot at the end of the recipe.

2 cups dry black beans

4 cups water

1 large green bell pepper, cored, seeded, and cut into thirds

1 bay leaf

2 large onions, peeled and quartered

3 garlic cloves, peeled

4 slices bacon (see Note)

2 teaspoons salt

¼ teaspoon freshly ground pepper

¼ teaspoon dry leaf oregano

¼ teaspoon ground cumin

2 cups Valencia (short-grain) rice

2 tablespoons olive oil

1. Place the beans in a colander and rinse them well under cold running water, removing any impurities.

2. Place the beans in the pressure cooker, add the water, and soak them for at least 8 hours.

3. Add ⅓ of the green pepper and the bay leaf to the pot. Lock the lid into place and put the pressure regulator on the vent pipe. Heat the cooker over high heat until the regulator starts to whistle and dance, indicating that high pressure has been reached. Reduce the heat to medium, maintaining high pressure, and cook for 20 minutes.

4. Remove the cooker from the heat and let the steam dissipate. After about 10 minutes, with your hand protected by an oven mitt, carefully remove the regulator. If no steam emerges from the vent pipe, remove the cover. (If it is still steaming, wait until it stops before opening.) The beans should be tender but still whole.

5. Strain the beans over a large measuring cup and set them aside. If you have more than 2½ cups liquid, return it to the pot and boil it, uncovered, over medium-high heat until it reduces to 2½ cups.

6. In a food processor, pulse the remaining green pepper, the onions, and the garlic until finely chopped.

7. Wash out the pressure cooker, return it to the stove, and fry the bacon in it over medium heat. When the bacon is crispy, transfer it to paper towels to drain.

8. Sauté the chopped vegetables in the bacon grease until the onion is translucent, about 3 minutes. Stir the salt, pepper, oregano, and cumin into this sofrito and cook for 1 minute more.

9. Add the rice, the reserved 2½ cups bean liquid, and the beans to the pressure cooker. Close pressure cooker securely, place the pressure regulator on the vent pipe, and raise the heat to high. When the regulator begins dancing and whistling, reduce the heat to medium-low and cook for 5 minutes.

10. Remove the pressure cooker from the stove and let the steam dissipate. When the pot has ceased to hiss, protect your hand with an oven mitt and remove the regulator to check whether all the steam has been released. Once it has, open the cooker and fluff the rice as you pour in the olive oil.

11. Transfer the moros y cristianos to a serving dish and crumble the bacon on top.

NOTE: When I was growing up, crispy pork cracklings (chicharrones) were used instead of the bacon, and pork lard instead of bacon fat.

VARIATION

Conventional Cooking Method: Rinse the beans as directed in Step 1. Place them in a large pot (at least 6 quarts), add 9 cups of water, and let them soak for 8 to 12 hours. Add the ⅓ green pepper and the bay leaf as directed in Step 3. Bring the beans to a boil, reduce the heat, cover the pot partially, and let the beans simmer until tender, about 1 hour. (Check them after 45 minutes, however, because some beans take less time.) Strain the beans as directed in Step 5 and add water if needed to make 4 cups. Chop the vegetables as directed in Step 6. Fry the bacon as directed in Step 7, using a skillet rather than the pressure cooker. Make the sofrito as directed in Step 8. Combine the sofrito, rice, and 4 cups bean liquid in the bean pot. Bring to a boil, reduce the heat, cover the pot, and simmer until the rice is al dente, about 20 minutes. Stir in the beans, return the mixture to a simmer, and cook until the rice is tender, about 10 minutes more. Fluff the rice and beans with olive oil and garnish with the bacon.

In Santiago de Cuba, and indeed the whole of Oriente—the eastern-most province of Cuba—in days gone by, black beans were not eaten as in the rest of Cuba. Instead of moros y cristianos (black beans with rice), congrí, or red beans with rice, was the favorite dish. This recipe was given to me by my dearest friend, the late Mancia Lee, who was from Santiago de Cuba and who never saw black beans until, as a young bride, she left the city of her childhood.

CONGRÍ

(RED BEANS WITH RICE)

8 servings

12 ounces red beans
2 quarts water
¼ pound salt pork
½ pound lean pork or ham
4 garlic cloves, peeled
2 teaspoons salt
½ teaspoon freshly ground pepper
½ teaspoon ground cumin

¼ cup vegetable oil
2 medium onions, peeled and chopped
1 small green bell pepper, cored, seeded, and chopped
⅛ teaspoon sugar
2¼ cups long-grain rice

1. Place the beans in a colander and rinse them under cold running water, removing any impurities. Put them in a large pot with the water and soak for at least 8 hours.

2. Place the pot on the stove and bring the beans to a boil. Reduce the heat, cover, and simmer until tender, about 1 hour and 45 minutes.

3. Meanwhile, cut the salt pork and ham into chunks, cover with cold water, and set them aside to soak.

4. When the beans are nearly cooked, mash the garlic, salt, pepper, and cumin into a paste. (A mortar and pestle works best, but you may mince the garlic finely with a knife or put it through a garlic press and mash the seasonings in with a fork.)

5. Warm the oil in a large skillet over medium heat. Sauté the onions and green pepper until the onions are translucent, about 3 minutes. Stir in the garlic paste and cook for 2 minutes more.

6. When they are tender, remove about 3 cups of the beans from the pot with a slotted spoon and set them aside.

7. Drain and rinse the salt pork and ham and add them to the bean pot. Stir in the cooked vegetables and sugar. Make sure you have at least 5 cups of liquid in the bean pot; add water if necessary.

8. Stir the rice into the bean mixture and bring it to a boil. Reduce the heat, cover, and simmer until the rice is al dente and there is still some liquid in the pot, about 20 minutes.

9. Return the reserved beans to the pot and simmer, uncovered, until all the liquid is absorbed.

ARROZ CON LENTEJAS
(RICE WITH LENTILS)

☙

6 to 8 servings

2 cups dry lentils	I teaspoon salt
I large green bell pepper, cut into thirds and seeded	½ teaspoon freshly ground pepper
I bay leaf	¼ teaspoon dry leaf oregano
4 slices bacon (see Note)	¼ teaspoon ground cumin
I large onion, peeled and cut up	2 cups Valencia (short-grain) rice
4 garlic cloves, peeled and roughly chopped	Dry white wine
	2 tablespoons vegetable oil (optional)

I. Place the lentils in a colander and rinse them well, removing any impurities.

2. Put the lentils in a large pot, add 4 cups of water, ⅓ of the green pepper, and the bay leaf. Bring to a boil, lower the heat, cover, and simmer, for about 30 to 35 minutes, until the lentils are tender but not mushy.

3. While the lentils are cooking, fry the bacon over medium heat in a paellera or other wide, shallow pan. Set it aside on paper towels to drain, reserving the bacon grease.

4. In a food processor, pulse the onion, garlic, and the remaining green pepper until finely chopped.

5. Reheat the bacon grease over medium heat and sauté the chopped vegetables for about 5 minutes. Add the salt, pepper, oregano, cumin, and rice, and stir lightly.

6. Strain the lentils and measure the cooking liquid. Add enough wine to make 4 cups of liquid, and pour it into the rice mixture. Discard the large piece of pepper and bay leaf.

7. Add the lentils to the pan and bring to a boil. Reduce the heat, cover, and simmer for 30 minutes, or until most of the liquid has been absorbed and the rice is tender.

8. Remove the pan from the heat and let the dish rest for 5 minutes. Before serving, fluff the rice and lentils with a fork, adding the optional oil to make it shiny and more delicious. Crumble the reserved bacon over it as a garnish.

NOTE: In my time, rather than bacon, homemade Chicharrones de Pellejo (see page 91) and pork lard were used. If you wish to omit the bacon, add ¼ cup of vegetable oil to replace the bacon grease.

Huevos (Eggs)

Huevos Fritos a la Cubana (Fried Eggs Cuban Style) 165

Revoltillo de Acelgas con Jamón (Scrambled Eggs with Swiss
    Chard and Ham) 165

Aporreado de Bacalao (Chopped Salted Codfish with Scrambled
    Eggs) 166

Huevos a la Malagueña (Eggs Malaga Style) 167

Huevos al Plato (Oven-poached Eggs) 168

Huevos con Almejas (Eggs with Clams) 168

Tortilla de Plátanos Maduros (Fried Ripe Plantain Omelet) 170

Tortilla Española Clásica (Classic Spanish Omelet) 171

HUEVOS (Eggs)

$\mathcal{W}$e did not eat eggs at breakfast in Cuba; we ate them at almuerzo, the midday meal. After the soup course, the cook might serve fried eggs with a plate of fluffy white rice, accompanied by picadillo, fried ripe plantains, and an avocado salad. Or the eggs might be combined with tasty vegetables and meats in a *revoltillo,* a scramble, or baked in little red clay *cazuelitas,* individual casseroles.

No matter how they were prepared, the eggs were always fertilized ones that had been laid by hens in our backyard or at some nearby farm. Those chickens were fed on corn, and that is why the yolks of Cuban eggs were so yellow and the eggs so especially delicious. In this country, one can purchase fertilized eggs at health food stores and in some Latin markets.

For a thoroughly Cuban presentation, serve a bowl of Mojo Criollo (Cuban Garlic Sauce, page 253) on the side.

½ cup vegetable oil or lard
2 fresh eggs

1. Warm the oil in a heavy skillet over medium heat.
2. Crack the eggs and slip them into the pan, one at a time. Gently spoon some of the hot oil up over the yolks until the egg white is thoroughly cooked and the yolk is soft and pink on top.

HUEVOS FRITOS A LA CUBANA

(FRIED EGGS CUBAN STYLE)

I serving

Swiss chard was plentiful in Cuba, and it was eaten often in a wide variety of ways. One of my favorites was with scrambled eggs.

2 pounds fresh Swiss chard
2 tablespoons vegetable oil
¼ pound jamón de cocinar (raw ham) or prosciutto, cut into I-inch cubes (see Note)
I small onion, peeled and finely chopped
I garlic clove, peeled and minced
4 eggs
½ teaspoon freshly ground pepper

1. Put about half a cup of water on to boil in a large pot.
2. Wash the Swiss chard under cold running water and place it, with its large, wide stems, in the pan. Cover the pan and steam the Swiss chard for a minute or two, just until it is wilted.
3. Drain the Swiss chard. When it is cool enough to handle, trim and remove the stems. Coarsely chop the leaves and set them aside.
4. Warm the oil in a large skillet over medium heat and sauté the ham for 5 minutes. Add the onion and sauté until it is translucent, about 3 minutes. Stir in the garlic and cook 2 minutes more. Stir in the Swiss chard.
5. Beat the eggs lightly with the pepper and pour them into the skillet. Stir constantly just until they are scrambled, so that the revoltillo remains moist.

REVOLTILLO DE ACELGAS CON JAMÓN

(SCRAMBLED EGGS WITH SWISS CHARD AND HAM)

4 servings

APORREADO DE BACALAO

(CHOPPED SALTED
CODFISH WITH
SCRAMBLED EGGS)

6 servings

The word *aporreado* is from a verb that means "to beat down." If a child is badly hurt in a fight or a fall, then he is aporreado. In cooking, it is used for dishes of beaten or crushed meat or fish.

Aporreado de bacalao is typically served with white rice and mashed boniato (Cuban sweet potato). Like all bacalao dishes, it requires advance planning because of the time needed to soak the salted codfish.

1 pound salted codfish
3 garlic cloves, peeled
⅛ teaspoon freshly ground pepper
½ cup olive oil
1 large onion, peeled and chopped
1 large green pepper, cored, seeded, and chopped

4 ounces (½ cup) tomato paste
½ cup dry white wine
1 bay leaf
One 6-ounce jar pimientos, sliced, with liquid reserved
6 eggs, lightly beaten

1. Soak the codfish as directed on page 48.

2. Place the codfish in a large pot, cover it with cold water, and bring to a boil. Lower the heat and simmer, uncovered, until the fish is tender, about 1 hour. Drain the fish in a colander and, when it is cool enough to handle, shred it with your fingers.

3. Mash the garlic and pepper into a paste. (A mortar and pestle works best, but you may mince the garlic finely with a knife or put it through a garlic press and mash the pepper in with a fork.)

4. In a large skillet, warm the oil over medium heat. Sauté the onion and green pepper until the onion is translucent, about 3 minutes. Stir in the garlic paste and then the tomato paste, cooking briefly after each addition.

5. Stir in the codfish, wine, bay leaf, and the liquid from the pimientos (save pimientos for garnish). Simmer, uncovered, over low heat for 15 minutes.

6. Add the eggs to the simmering sauce, stirring continuously about 3 to 4 minutes, until they solidify.

7. Transfer to a serving dish and garnish with the pimientos.

Though it originated in the south of Spain, this dish is, to me, typically Cuban. Often, if we had company for almuerzo, it was served as a special first course instead of soup. Asparagus tips and tiny peas—always canned in Cuba and considered delicacies—lent it an elegant touch. It was baked in individual cazuelitas.

HUEVOS A LA MALAGUEÑA
(EGGS MALAGA STYLE)

6 servings

About 3 tablespoons butter
12 medium shrimp
1 dozen eggs
6 tablespoons ketchup
¼ pound jamón de cocinar (raw ham) or prosciutto, coarsely chopped

6 asparagus tips
One 8-ounce can petit pois (tiny peas), or small frozen peas, thawed
Salt
Freshly ground pepper

1. Put a large pot of water on to boil. Preheat the oven to 325 degrees. Grease 6 individual 4- or 5-inch-diameter casserole dishes or ramekins with some of the butter.

2. Drop the shrimp into the boiling water, then lower the heat and simmer for about 4 minutes, just until they turn pink. Drain the shrimp and, when cool enough to handle, shell and devein them.

3. Break 2 eggs into each casserole. Place 2 shrimp in each dish, and pour 1 tablespoon of ketchup over them. Arrange equal amounts of ham, asparagus, and peas on top. Dot each casserole with butter and sprinkle with salt and pepper.

4. Bake for about 15 minutes, until the whites are set but the yolks are still soft. Serve immediately.

HUEVOS AL PLATO

(OVEN-POACHED EGGS)

4 servings

Simpler than huevos a la malagueña, these eggs were a favorite among children. Sometimes they were dressed up with chopped ham or, when served to my father, a spoonful of *encurtido* or pickle relish.

About 2 tablespoons butter	Salt
8 eggs	Freshly ground black pepper
¼ cup milk	¼ cup finely chopped parsley

1. Preheat the oven to 325 degrees. Grease four 4- to 5-inch-diameter individual casserole dishes or ramekins with some of the butter.

2. Break 2 eggs into each dish. Place 1 teaspoon of butter and 1 tablespoon of milk on the eggs in each casserole. Sprinkle with salt, pepper, and parsley.

3. Bake for 15 minutes, until the whites are set but the yolks are still soft. Serve immediately.

HUEVOS CON ALMEJAS

(EGGS WITH CLAMS)

6 servings

This recipe is for one large casserole, but like huevos al plato and huevos a la malagueña, it may be prepared in individual casseroles.

12 small to medium clams	½ cup strong Fish Broth (page 13)
4 tablespoons (½ stick) butter	or canned clam juice, heated
¼ cup chopped parsley	6 whole eggs
1 tablespoon flour	Salt
1 beaten egg yolk	Freshly ground pepper

1. Scrub the clams well under cold running water. Place them in a heavy saucepan or steamer with 1 inch of water, turn heat to high, and cover. As soon as the clams open, remove them from the heat. When they are cool enough to handle, remove them from their shells and set them aside. Strain the cooking liquid through a sieve lined with cheesecloth or paper towel to catch any remaining sand and grit. Discard the shells.

2. Preheat the oven to 325 degrees.

3. In the same saucepan, melt the butter and cook the parsley until it wilts. Stir in the flour and the cooking liquid, and simmer for a few minutes.

4. Remove the saucepan from the heat. Stir in the egg yolk and hot broth until smooth. Pour this mixture into a large casserole, and carefully break the eggs into it.

5. Arrange the clams evenly between the floating eggs. Season them with salt and pepper.

6. Bake for 15 minutes, until the whites are set but the yolks are still soft.

TORTILLAS (Omelets)

In Cuba, we had no Indian tortillas like those in Mexico. To us, as to the Spanish, the word *tortilla* means omelet. There are a great variety of omelets in Cuban cuisine, made either a la española or a la francesa—that is, Spanish style (flat, firm, and dry) or French style (rolled up or turned over, and not so well cooked inside).

Of all our cooks, the best omelet maker was Sisto, who proudly called himself Betún, or shoe polish, because his skin was so shiny and black. To this day, when making French-style omelets I use his method of beating the egg whites and yolks separately for a more tender result.

The pan in which an omelet is made is very important. In Cuba, iron skillets were used almost exclusively. Iron pans are still my favorite, and I have them in various sizes. Pans with nonstick finishes are also excellent for omelet making. For a small, 2- to 3-egg omelet, the pan's bottom should be no more than 7 inches across. For an omelet of 6 to 8 eggs, use a 10- to 11-inch pan.

TORTILLA DE PLÁTANOS MADUROS

(FRIED RIPE PLANTAIN OMELET)

4 servings

Though it is a la francesa, this omelet, with its ripe plantain filling, couldn't be more typically Cuban. Have all of your ingredients ready and work quickly; the omelet itself cooks in about 10 minutes.

¼ cup vegetable oil
1 large ripe plantain, peeled and
   sliced thinly on the diagonal
6 egg whites, at room temperature

6 egg yolks, at room temperature
⅛ teaspoon salt
2 tablespoons butter

1. Warm the oil in a 10-inch skillet over medium heat and fry the plantain slices until dark, being careful not to burn them. Drain them on paper towels and wipe out the skillet, discarding the oil.

2. In a bowl, beat the egg whites until stiff but not dry. Lightly whisk the yolks and fold into the beaten whites with the salt.

3. In the 10-inch skillet, melt the butter over medium-high heat. Pour the egg mixture into the pan and when the eggs begin to set, place the plantains in the center. If some of the egg mixture is still runny, move it with a spatula toward the center.

4. When the eggs are set enough to hold their shape, fold the omelet into thirds: Tilt the pan and use a spatula to turn the right side of the omelet all the way across to the left side. Tilt the pan the other way and fold the left side back all the way across to the right, wrapping up the filling in a neat package. Serve immediately.

VARIATION

Tortilla de Tasajo: Tasajo, jerked beef, makes a very tasty tortilla. Substitute 2 cups of Aporreado de Tasajo (Hash of Jerked Beef, page 77) for the plantains, and omit the salt and vegetable oil.

There is no more famous omelet than this classic tortilla española. In Cuba we ate it at our midday meal and sometimes, cut into tiny wedges, as appetizers at parties. It was a great surprise to me, years later, when we spent the summer at Pedernales, a beach resort in the Spanish province of Vizcaya, to find the dish served so differently. There, wedges of tortilla española were eaten sandwich-style, between pieces of crusty bread.

The variation, tortilla guisada, is a delightful dish from the old days when economy was a way of survival.

TORTILLA ESPAÑOLA CLÁSICA

(CLASSIC SPANISH OMELET)

4 to 6 servings

¾ cup olive oil
I pound potatoes, peeled and
    thinly sliced
I large onion, peeled and thinly
    sliced

5 eggs
¼ teaspoon salt

I. In a deep 9- or I0-inch skillet, warm the oil over medium heat. Drop the potato slices in one by one. Keep them loose by gently turning them with a fork in the oil. Reduce the heat to low. Maintain the oil just at the boiling point and continue cooking for about I5 minutes. Do not allow the potatoes to brown.

2. Add the onion slices to the pan, turning the potatoes and onions frequently to prevent them from sticking together. Cook a few minutes, until the potatoes are tender and the onions are translucent.

3. Place a colander over a bowl and drain the potatoes and onions, reserving the oil. Wipe out the skillet and set it aside.

4. Beat the eggs and salt together thoroughly in a large mixing bowl. Add the potatoes and onions and push them down until they are covered by the eggs. Let them settle for I5 minutes.

5. Pour ¼ cup of the reserved oil back into the skillet and heat it over high heat. Pour in the egg mixture, arranging it to surround the potatoes and onions. Lower the heat to medium-high, and shake the pan gently to keep the eggs from sticking to the bottom.

6. When the eggs have set enough to hold their shape, place a plate or pan lid over the skillet and flip the omelet onto it. Add 2 more tablespoons of oil to the pan, and slide the omelet back into place, cooked side up. Repeat this flipping and sliding procedure several times, adding more oil as needed, until the omelet is firm in the center and golden brown on both sides. (Rather than flip the omelet, you may place it under a hot broiler for 1 minute to brown the top.)

7. Cut the omelet into wedges and serve hot with crusty bread.

VARIATION

Tortilla Guisada (Stewed Omelet): For 4 servings, place 4 wedges of leftover tortilla española clásica in a large skillet or flameproof casserole and cover with 2 cups of Salsa Española (page 253). Cook gently, uncovered, over very low heat for about 10 minutes, just until heated through.

FRITURAS (FRITTERS)

FRITURAS (Fritters)

*M*early every vegetable and meat imaginable was used to make fritters in Cuba, and nearly every meal included *frituritas de ésto o de lo otro* (fritters of this or that). Fritters were a side dish—never an entrée—but they were a very important one. When dinner was almost ready, the lady of the house announced to the cook, "*Ya puedes empezar a freir,*" "You may begin to fry," and the fritters would be fried quickly and brought to the table crispy and succulent.

In Cuba of yore, frying was usually done in pork lard, often home-made. For those who wonder how Cubans maintained their health, it must be noted that our cooks were experts at the art of deep-frying. They heated the oil to just the right temperature. Our fritters were always crisp and never greasy.

Croquettes, which are a type of fritter, are the perfect use for bits of beef, chicken, or seafood salvaged from bones used to cook broth. After dining at our home one evening on baked red snapper, my friend Lucy Fiallo looked at the leftovers and said, "*Con esas masitas puedes hacer unas croquetas riquísimas.*" ("With those morsels you can make the most delicious croquettes.") And she began making them for me right then and there!

How to Fry Fritters

No matter what kind of fritters you are making, the procedure for frying them is the same once you have mixed the batter:

1. In a deep, heavy skillet or a deep fryer, heat the oil until fragrant (about 375 degrees).

2. Drop the batter into the hot oil by the tablespoonful or, for appetizer servings, the teaspoonful.

3. Fry the fritters, no more than 4 at a time, until they are golden on all sides.

4. Drain the fritters on paper towels and place them in a warm oven until you have fried all the batter. (Be sure to keep the oil very hot to minimize the amount the fritters absorb.) Serve them hot.

Years ago, these fritters were made with fresh yucca that had to be peeled and boiled the way I describe in the recipe for Yuca con Mojo (page 190). When very tender and still hot, the yucca was mashed using a mortar and pestle to make the "paste." These days, this task is easier and quicker with frozen yucca and a food processor.

1 pound frozen yucca
2 eggs, separated
2 small garlic cloves, peeled
2 tablespoons freshly squeezed
    lime juice

1 teaspoon salt
1½ to 2 cups vegetable oil

1. Following the instructions on the package, boil the yucca until it is very tender.

2. Carefully remove and discard the wicklike *palitos* from the center of the vegetable and quickly place the hot yucca in a food processor. (If the yucca cools, it hardens and becomes unmashable.) Pulse it until it becomes a thick paste.

3. Add the egg yolks, garlic, lime juice, and salt. Pulse until well mixed.

4. Beat the egg whites until stiff but not dry and fold them into the yucca batter.

5. Fry the fritters in the oil as directed on page 176.

VARIATION

Dessert Fritters: For a delicious dessert, omit the garlic, add 1 teaspoon ground anise, and proceed as directed. Serve the fritters with Almíbar No. 2 (page 255).

FRITURAS DE MALANGA CRUDA

(RAW MALANGA FRITTERS)

8 servings

These fritters are lovely as a side dish or as appetizers.

3 or 4 malangas (about 2 pounds total)
2 garlic cloves, peeled and minced
1 teaspoon salt
½ teaspoon freshly ground pepper
2 eggs, beaten
1 tablespoon chopped parsley
1½ to 2 cups vegetable oil

1. Cut each malanga into 3 or 4 pieces for easier peeling. Peel and chop into smaller chunks. Grate the malanga in a food processor quickly, making sure it doesn't turn gummy.

2. In a mixing bowl, stir together the malanga, garlic, salt, pepper, eggs, and parsley until well blended.

3. Fry the fritters in the oil as directed on page 176.

VARIATION

Dessert fritters: For a delicious dessert, omit the garlic, pepper, and parsely and serve them hot or cold, with Almíbar No. 1 (page 255).

FRITURAS DE PAPAS

(POTATO FRITTERS)

8 servings

1½ pounds potatoes, peeled and quartered
3 eggs
1 cup flour
¼ cup grated Cheddar cheese
2 tablespoons finely chopped parsley
1 teaspoon salt
½ teaspoon fresh ground pepper
1½ to 2 cups vegetable oil

1. Cover the potatoes with water in a heavy saucepan and cook them until tender, about 30 minutes.

2. While they are still hot, drain the potatoes and purée them in a food processor.

3. Add the eggs, one by one, pulsing each time. Continue pulsing as you gradually add the flour, cheese, parsley, salt, and pepper.

4. Fry the fritters in the oil as directed on page 176.

6 ears of fresh corn (see Note), or
   3 cups canned and drained or
   frozen and thawed corn
1 medium onion, peeled and quartered
3 tablespoons tomato purée

2 tablespoons chopped parsley
2 eggs
1 teaspoon salt
½ teaspoon freshly ground pepper
1½ to 2 cups vegetable oil

FRITURAS DE MAÍZ

(CORN FRITTERS)

4 servings

1. Husk the corn and cut off the kernels with a sharp knife.

2. Place the corn, onion, tomato purée, parsley, eggs, salt, and pepper in a food processor. Pulse them into a coarse batter.

3. Fry the fritters in the oil as directed on page 176.

NOTE: Autumn corn, which is tougher, drier, and less sweet than summer corn, is best for this purpose.

This fritter dish is not Spanish, nor is it Texan, though Texans love their black-eyed peas. It was not invented by the African slaves, and it is certainly not an inheritance from Cuba's native Siboneyes. It is of Chinese origin, handed down by the Chinese who came to Cuba as laborers in the nineteenth century. So these fritters are really *bollitos chinos.* Garnish them with lime wedges.

1 pound dry black-eyed peas,
   picked over and washed
10 garlic cloves, peeled

1 teaspoon salt
½ teaspoon freshly ground pepper
1½ to 2 cups vegetable oil

BOLLITOS DE FRIJOLES DE CARITAS

(FRIED LITTLE ROLLS OF BLACK-EYED PEAS)

4 servings

1. Place the black-eyed peas in a large pot and cover them with water. Soak them for at least 8 hours, changing the water twice.

2. Discard all but ¼ cup of the soaking water, and rinse the peas well under cold running water. Rub each one between your fingers to remove the skin (it will be loose and blistered from the soaking). Discard the skin.

3. Using a mortar and pestle or a food processor, mash the peas into a paste. Add the garlic and continue mashing just until smooth.

4. Stir in the salt and pepper. Add the reserved soaking water and beat vigorously until you have a soft batter.

5. Fry the bollitos in the oil as directed on page 176.

FRITURAS DE BACALAO
(CODFISH FRITTERS)

4 servings

In Cárdenas, my hometown, one could buy frituras de bacalao warm and ready to eat at La Plaza del Mercado, a huge marketplace that in the 1920s and '30s was already a shopping mall of the future. Made bite-size, these are excellent appetizers.

I pound dry salted codfish
I large onion, peeled
4 eggs
3 tablespoons flour
I tablespoon milk

¼ teaspoon freshly ground black pepper
Salt (optional)
2 tablespoons minced parsley
I½ to 2 cups vegetable oil

1. Prepare the codfish as directed on page 48.

2. Place the fish and the onion in a large pot, cover them with cold water, and bring to a boil. Reduce the heat and simmer, uncovered, until the fish is tender, about I hour.

3. Drain the codfish, reserving the onion and discarding the water. When it is cool enough to handle, shred the codfish into slivers with your fingers.

4. In a food processor, pulse the onion, eggs, flour, milk, pepper, and, if needed, salt (the codfish may supply enough) until blended.

5. Stir the onion mixture and the parsley into the shredded codfish.

6. Fry the fritters in the oil as directed on page 176.

Vegetales y Viandas (Vegetables)

VEGETALES Y VIANDAS (Vegetables)

Cuba's fertile soil and hospitable climate produce such lush vegetation that it is no wonder that Christopher Columbus wrote in his journal: "This is the most beautiful land that human eyes have ever seen."

Only a touch of the hoe prepared the land for planting, as the Chinese who were brought to Cuba as laborers in the mid-nineteenth century discovered. Chinese farmers soon came to dominate vegetable gardening in Cuba, and I well remember how their neat plots dotted the landscape around Cárdenas.

In Cárdenas and later Varadero, a Chinese vegetable vendor would call at our back door early each morning before the sun was too strong. Balancing a basket of produce on either end of the *palo* or stick on his shoulders, he would announce that everything was *"flesquecito,"* his Chinese-accented version of *fresquecito* or "fresh." The cook, supervised by my great-grandmother Chicha (or, if Chicha was inclined to share her power, my mother), would select the day's vegetables. I can still see those sweet, crispy greens, whether leafy lettuce, watercress, parsley, or Swiss chard; those crunchy, bright orange carrots; those red-skinned potatoes; and those succulent tomatoes, little red ones for cooking and large green and pink ones for salads. And then there were the hearty *viandas,* the native root vegetables such as yucca, malanga, boniato, and ñame that were and are so indispensable to Cuban cooking.

In my childhood home and in my own kitchen today, cooking vegetables yields not only a delicious dish for that day's table but a tasty and nutritious broth for a future soup or sauce. Gaylord Hauser, a health and fitness "guru" of the 1940s, used to say, "If you must discard something when cooking vegetables, discard the vegetable." I would not, of course, suggest that you go that far, but you will be delighted to find how such broths enhance your cooking.

Vegetables also were the basis for many delicious and uniquely Cuban entrées in our home. Some, such as stuffed vegetables and meat and vegetable pies, evolved from the universal desire of thrifty cooks to make imaginative use of leftovers. Others, such as okra with plantain dumplings, are evidence of the ways in which African slaves brought their heritage to bear on the island's tropical vegetables. Still others incorporate corn, a staple of Cuba's native Siboneyes.

Fresh corn never became popular in Spain as did such New World products as tomatoes, potatoes, and coffee. Even in contemporary Spain, fresh corn is considered fit only for pig feed. But in Cuba, as throughout Latin America, corn has always been essential.

Corn was one of my grandfather's favorite crops, and when we were poor we had wonderful meals of tamales, *tamal en cazuela, guiso de maíz,* and *albóndigas de maíz.* When I think of those delicious dishes, I cannot help but recall a friendly (not to say fresh) family of seven who for a whole summer season came by bus from Cárdenas and invaded our house nearly every day to use the bathrooms to change into their bathing suits. They would walk to the north beach, have their swim, and invade our privacy again after a couple of hours to change clothes just about the time when we were sitting down to eat our midday meal. One day one of the children—a fat little boy, as I recall—blurted out: *"Oye, pero ustedes no comen nada más que maíz todos los días?"* ("Hey, don't you eat anything but corn every day?")

PLÁTANOS (Plantains)

Although plantains are used widely throughout the Caribbean, Cubans regard them as a sort of national symbol. In fact, when a non-Cuban becomes thoroughly "Cubanized," he is described as *aplatanado* or "plantainized." My freckled, fair-skinned Irish-American husband, for example, who wears guayaberas (Cuban shirts) and is his charming, corny self to exactly the same degree in Spanish as in English, is regarded as very aplatanado.

The following recipes use plantains in their three forms. You will note that ripe plantains may be peeled like bananas, while semiripe ones are cooked with their skins on to preserve their sweetness. Hard green plantains require a special peeling procedure, which I describe in detail.

Sweet, succulent maduros are universally loved by Cubans, and are served as a side dish with any entrée whatsoever.

3 large, very ripe (black-skinned)
　　plantains
Vegetable oil

1. Peel the plantains as you would bananas, and cut each one on the diagonal into ½-inch slices.
2. Pour about 1 inch of oil into a large skillet and heat it over medium-high heat. (You must keep it hot or the plantains will absorb too much oil.)
3. Fry the plantain slices until they are almost black but not burned.
4. Drain them on paper towels. Serve them immediately, or keep them in a warm oven until serving time.

PLÁTANOS MADUROS FRITOS
(FRIED RIPE PLANTAINS)

6 to 8 servings

PLÁTANOS EN TENTACIÓN
(TEMPTATION PLANTAINS)

12 to 16 servings

This rich dish can be served hot, cold, or at room temperature; it is always ambrosial. In Cuba it was sometimes made with bananas, which were called "plátanos Johnson," and served flambé as dessert.

About 6 teaspoons butter
4 very ripe plantains, each about 10 inches long
¼ cup granulated sugar
⅓ cup dark brown sugar

5 tablespoons dry white wine (see Note)
2 cinnamon sticks
¼ teaspoon ground cinnamon

1. Preheat the oven to 375 degrees. Butter a large baking dish.
2. Peel the plantains as you would bananas. Lay them in the baking dish and dust them with half the granulated and brown sugars.
3. Pour on the wine and add the cinnamon sticks. Dust the plantains with the remaining sugar and the ground cinnamon. Place a teaspoon of butter on each plantain and bake for 40 minutes.
4. Remove the plantains from the oven and slice each one into 3 or 4 portions.

NOTE: Some Cuban cooks use white vermouth or red wine instead.

PLÁTANOS PINTONES SALCOCHADOS
("BOILED" SEMIRIPE PLANTAINS)

6 to 8 servings

The best way to cook semiripe plantains is in a pressure cooker or microwave; less water is required than with conventional boiling, and there is therefore less waste of the plantains' sweetness. Semiripe plantains must be cooked in their skins; otherwise they lose their flavor. Serve them with butter as you would mashed potatoes, or use them in other recipes such as Fufú de Plátano Pintón (page 188) or Quimbombó con Bolas de Plátanos (page 199).

3 large, semiripe plantains

PRESSURE COOKER METHOD:
1. Cut the plantains into 2- or 3-inch chunks.
2. Place them in a pressure cooker and add 1 inch of water. Lock the lid into place and put the pressure regulator on the vent pipe.

Heat the cooker over high heat until the regulator starts to whistle and dance, indicating that high pressure has been reached. Reduce the heat to medium, maintaining high pressure, and cook for 3 minutes.

3. Remove the cooker from the heat and let the steam spend itself. After about 10 minutes, with your hand protected by an oven mitt, carefully remove the regulator. If no steam emerges from the vent pipe, remove the cover. (If it is still steaming, wait until it stops before opening.)

4. Drain the plantains in a colander. When they are cool enough to handle, slash the skins lengthwise with a sharp knife or kitchen scissors and peel the plantains.

MICROWAVE METHOD:

1. Cut the plantains into 2- or 3-inch chunks.

2. Place the plantains in a single layer in a glass baking dish. Add ¼ inch of water and cover the dish tightly with plastic wrap.

3. Microwave on high for 3 minutes per plantain.

4. Remove the dish from the microwave and remove the plastic wrap to allow the steam to escape.

5. When the steam has dissipated, test the plantains with a fork; if they are not tender, re-cover them and microwave on high for 1 minute at a time until done.

6. Drain the plantains in a colander. When they are cool enough to handle, slash the skins lengthwise with a sharp knife or kitchen scissors and peel the plantains.

Lilí, one of our maids, buying from a Chinese vegetable vendor. Varadero, 1946.
Author's collection

FUFÚ DE PLÁTANO PINTÓN

(MASHED SEMIRIPE PLANTAINS)

6 to 8 servings

Fufú can be served as is or used in a number of interesting dishes, including Bolas de Plátano Pintón (Semiripe Plantain Balls, page 200).

3 semiripe (yellow) plantains
2 tablespoons vegetable oil

1. Peel and cook the plantains as directed on pages 186-87.
2. Mash them with a potato masher, adding the vegetable oil as you do so, until they have the consistency of lumpy mashed potatoes.
3. Serve the fufú as a hot side dish or use it to make a Tambor (see page 198 for guidance).

MACHUQUILLO

(MASHED PLANTAINS WITH PORK)

6 to 8 servings

Machuquillo was served much as one would serve mashed potatoes in this country. It was also called *migas de plátano*, or plantain crumbs, because it was thought of as poor people's food, but in my house we enjoyed it often, regardless of our circumstances.

2 quarts water
1 tablespoon salt
3 green plantains
1 tablespoon lime juice

6 cloves garlic, peeled and minced
1 cup Chicharrones (page 91; see Note)
1 tablespoon vegetable oil

1. Combine the water and salt in a large saucepan and put it on to boil.
2. With a sharp knife, slash the skin of each plantain once lengthwise. Cut the plantains into 2-inch pieces. Take the skin off each piece by opening it away from the center as if you were taking off a coat. Discard the skins. In a shallow glass or ceramic dish, paint the plantain pieces with the lime juice.
3. Mash the garlic and the chicharrones together into a fine paste with a mortar and pestle or food processor.
4. When the water reaches a full boil, add the plantains and lime juice. Boil for about 25 minutes, until the plantains are tender, and drain them.

5. While they are still warm and malleable, mash the plantains with a potato masher until they have the consistency of lumpy mashed potatoes.

6. Add the garlic mixture to the plantains and blend well.

7. Heat the oil in the saucepan over medium heat. Add the plantain mixture and stir for a minute or two, until any excess moisture has evaporated. Serve hot.

NOTE: If you prefer not to make your own cracklings you can find the packaged variety in most Latin markets. For a different but tasty result, you may substitute half a pound of bacon, fried crisp and crumbled.

TOSTONES
(PLANTAIN PATTIES)

6 to 8 servings

Traditionally, tostones, twice-fried green plantain patties, were prepared for their second frying by pressing them between two sheets of brown paper, or inside a paper bag. Today one can buy a kitchen tool made expressly for this purpose called a *tostonera*—a kind of press made of two hinged pieces of wood. Its makers would have you believe that one press of the tostonera will produce a perfect tostón, but I much prefer the old method. It allows you to feel how fragile the plantain is and to adjust your pressure accordingly so that the tostón does not break.

3 large green plantains
1 cup vegetable oil
Salt

1. With a sharp knife, slash the skin of each plantain once lengthwise. Cut the plantains into 1½-inch pieces. Take the skin off each piece by opening it away from the center as if you were taking off a coat.

2. Warm the oil over medium heat in a large, heavy skillet. Sauté the plantain pieces until slightly golden on all sides. Drain them on paper towels. Remove the skillet from the heat.

3. While the pieces are still warm, slip them, one at a time, between two thicknesses of brown paper (a paper bag works well) and press them gently but firmly until they are about half their original thickness. (You may freeze them for future use at this point.)

4. Mix a little salt with some warm water in a bowl or pan, and soak the tostones for about 5 minutes. (This keeps them moist and makes them much more delicious.) Drain them on paper towels.

5. Reheat the oil over medium heat and fry the tostones until they are warmed through and just a bit darker gold. Drain them on paper towels again, sprinkle them with salt, and serve. (After frying, you may set them aside until serving time and reheat them for about 5 minutes in a warm oven, but they are at their best when just fried.)

YUCA CON MOJO

(YUCCA WITH GARLIC SAUCE)

6 to 8 servings

When something is really tough, Cubans are likely to exclaim, "*¡Esto está de yuca y ñame!*" likening the experience to two very tough root vegetables. However, when boiled, both yucca and ñame turn soft and delicious. Swimming in mojo, they become potent side dishes. As you can see from the second variation, yellow malanga is also served this way. All of these vegetables must be served immediately after cooking, lest they harden as they cool into a virtually inedible mass.

This cooking method, with its interrupted boiling, ensures that the yucca will "open up" properly and expose its wicklike core.

3 pounds (6 medium) yucca (see Note)

I teaspoon salt
I cup Mojo Criollo (page 253)

I. Slit the yucca lengthwise and peel off the barklike skin. Cut the yucca into chunks.

2. Place the yucca in a large pot, cover it with cold water, and put it on to boil. Measure 2 cups of cold water and set it aside. When the yucca reaches a vigorous boil, pour the additional cold water into the pot. Return it to a boil and cook the yucca, uncovered, until very tender, about 15 minutes.

3. Remove the pot from the heat and add the salt. Allow the yucca to soak for 3 minutes in the hot, salty water. Drain it, place it in a serving dish, and douse it with the mojo.

NOTE: Frozen yucca, available in many Latin markets, is a convenient substitute for fresh. Cook it according to the package directions.

VARIATIONS

Ñame Salcochado con Mojo (Boiled White Yam with Garlic Sauce): Substitute 3 pounds ñame for the yucca. Cut it into 1-inch slices and then peel each slice. Cover the ñame with water and cook it for 30 minutes. Proceed as directed above beginning with Step 3.

Malanga Amarilla con Mojo (Yellow Malanga with Garlic Sauce): Substitute 3 pounds yellow malanga for the yucca. Proceed as directed in the ñame variation above.

BONIATOS FRITOS
(FRIED TROPICAL SWEET POTATO)

6 servings

While not so sweet as American sweet potatoes or yams, boniatos have a delicately sweet flavor of their own. Some Cuban cooks sprinkle these "fries" with sugar—never salt—to further bring out their flavor.

2 pounds (4 medium) boniato
½ cup vegetable oil

1. Peel the boniatos and cut them into the desired shape: 1-inch-thick rounds, 1-inch cubes, or "fingers" 3 inches long and 1 inch thick.
2. In a large, heavy skillet or a deep fryer, heat the oil over medium-high heat.
3. Fry the boniatos just as you would fry potatoes, until they are golden. Drain them on paper towels and serve hot.

BONIATOS SALCOCHADOS CON CEBOLLAS AMORTIGUADAS

(BOILED TROPICAL SWEET POTATOES WITH LIMP ONIONS)

6 servings

Boniato was often served this way in our home when I was a child, and I still enjoy the combination of the sweet sautéed onion and the even sweeter boniato.

2 pounds (4 medium) boniato
2 tablespoons vegetable oil

I large yellow onion, peeled and cut into ½-inch rings

I. Place the unpeeled boniatos in a large pot, cover them with water, and bring to a boil. Reduce the heat, cover, and simmer until tender, 35 to 40 minutes.

2. In a large skillet, warm the oil over medium heat and sauté the onion slices until limp, about 5 minutes.

3. Drain the boniatos into a colander. When they are cool enough to handle, peel them and slice them into I-inch-thick rounds. Transfer them to a serving dish and arrange the onion slices over them. Serve immediately.

PURÉ DE MALANGA

(MALANGA PURÉE)

4 servings

When puréeing malanga, it is essential to work fast because malanga hardens, almost petrifies, when it cools. A potato masher works best because it can be used right in the pot before the malanga has a chance to cool. (A food processor makes the malanga gummy rather than creamy and smooth.) The variation with milk produces an even creamier purée.

2 pounds (4 medium) malanga
⅓ cup Spanish olive oil
I teaspoon salt

I. Cut the unpeeled malanga into I-inch rounds, and peel each slice.

2. Place the malanga in a large saucepan and cover it with cold water. Bring to a boil, reduce the heat, cover, and simmer until the malanga is tender, about 20 minutes.

3. Pour all but about ⅓ cup of the cooking water from the pot. (Save the excess for a future soup.) Quickly mash the malanga with a

potato masher, simultaneously adding the olive oil and the salt. Serve immediately.

VARIATION

Puré de Malanga con Leche (Malanga Purée with Milk): Substitute 3 tablespoons of butter for the olive oil. Heat it together with ¼ cup milk while the malanga is cooking. Drain the cooked malanga completely, add the milk mixture, and mash.

PURÉ DE CALABAZA

(CALABAZA PURÉE)

6 to 8 servings

When a calabaza is good, it is better than any kind of pumpkin, but you must select calabazas that are a deep orange color. When buying one, try to insert your thumbnail into its skin. If you cannot, then the calabaza is sweet and *amazada*, which is to say firm and densely textured rather than bland, watery, and stringy.

Of the many ways to cook calabaza, I find a pressure cooker the most efficient. Alternatively, steam or boil it until it is tender, about 30 minutes.

2 pounds (I medium) calabaza
3 tablespoons vegetable oil or
   unsalted butter

I large onion, peeled and
   chopped

I. Using a large, sturdy butcher knife, cut the calabaza into chunks. Remove the seeds but not the skin.

2. Put I cup of water in a pressure cooker and place the calabaza on the cooking rack. Lock the lid into place and put the pressure regulator on the vent pipe. Heat the cooker over high heat until the regulator starts to whistle and dance, indicating that high pressure has been reached. Reduce the heat to medium, maintaining high pressure, and cook for 2 minutes.

3. Remove the cooker from the heat and let the steam dissipate. After about I0 minutes, with your hand protected by an oven mitt, carefully remove the regulator. If no steam emerges from the vent pipe, remove the lid. (If it is still steaming, wait until it stops before opening.)

4. While the pressure cooker is cooling, warm the oil in a large skillet over medium heat. Sauté the onion until translucent, about 3 minutes, and remove it from the heat.

5. Drain the calabaza, and when it is cool enough to handle, peel it.

6. Stir the calabaza into the onion, and mash it in the skillet with a potato masher. Heat it over medium heat and allow it to simmer until thick.

VARIATION

Puré de Calabaza con Ajo (Calabaza Purée with Garlic): Substitute 4 peeled, minced garlic cloves for the onion, and olive oil for the vegetable oil. Sauté the garlic for only about 3 minutes.

COL ESPAÑOLA
(SPANISH CABBAGE)

6 servings

This recipe was a favorite of Agustina, the cook and housemaid who was our only hired help when we were poor. She called it Spanish cabbage because she claimed it was from *El Tiempo de España*, or colonial times.

2 tablespoons vegetable oil
I large onion, peeled and chopped
I large green bell pepper, cored, seeded, and chopped
¾ cup tomato sauce

I small cabbage (about I pound)
I teaspoon salt
½ teaspoon freshly ground pepper
¼ cup grated Cheddar cheese
2 tablespoons dry bread crumbs

I. In a large skillet, warm the oil over medium heat. Sauté the onion and green pepper until the onion is translucent, about 3 minutes. Stir in the tomato sauce and cook for a few minutes more. Remove the sauce from the heat.

2. Put 2 or 3 inches of water in a steamer and bring it to a boil. Preheat the oven to 350 degrees.

3. Cut the cabbage into quarters, and cut each quarter in half crosswise. Steam the cabbage for about 5 minutes, until the heart is tender when pierced with a fork.

4. Place the cabbage wedges in a large casserole and season with salt and pepper. Top them with the cheese and sauce. Sprinkle with bread crumbs.

5. Bake the cabbage for 15 to 20 minutes, until the crumbs are golden.

"Cuando no hay pan, se come casabe." ("If we don't have bread, then we will use Casabe") —an old Cuban saying comparable to "If you can't be with the one you love, love the one you're with."

CASABE
(BREAD OF THE INDIANS)

12 servings

Cuba's native Indians, the Siboneyes, were nearly obliterated by the Spanish colonization. Within a century of Columbus's arrival, only a few Indians remained in the eastern end of the island, around Santiago. It follows that casabe, the vegetable dish eaten as a bread and called bread of the Indians, was not eaten on the western end of the island where I grew up. In fact, I never saw casabe until I was an adult living in Venezuela, where it was often served at barbecues in the form of a large, round cracker that was cut into small pieces to accompany the meat. (It resembled a piece of the fiberboard used in construction, and that is what my husband dubbed it!)

Sarita Bueno, a friend from Santiago, gave me this recipe. Since it requires many hours of exposure to the natural heat of the sun, casabe can only be made during the summer months in most parts of this country.

8 fresh yuccas (about 2 pounds)

1. Peel the yucca and grate it finely. (You may use a food processor for grating.)

2. Line a large colander with 6 thicknesses of cheesecloth, and pour the grated yucca into it. Press and twist the cheesecloth to extract as much liquid as possible.

3. Outdoors, on a large wooden or stone surface, spread the yucca pulp, still on the cheesecloth, to a thickness of ⅛ inch and leave it in the full sun and *sereno* for 14 to 16 hours.

4. Preheat the oven to 200 degrees.

5. Press the yucca into two 14-inch pizza pans. Bake it for about 30 minutes, until the casabe is perfectly dry but not toasted. It should look like a large, white cracker.

6. To serve, break the casabe into small pieces and eat it, like a corn chip, with your favorite dip.

AJÍES RELLENOS
(STUFFED PEPPERS)

6 servings

Cubans call green bell peppers *ajíes*. Spainiards call them *pimientos,* a word that to us, as to most Americans, means peppers of the canned red variety. From the Spaniards, though, Cubans learned to peel sweet peppers, a procedure that, as in this recipe, yields a delicious and delicate result—perfect for dinner parties. Serve ajíes rellenos with fluffy white rice, and encourage your guests to spoon the sauce over the peppers and rice.

6 medium green bell peppers
½ cup milk
½ cup bread crumbs, plucked from a fresh loaf
6 tablespoons vegetable oil
I medium onion, peeled and chopped
2 garlic cloves, peeled and minced
I tablespoon tomato paste
2 cups finely chopped cooked pork (see Note)

I cup finely chopped jamón de cocinar (raw ham) or prosciutto
½ cup raisins
⅓ cup pitted green olives
2 eggs
½ teaspoon salt
¼ teaspoon freshly ground pepper
½ cup dry bread crumbs
2 cups Salsa Española (Spanish Sauce, page 253)

I. Preheat the broiler.

2. Cut off the tops of the peppers and remove the seeds and membranes, being careful not to pierce the shells. Place the peppers under the broiler, turning them every few minutes, until they are blistered on all sides (about 5 minutes). Transfer them to a cooling rack. When the peppers are cool enough to handle, pull off the blistered skin. (If you want to use a paring knife rather than your fingers, take care not to puncture the peppers.) Set them aside.

3. Pour the milk over the fresh bread crumbs and set them aside to soak.

4. In a large, heavy skillet, heat 2 tablespoons of the oil over medium heat and sauté the onion until translucent, about 3 minutes. Add the garlic and cook 2 minutes more. Stir in the tomato paste, pork, ham, and the bread mixture, and simmer for 10 minutes. Stir in the raisins and olives.

5. Preheat the oven to 350 degrees. Beat the eggs with the salt and pepper in one dish and place the dry bread crumbs in another.

6. Gently pack the meat mixture into the hollow peppers.

7. Being careful that the stuffing doesn't fall out, dip the top of each pepper in the egg and then in the bread crumbs.

8. Pour the salsa española into an attractive casserole large enough to hold all the peppers upright.

9. Wipe out the pan in which you made the meat filling, and heat the remaining ¼ cup of oil in it over medium-high heat. Sauté the peppers, crumb side down, for about a minute, just to set the crumbs.

10. Place the peppers, right side up, in the casserole. Bake them, uncovered, for 15 or 20 minutes, until the tops are crisp and golden.

11. Spoon the sauce over the peppers and serve in the casserole.

NOTE: Leftover roast pork or Masitas de Puerco Fritas (page 92) would typically be used in this dish.

This captivating dish makes a much more dramatic presentation than the stuffed cabbage leaves of Eastern European origin. Bring it to the table whole in a large, deep serving dish surrounded by its rich sauce. As you cut it into wedges it will open, petallike, spilling the filling into the serving dish to mingle with the rich sauce. Serve each guest a wedge of cabbage with a brimming ladleful of saucy filling poured over a bed of fluffy white rice.

COL RELLENA
(STUFFED CABBAGE)

6 to 8 servings

One 2-pound cabbage
2 cups Picadillo Clásico (page 71)
1 cup Beef Broth (page 13)

2 cups Salsa Española (Spanish
   Sauce, page 253)

1. Trim the outer leaves from the cabbage. With a sharp knife, cut a "lid" about 4 inches square from the top and set it aside.

2. Scoop out most of the inside of the cabbage with a paring knife, reserving the pulp and leaving a ¾-inch shell. Be careful not to puncture the sides of the cabbage.

3. Fill the cabbage shell with the picadillo. Put the "lid" on and tie it onto the cabbage securely with kitchen string. Place the cabbage in a dutch oven or other large, heavy pot. Arrange the cabbage pulp around it.

4. Combine the broth and salsa española and pour it over the cabbage. Cover the pot and simmer the cabbage for at least 2 hours. (If the sauce is still watery at that point, uncover the pot and continue cooking until it reduces to the consistency of a creamy soup.)

5. Transfer the cabbage to a deep serving dish. Remove the string and pour the sauce around the cabbage.

TAMBOR DE BONIATO

(MEAT AND CUBAN
SWEET POTATO PIE)

4 to 6 servings

This dish is a wonderful way to use leftover boniatos and picadillo clásico.

1 teaspoon butter or margarine
2 cups mashed boniatos
1½ cups Picadillo Clásico
   (page 71)

¼ cup dry bread crumbs
¼ cup grated Cheddar cheese
   (optional)

1. Preheat the oven to 350 degrees.

2. Grease a 1-quart casserole or a deep pie plate with the butter.

3. Spread half the mashed boniatos in the bottom of the casserole and spoon in the picadillo in an even layer. Spread the remaining mashed boniatos on top and sprinkle with bread crumbs and grated cheese.

4. Bake until a golden crust forms on top, about 30 minutes.

VARIATIONS

Tambor de Plátano Pintón (Meat and Semiripe Plantain Pie): Substitute 2 cups of Fufú de Plátano Pintón (page 188) for the boniatos.

Tambor de Malanga (Meat and Malanga Pie): Substitute 2 cups of Puré de Malanga (page 192) for the boniatos.

This mouth-watering Afro-Cuban dish is my favorite way to serve okra.

I pound fresh okra
⅓ cup vegetable oil
I chorizo, sliced
I large onion, peeled and chopped
I large green bell pepper, cored, seeded, and chopped
3 cloves garlic, peeled and minced

I cup tomato sauce
4 cups Chicken Broth (page 13)
2 cups dry white wine
I tablespoon white wine vinegar
I teaspoon salt
½ teaspoon freshly ground pepper
24 plantain balls (recipe follows)

QUIMBOMBÓ CON BOLAS DE PLÁTANOS

(OKRA WITH PLANTAIN DUMPLINGS)

6 to 8 servings

1. Rinse the okra and dry it well. Cut it crosswise into ¼-inch rounds, taking care to keep it dry. This is very important. If wet, okra turns slimy when cut.

2. In a large soup pot, warm the oil over medium heat and lightly sauté the chorizo. Add the onion and green pepper, and sauté until the onion is translucent, about 3 minutes. Stir in the garlic and cook 2 minutes more.

3. Stir in the okra and cook for about 5 minutes longer. Add the tomato sauce, chicken broth, wine, vinegar, salt, and pepper. Bring to a boil, reduce the heat, cover, and simmer for about 45 minutes, until the okra is tender.

4. While the stew is cooking, make the plantain balls.

5. Just before serving, carefully drop the plantain balls into the stew and cook them gently just until heated through, about 5 minutes.

BOLAS DE PLÁTANO PINTÓN

(SEMIRIPE PLANTAIN BALLS)

🌿

24 balls

These dumplinglike balls are typically served in quimbombó, but they are good in other stews as well. They are extremely delicate, and should be added to the stew just before serving to heat them through. They disintegrate so easily that they are not good leftovers, so encourage everyone at the table to eat them up at one sitting. Urge your guests, as my brother Pancho would say, *"Sacrifícate!"* ("Sacrifice yourself!") But believe me, eating these tasty morsels is no sacrifice!

3 semiripe (yellow) plantains
2 tablespoons liquid reserved from
    cooking the plantains

Oil or butter

1. Cook and peel the plantains as directed on pages 186–87, reserving 2 tablespoons of the cooking liquid.

2. Mash the plantains with a potato masher or in a food processor, gradually adding just enough of the cooking liquid to achieve a thick, doughlike consistency.

3. Grease your hands, take 1 heaping tablespoon of the plantain mixture at a time, and form each into a ball about 1½ inches in diameter. Set the balls aside until it is time to add them to the stew.

GUISO DE BERENJENA

(EGGPLANT STEW)

🌿

6 servings

The authoritative Cuban cookbook of my mother's generation was *Delicias de la Mesa* (*Delights of the Table*), a huge tome by María Antonia de los Reyes y Gavilán. My mother once handed the book to a cook she had just hired, recommending that she consult it often. "Never have I worked for anyone who made me cook by the book!" the woman exclaimed as she stomped out of our kitchen, never to return. The ex-cook's opinion notwithstanding, María Antonia de los Reyes y Gavilán was considered the cooking authority of her time, a veritable Julia Child of Cuban cuisine. This is a variation on one of her recipes. Note that you do not peel the eggplant.

2 large eggplants (3½ to 4 pounds total)
salt
¼ cup Spanish olive oil
I large onion, chopped
I small green pepper, chopped
3 cloves garlic, minced
3 plum tomatos, chopped

2 tablespoons chopped parsley
2 tablespoons freshly squeezed lime juice
I cup cubed jamón de cocinar (raw ham) or prosciutto
½ teaspoon freshly ground pepper
½ cup dry white wine

I. Slice the eggplants into ¼-inch rounds. Salt the slices liberally and place them in a colander over a large bowl or in the sink. Place another heavy bowl on top of the eggplant to help squeeze out the liquid. Allow it to drain for 30 minutes. Pat the slices dry.

2. Meanwhile, warm the oil over medium heat in a large skillet and sauté the onion and green pepper until the onion is translucent, about 3 minutes. Stir in the garlic and cook 2 minutes more.

3. Cube the slices of eggplant and add them to the skillet. Cook them over medium heat, stirring often and watching closely, for about 10 minutes. (Add more oil if necessary, I tablespoon at a time.) Stir in the tomatoes, parsley, and lime juice, and simmer for 5 minutes.

4. Add the ham, pepper, and wine, and bring just to a boil. Reduce the heat, cover, and simmer until the eggplant is tender, about 30 minutes.

NOTE: This recipe is equally good with beef or pork, but as they are not cured, they need to be browned in the oil before the sofrito is made.

MAÍZ (Corn)

The sweet corn available in this country is too tender for making albóndigas de maíz, tamal en cazuela, and guiso de maíz tierno. Look instead for autumn corn (my husband calls it horse corn), which is tougher, drier, less sweet, and altogether more like the corn we had in

Cuba. The ground fresh corn (*maíz molido*) sold in Latin grocery stores also works well in most of these recipes. Frozen corn is not a good substitute.

ALBÓNDIGAS DE MAÍZ

(CORN DUMPLINGS)

6 servings

Served with fluffy white rice, this dish is absolutely scrumptious; my mouth waters when I think of it.

FOR THE DUMPLINGS:

12 ears fresh autumn corn, or 3 cups ground corn (found in Latin markets)
2 garlic cloves, peeled and minced
2 tablespoons lard or vegetable shortening

I teaspoon salt
½ teaspoon freshly ground pepper
I whole egg
I egg white

FOR THE SAUCE:

¼ cup vegetable oil
I large onion, peeled and chopped
I medium green bell pepper, cored, seeded, and chopped

I garlic clove, peeled and minced
½ cup tomato purée
2 cups Chicken Broth or Beef Broth (page 13)

MAKE THE DUMPLINGS:

1. Husk the corn and slice off the kernels with a sharp knife. Grind them in a food processor.

2. Add the garlic, lard, salt, pepper, egg, and egg white to the food processor, and pulse until everything is well blended.

3. Form the dumplings as you would meatballs, making each one no larger than a golf ball. Set them aside.

MAKE THE SAUCE:

1. In a large saucepan, heat the oil over medium heat. Sauté the onion and green pepper until the onion is translucent, about 3 minutes. Add the garlic and cook 2 minutes more. Add the tomato purée and broth, and bring to a boil.

2. Carefully place the dumplings in the boiling sauce, one by one. Lower the heat and simmer, uncovered, until the sauce thickens, about 30 minutes.

Unlike polenta in italy, this one is made with fresh corn rather than cornmill. I have fond memories of eating this dish often when we ate "nothing but corn" in our house.

TAMAL EN CAZUELA

(SPICY FRESH POLENTA WITH PORK)

🌿

10 to 12 servings

6 garlic cloves, peeled
1 tablespoon salt
½ teaspoon freshly ground pepper
1 teaspoon dry leaf oregano
¼ cup sour orange juice (or a 50-50 mixture of sweet orange juice and lime juice)
2 pounds lean pork, cut into 2-inch cubes
16 ears fresh autumn corn or 4 cups ground corn (sold in Latin markets)

6 cups warm water
½ cup vegetable oil
1 large onion, peeled and finely chopped
1 large green bell pepper, cored, seeded, and finely chopped
⅔ cup tomato purée
½ cup dry white wine

1. Mash the garlic, salt, pepper, and oregano into a paste. (A mortar and pestle works best, but you may mince the garlic finely with a knife or put it through a garlic press and mash the seasonings in with a fork.) Stir in the orange juice. Pour this marinade over the pork and set it aside.

2. Husk the corn and slice off the kernels with a sharp knife. Place the corn cobs in a pan with the warm water and let them soak.

3. Grind the kernels coarsely in a food processor.

4. Squeeze the corn cobs over the soaking water so as to wring out all the "milk" they contain, and discard them.

5. Add the ground corn to the milky water and pour the mixture through a colander. Discard the coarse particles and set aside the liquid.

6. Blot the pork on paper towels. Reserve the marinade.

7. Warm the oil over medium heat in a large dutch oven or a

flameproof earthenware casserole. Brown the pork and remove it from the pan.

8. In the same pan, sauté the onion and green pepper until the onion is translucent, about 3 minutes. Stir in the tomato purée, wine, reserved marinade, meat, and corn liquid. Cover the pan, reduce the heat, and simmer for at least an hour, stirring occasionally so that the porridgelike mixture does not stick to the pan.

9. Serve with a green salad and crusty bread.

GUISO DE MAÍZ TIERNO

(FRESH CORN STEW)

8 to 10 servings

10 ears fresh autumn corn
½ cup vegetable oil
½ pound jamón de cocinar (raw ham) or prosciutto, cubed
I chorizo, skinned and thinly sliced
2 medium onions, peeled and chopped
I large green bell pepper, cored, seeded, and chopped
4 garlic cloves, peeled and minced
I cup tomato sauce
2 cups Beef Broth (page 13)

¼ cup dry white wine
I teaspoon white wine vinegar
½ pound potatoes, peeled and cubed
¼ pound calabaza, peeled, seeded, and cubed
¼ cup chopped parsley
I teaspoon dry leaf oregano
I teaspoon salt
½ teaspoon freshly ground pepper

1. With a sharp knife, slice the kernels from the ears of corn into a bowl. Using the back of the knife, press the corn "milk" from the cobs into the bowl and discard the cobs.

2. Warm the oil in a large dutch oven over medium heat, and brown the ham and chorizo.

3. Add the onions and green pepper to the meat and sauté until the onions are translucent, about 3 minutes. Stir in the garlic and cook 2 minutes more.

4. Stir in the tomato sauce, broth, wine, vinegar, potatoes, calabaza, parsley, oregano, salt, pepper, corn, and corn "milk." Bring just to a boil, reduce the heat, cover, and simmer for an hour, stirring occasionally.

Ensaladas (Salads)

Ensaladas (Salads)

$\mathcal{A}$lfredo Viazzi says that "a good salad is poetry." In our house in Cuba it was more: It was music, poetry, and the visual arts all in one, a veritable opera of dazzling color and flavors, abundant, varied, and eaten all year round.

My father was a fanatic about salad and insisted that it be served at every meal. I remember some neighborhood children remarking to their mother after eating with us, *"En casa de Lluriá el plato fuerte es la ensalada."* ("At the Lluriás' the main dish is the salad.")

That was, of course, an exaggeration, but it must have seemed that way to them because most Cubans did not eat salad as Americans know it. In most Cuban homes, cooked salads were served instead of fresh, leafy greens and other raw vegetables. Our family was accustomed to having both, and it seemed odd to us that anyone could regard this as strange.

The vegetables came from the Chinese vegetable vendor who called at our house each morning, and also from the garden of my maternal grandfather, Cipriano Carol y Sicard, whom we called Papabuelo. He was a horticulturist at heart, and at his Cárdenas *quinta* (villa) he grew not only tropical produce but also vegetables and fruits native to temperate zones. (His succulent peaches were a source of wonder, and people used to come from near and far to see if the "Carol peaches" really existed.)

Papabuelo built his summer home (the eight-bedroom house where we lived for many years) on the south shore of Varadero because the winds and surf of the north shore would have hurt his precious plants. And in Varadero, where no one else could grow anything except sea grapes and cocoplums, he had topsoil trucked in from Cárdenas for his garden, and cultivated vegetables and fruits that were even better and fresher than the ones the vegetable vendor sold us from his basket.

Mustard and pepper are not typically Cuban, but they add a nice touch to this salad.

2 large or 4 small ripe avocados
¼ cup Spanish olive oil
¼ cup freshly squeezed lime juice
⅛ teaspoon prepared mustard
   (optional)
⅛ teaspoon salt
⅛ teaspoon freshly ground pepper
   (optional)

ENSALADA DE AGUACATES

(AVOCADO SALAD)

4 to 6 servings

1. Cut the avocados in half lengthwise, remove the pits, and cut in half again. Carefully remove the skin and cut the avocados into bite-size pieces.

2. In a salad bowl, whisk together the oil, lime juice, mustard, salt, and pepper. Add the avocados and toss gently, being careful not to mash them.

Cuban guacamole is as different from the Mexican version as Cuban tortillas, or omelets, are from the Mexican corn pancake of the same name.

Lettuce leaves (optional)
1 large ripe pineapple
2 large or 4 small avocados
¼ cup Spanish olive oil
¼ cup freshly squeezed lime juice
⅛ teaspoon salt
¼ cup red onion, peeled and cut
   into slivers (optional)

GUACAMOLE CUBANO

(AVOCADO SALAD WITH PINEAPPLE)

4 to 6 servings

1. Wash and dry the lettuce leaves, if using, and line a salad bowl with them.

2. Slice the pineapple lengthwise into quarters. Peel it and remove the fibrous core. Cut the pineapple meat into 1-inch cubes and place it in the salad bowl.

3. Cut the avocados in half lengthwise, remove the pits, and cut in half again. Carefully remove the skin and cut the avocados into bite-size pieces. Add them to the pineapple.

4. Whisk together the oil, lime juice, and salt, and pour it over the fruit. Add the onion and toss gently, being careful not to mash the avocado.

ENSALADA DE TOMATES DE PAPABUELO

(GRANDFATHER'S TOMATO SALAD)

6 to 8 servings

This is how the luscious tomatoes grown by Papabuelo, my maternal grandfather, were served.

4 large, semiripe tomatoes (see Note)
¼ cup Spanish olive oil
¼ cup white wine vinegar
1 tablespoon freshly squeezed lime juice

¼ teaspoon salt
¼ teaspoon freshly ground pepper
⅛ teaspoon sugar
¼ teaspoon dry leaf oregano
Lettuce leaves or watercress

1. Bring a large pot of water to a rapid boil.

2. Put the tomatoes in the boiling water for 1 minute to facilitate peeling. Remove them with a slotted spoon and plunge them into cold water.

3. Peel the tomatoes and slice them into ½-inch rounds. With the point of a thin, sharp knife, remove all the seeds, putting them in a small bowl, and place the slices in a single layer on a large platter.

4. Place the tomato seeds and the gelatinous substance that surrounds them into a fine colander. Squeeze the juice from the colander into a small bowl, adding a little water in order to get it all.

5. Add the oil, vinegar, lime juice, salt, pepper, sugar, and oregano to the tomato juice, and whisk it all together.

6. Pour this vinaigrette over the tomatoes, cover them with plastic wrap, and refrigerate until serving time.

7. Serve the tomatoes on a bed of crispy lettuce leaves or watercress.

NOTE: In those days, salad tomatoes were always large, and were eaten before they ripened fully. They were still full of flavor, though.

Calabaza, calabaza, cada uno pa' su casa. Y el que no tenga casa, que se vaya pa' la plaza. (Pumpkin, pumpkin, be off you country bumpkins, off to your houses or your lairs. And if you have none, then go to the square!)

As children we used to chant this rhyme when we tired of our playmates and wanted to let them know they had overstayed their welcome. What the ditty lacked in politeness was amply compensated for by its effectiveness; most children took the hint and moved on!

This pumpkin salad is typical of the cooked salads served in most Cuban homes years ago.

ENSALADA DE CALABAZA
(CUBAN PUMPKIN SALAD)

6 to 8 servings

1 pound calabaza
1 large onion, peeled and sliced
  into paper-thin rings
1 cup Spanish olive oil
2 tablespoons white wine vinegar

⅛ teaspoon dry mustard (optional)
½ teaspoon salt
½ teaspoon freshly ground pepper
Lettuce leaves (optional)

1. Cut the calabaza into 1½-inch cubes and remove the seeds. (Do not peel it; that job is much more easily accomplished once it is cooked.)

2. Place the calabaza in a large saucepan, cover it with water, and bring it to a boil. Reduce the heat to medium and cook until the calabaza is tender but not mushy, about 20 minutes.

3. Drain the calabaza and, when it is cool enough to handle, remove the skin. (Save the cooking water, rich in nutrients, for a future soup.)

4. Arrange the calabaza and the onion rings in a serving bowl.

5. Whisk together the oil, vinegar, mustard, salt, and pepper, and pour it over the vegetables. Cover with plastic wrap and refrigerate for at least an hour. If desired, serve the salad over lettuce leaves.

ENSALADA DE BERENJENAS

(EGGPLANT SALAD)

8 servings

2 medium eggplants
½ cup Spanish olive oil
3 tablespoons white wine vinegar
  (see Note)
½ teaspoon salt
¼ teaspoon freshly ground pepper
2 tablespoons chopped fresh basil
  (optional)

1. Preheat the oven to 375 degrees.

2. Cut each eggplant in half lengthwise and pierce here and there with a sharp knife. Place the halves, cut sides down, on a greased cookie sheet. Brush with a little of the oil and bake until tender, about 30 minutes.

3. Transfer the eggplant to a cooling rack. When cool enough to handle, skin it, cut it into strips, and place it in a serving dish.

4. Whisk together the remaining oil, the vinegar, salt, and pepper, and pour it over the eggplant. Garnish the salad with the basil if desired, cover it with plastic wrap, and refrigerate it until chilled.

NOTE: Although not Cuban, balsamic vinegar is frequently used by Cubans in exile. If you prefer it, reduce the amount to 2 tablespoons.

ENSALADA DE QUIMBOMBÓ

(OKRA SALAD)

6 to 8 servings

2 pounds small, fresh okra
¼ cup Spanish olive oil
1½ tablespoons white wine vinegar
  (see Note)
½ teaspoon salt
⅛ teaspoon freshly ground pepper
2 small onions, peeled and sliced
  paper-thin

1. Bring about 1 inch of water to a rapid boil in a large pot.

2. Wash the okra and drop the pods into the boiling water. Cook them, covered, for about 8 minutes, until the pods are tender but still bright green.

3. Drain the okra and place them on paper towels. When they are dry, cut off the little stems. (If the pods are more than 2 inches long, cut them in half lengthwise.) Transfer the okra to a salad bowl.

4. Whisk together the oil, vinegar, salt, and pepper. Pour this vinaigrette over the okra and toss. Garnish the salad with onion rings.

5. Serve chilled.

NOTE: Although not Cuban, balsamic vinegar is frequently used by Cubans in exile. If you prefer it, reduce the amount to I tablespoon.

This is one of the salads made from the fresh produce that our Chinese vegetable vendor brought around every day. The potatoes were flawless littled red-skinned ones, the carrots were bright orange with fresh green tops, and the crisp green beans would snap, crackle, and pop when they were broken into pieces for the salad.

ENSALADA DE HABICHUELAS, PAPAS Y ZANAHORIAS

(GREEN BEAN, POTATO, AND CARROT SALAD)

6 servings

I pound new potatoes, peeled and cut into I-inch cubes
6 medium carrots, peeled and cut into ½-inch cubes
¾ pound green beans, stemmed and cut into 2-inch pieces
½ cup Spanish olive oil
¼ cup white wine vinegar

I teaspoon salt
½ teaspoon freshly ground pepper
⅛ teaspoon sugar
¼ cup chopped parsley (optional)
I small onion, peeled and cut into thin rings
Lettuce leaves

I. Place the potatoes and carrots in a large pot, cover them with water, and bring to a boil. Reduce the heat, cover, and cook for 15 minutes.

2. Add the beans and cook another 5 minutes, until the vegetables are barely tender. Drain the vegetables into a colander and set them aside to cool. (Save the water for a future soup.)

3. Whisk together the oil, vinegar, salt, pepper, sugar, and parsley.

4. Place half the cooled vegetables in a serving dish and pour half the vinaigrette over them. Add the rest of the vegetables and the remaining vinaigrette.

5. Cover the bowl with plastic wrap and refrigerate the salad until chilled. Garnish with onion rings and lettuce leaves, and serve.

ENSALADA DE REMOLACHA CRUDA CON PAPAS HERVIDAS

(RAW BEET AND BOILED POTATO SALAD)

4 to 6 servings

1 pound potatoes
½ pound fresh beets (about 3 small ones), washed and peeled
2 tablespoons freshly squeezed lime juice
½ teaspoon salt
¼ teaspoon freshly ground pepper
½ cup mayonnaise
½ cup chopped parsley (optional)
Lettuce leaves

1. Cut the potatoes into quarters, place them in a large pot, and cover them with water. Bring them to a boil, reduce the heat, cover, and cook until tender, about 30 minutes. Drain the potatoes, and when they are cool enough to handle, skin them and slice them into 1-inch cubes.

2. While the potatoes are cooling, cut the beets into chunks and pulse them in a food processor until shredded. Sprinkle them with the lime juice.

3. Place the potatoes in a salad bowl. Sprinkle them with the salt and pepper and toss them gently with the mayonnaise.

4. Add the beets with the lime juice and toss gently. Cover the salad with plastic wrap and refrigerate it for at least 4 hours.

5. Sprinkle the salad with parsley and serve it, chilled, on lettuce leaves.

ENSALADA DE BACALAO CON PAPAS Y HUEVOS

(CODFISH SALAD WITH POTATOES AND EGGS)

6 servings

Lovers of bacalao will enjoy this traditional salad. As always with dried salted codfish, you must plan ahead to allow time for soaking.

1 pound salted codfish
2 large potatoes, peeled and cut into ¼-inch rounds
1 large sweet onion, peeled and thinly sliced
2 hard-boiled eggs, cut into wedges
⅓ cup Spanish olive oil
2 tablespoons white wine vinegar
½ teaspoon freshly ground pepper
4 sprigs parsley

1. Prepare the codfish as directed on page 48.

2. Put the codfish in a large pot and cover it with cold water. Bring to a boil, lower the heat, cover, and simmer until tender, about 1 hour.

3. Remove the codfish from the pot with a slotted spoon and set it aside in a colander to drain and cool.

4. In the same water, bring the potato slices to a boil and cook them until they are tender but not mushy, no more than 15 minutes. Drain and set aside.

5. Arrange the potato slices in a layer at the bottom of a large, attractive serving bowl.

6. Create a second layer with the codfish.

7. Arrange the onion and egg wedges neatly on top.

8. Whisk the oil and vinegar together, and pour it over the salad. Grind on the pepper and refrigerate the salad until well chilled.

9. Garnish with parsley and serve.

ENSALADA DE JUDÍAS BLANCAS
(WHITE BEAN SALAD)

6 to 8 servings

This bean salad is delicious, as is the variation with lentils and the one with black-eyed peas—which are called *frijoles de carita* or "beans with faces."

I pound dry white beans	½ cup Spanish olive oil
I clove garlic, peeled	3½ tablespoons white wine vinegar
½ pound potatoes, quartered	½ teaspoon salt
I medium onion, peeled and sliced into paper-thin rings	½ teaspoon freshly ground pepper
¼ cup chopped parsley	Lettuce leaves

1. Place the beans in a large pot, cover them with cold water, and let them soak for about 8 hours. Drain them and remove any impurities.

2. Return the beans to the pot and cover them with fresh water. Add the garlic, bring the water to a boil, reduce the heat, and simmer the beans, covered, for about I hour, until they are tender but still whole.

3. Add the potatoes and cook for 30 minutes more.

4. Drain the beans and potatoes. When they are cool enough to handle, skin and cube the potatoes.

5. Place the beans, potatoes, onion, and parsley in a salad bowl.

6. Whisk together the oil, vinegar, salt, and pepper, and pour it over the bean mixture. Toss the salad gently, cover it with plastic wrap, and refrigerate it until chilled. Serve it on a bed of lettuce.

Ensalada de Lentejas (Lentil Salad): Substitute 1 pound of dry lentils for the white beans. Do not soak the lentils, and cook them for only 1 hour. Proceed as directed starting with Step 3. Garnish the salad with 2 hard-boiled eggs cut into wedges.

Ensalada de Frijoles de Carita (Black-eyed Peas Salad): Substitute 1 pound of dry black-eyed peas for the white beans and omit the potatoes. Garnish the salad with 2 hard-boiled eggs cut into wedges.

My great grandmother, María Wencesla Rosell (whom we called Chicha), seated with my uncle, Julio Lluriá y García, his mother, my Abuela Carmela García y Rodríguez, and my cousin, Cuchita Lluriá y Aragón, with her little daughter Lilian Sánchez y Lluriá. Chicha was one hundred years old when this photo was taken. Varadero, 1941. *Author's collection*

Ensaladas Festivas (Party Salads)

In this country, the following salads might be served as luncheon entrées, but in Cuba they were most often seen on the buffet table at parties. Seafood and chicken, which were usually served hot, took on a new character when chilled and tossed with homemade mayonnaise, or with oil and lime juice or vinegar.

AGUACATES RELLENOS (STUFFED AVOCADOS)

4 servings

If you prepare the stuffing ahead of time, this delicious and satisfying salad can be put together in minutes.

Be sure to wash the avocados thoroughly since they are served with their skins on. If you prefer them peeled, slice a thin sliver from the bottom of each half so that the avocado does not topple over once filled.

2 large ripe, avocados, chilled
Juice of 1 lime
Stuffing of your choice (recipes follow)

Large, whole lettuce leaves, washed and chilled

1. Wash the avocados, cut them lengthwise in half, and remove the pits.
2. Sprinkle each half with lime juice immediately to prevent discoloration.
3. Fill each half with stuffing. Garnish as suggested below, and serve cold on a bed of lettuce.

RELLENO DE LANGOSTA (LOBSTER STUFFING)

⅓ cup mayonnaise
¼ cup freshly squeezed lime juice
3 cups chopped, cooked lobster meat
¼ cup chopped sweet pickle
2 hard-boiled eggs, chopped
¼ teaspoon salt

⅛ teaspoon freshly ground pepper
One 8-ounce can petit pois (tiny peas), drained, or ¾ cup cooked fresh or frozen and thawed tiny peas
One 6-ounce jar pimientos, drained and cut into thin strips

1. In a large mixing bowl, stir together the mayonnaise and lime juice.

2. Add the lobster, pickle, eggs, salt, and pepper, and mix well.

3. Add the peas and toss lightly. Refrigerate the stuffing until needed.

4. After stuffing the avocados, garnish them with the pimiento strips.

RELLENO DE ATÚN
(TUNA STUFFING)

8 ounces (I cup) cream cheese, softened
2 tablespoons mayonnaise
¼ cup freshly squeezed lime juice
Two 7-ounce cans white tuna, drained and flaked

2 teaspoons capers
2 tablespoons minced onion
2 tablespoons minced parsley
2 hard-boiled eggs, chopped

1. In a large mixing bowl, stir together the cream cheese, mayonnaise, and lime juice.

2. Add the tuna, capers, and onion, and mix well. Refrigerate the stuffing until needed.

3. After stuffing the avocados, garnish them with the parsley and eggs.

RELLENO DE POLLO
(CHICKEN STUFFING)

¼ cup mayonnaise
¼ cup freshly squeezed lime juice
3 cups diced, cooked chicken breast meat
I apple, peeled and diced
¼ cup chopped celery
2 tablespoons minced onion

2 tablespoons minced parsley
¼ teaspoon salt
⅛ teaspoon freshly ground pepper
One 6-ounce jar pimientos, drained and cut into thin strips
One 8-ounce can petit pois (tiny peas), drained

1. In a large mixing bowl, stir together the mayonnaise and lime juice.

2. Add the chicken, apple, celery, onion, parsley, salt, and pepper, and mix well.

3. After stuffing the avocados, garnish them with the pimiento strips and peas.

This recipe was given to me by Dulce Zúñiga.

1 ripe pineapple, about 12 inches long including the leaves

½ cup mayonnaise

2 tablespoons freshly squeezed lime juice

1 cup cubed, cooked chicken breast meat

½ cup chopped walnuts

2 cups watercress leaves

1. Cut the pineapple in half lengthwise, keeping the leaves intact on each side.

2. Using a sharp paring knife, carefully cut around the inside of each half, leaving about ½ inch of meat and being careful not to pierce the shell. Scoop out the meat, cut out and discard the fibrous center core, and chop the meat into 1-inch cubes.

3. Stir together the mayonnaise and lime juice in a large mixing bowl. Add the pineapple meat, chicken, and walnuts, mixing well.

4. Divide this filling between the pineapple shells, and refrigerate them until well chilled.

5. At serving time, arrange the watercress leaves on a large platter. Place the pineapple halves on it and serve.

ENSALADA DE POLLO CON PIÑA

(CHICKEN AND PINEAPPLE SALAD)

6 servings

POSTRES (DESSERTS)

Flan de Leche Clásico (Classic Flan) 225

Flan de Chocolate (Chocolate Flan) 226

Flan de Calabaza (Cuban Pumpkin Flan) 227

Dulce de Leche (Sweet Milk Dessert) 228

Natilla (Spanish Custard) 229

Merengón con Natilla (Meringue Ring with Custard) 230

Arroz con Leche Vasco (Basque Rice Pudding) 230

Pudín Diplomático (Cuban Bread Pudding with Fruit) 231

Boniatillo (Sweet Potato Dessert) 232

Pudín de Malanga (Malanga Pudding) 234

Casquitos de Guayaba (Guava Shells) 235

Dulce de Hicacos (Cocoplums in Syrup) 236

Yemas Dobles (Medallions of Egg in Syrup) 237

Panetela Borracha (Drunken Sponge Cake) 238

Pastel de Limones Criollos de Cayo Hueso (Key Lime Pie) 239

Pastel de Mango Verde (Green Mango Pie) 240

POSTRES (Desserts)

Cubans have a sweet tooth, which they come by naturally enough. It has to do with our homeland's fertile soil and, odd as it may sound, with patriotism.

When the Spaniards who colonized the island in the sixteenth century failed to find the gold mines they had so avariciously expected, they turned to the practical pursuit of agriculture. With their African slaves, they cultivated the crops that were most coveted in that era, especially tobacco and sugarcane.

Cuba proved to be an ideal place to grow sugarcane, and in time the island became the world's "Sugar Bowl." Early in this century, the fabulous wealth generated by sugar production gave rise to a fevered period of prosperity that extended from World War I to the 1920s referred to both as *La Danza de los Millones* (the Dance of the Millions) and *Las Vacas Gordas* (the Fat Cows).

It is easy to understand, then, how consuming sweets came to be seen as a virtual act of patriotism. It is not uncommon, still, to hear a Cuban of my generation say, *"Dos para mí y tres para Cuba"* ("Two for me, three for Cuba") while pouring five heaping teaspoons of sugar into a cup of café con leche. There was even a popular song about the *Azuquitar en el Fondo* (The Little Sugar at the Bottom) that did not dissolve and was always spooned out of the cup with such gusto.

So it is no wonder that our desserts are so sweet. Some, like flan and *natilla* (custard) are interpretations of Spanish classics. Others, like *boniatillo* (Cuban sweet potato dessert) and *casquitos de guayaba* (guava shells) are made with tropical vegetables and fruit. Always, though, they are sweet.

You will also find in this chapter recipes for a few of the treats such as *frangollo* (little rolls of plantain and molasses) that were special childhood delights in our home years ago.

A *carreta* (cart) loaded with sugarcane traveling through the Cuban countryside to the sugar mill, circa 1900. *Elenita Cora Johnson*

How to Caramelize a Mold

Caramelizing a mold is the first step in all flan recipes, and here are two ways to do it.

Whichever method you choose, it is best to caramelize the mold just before you intend to fill it. If it is done too far in advance, the caramel tends to crack. When hot filling is poured into a mold, the caramel sometimes makes a crackling sound, but this is not an indication of trouble.

Stovetop Method: Put the sugar in a metal mold and place it directly on the burner over medium heat. Using pot holders, grasp the mold with both hands, turning and tipping it gently until the sugar melts and becomes amber-colored. Continue to tip the pan back and forth until the caramel is spread evenly throughout the inside of the mold.

Saucepan Method: Put the sugar in a heavy, medium-sized saucepan and place it over medium heat. Grasping the pan by the handle, turn and tip it gently until the sugar melts and becomes amber-colored. Pour the caramel into the mold, and tip the mold back and forth to spread it evenly over the sides and bottom.

Though not unique to Cuba, flan is a great favorite among Cubans, and no Cuban cookbook would be complete without it. There are many ways to make this delectable dessert, but this one, which I have known since childhood, is the most common.

FLAN DE LECHE CLASÍCO
(CLASSIC FLAN)

6 servings

1¾ cups sugar	Pinch of salt
3 eggs	1 teaspoon vanilla extract
3 egg yolks	1 cinnamon stick
2 cups milk	2-inch strip of lime rind

1. Preheat the oven to 350 degrees.

2. Use 1 cup of the sugar to caramelize a 3- or 4-cup mold as directed above. Set it aside.

3. With a wire whisk, lightly beat the eggs and egg yolks together.

4. Add the milk, the remaining ¾ cup sugar, the salt, vanilla, cinnamon stick, and lime rind, whisking just enough to mix them.

5. Pour the mixture into the mold. Place the mold in a large pan, and pour enough hot water into the larger pan to come halfway up the sides of the mold.

6. Bake for about 1¼ hours, until a toothpick inserted in the flan comes out clean.

7. Remove the mold from the hot water, allow it to cool on a wire rack for 30 minutes, and refrigerate it until chilled.

8. When ready to serve, turn the flan over onto a serving plate that is deep enough to hold the caramelized sugar. Slice it into portions and spoon the caramel over each serving.

FLAN DE CHOCOLATE
(CHOCOLATE FLAN)

8 servings

This recipe is from my cousin Graciela Carol, who, like her husband, Juan Argüelles, is a superb cook. While his specialty is fanciful entrées, hers is rich desserts.

1 cup plus 6 tablespoons sugar
Two 12-ounce cans evaporated milk
1 cup fresh milk
Pinch of salt
2 heaping tablespoons cocoa powder
5 eggs
1 teaspoon vanilla extract

1. Use 1 cup of the sugar to caramelize a 3- or 4-cup mold as directed on page 225. Set it aside.

2. Pour the evaporated and fresh milk into a heavy saucepan, add the salt, and bring to a boil. Set aside to cool.

3. In a small bowl, mix the cocoa with the remaining 6 tablespoons of sugar.

4. In a large mixing bowl, beat the eggs with a whisk until lemon-colored. Add the cocoa mixture and continue beating until well blended. Stir in the cooled milk and the vanilla.

5. Strain this mixture into the caramelized mold. Place the mold in a large pan, and pour enough hot water into the pan to come halfway up the sides of the mold.

6. Bake for about 1¼ hours, until a toothpick inserted in the flan comes out clean.

7. Remove the mold from the hot water, allow it to cool on a wire rack for 30 minutes. Refrigerate until chilled.

8. When ready to serve, turn the flan over onto a serving plate that is deep enough to hold the caramelized sugar. Slice it into portions and spoon the caramel over each serving.

This unusual flan is made with one of my favorite vegetables, and is rich in nutrients as well as calories. Unlike other flans, this one is refrigerated once it is put into its mold, and is not cooked further.

FLAN DE CALABAZA
(CUBAN PUMPKIN FLAN)

&

8 servings

1½ cups sugar
1½-pounds (¾ medium)
   calabaza (see Note)
One 14-ounce can sweetened
   condensed milk

I cinnamon stick
¼ teaspoon salt
6 tablespoons cornstarch
I teaspoon vanilla extract

1. Use I cup of the sugar to caramelize a 1½- or 2-quart mold as directed on page 225. Set it aside.

2. With a heavy butcher knife, cut the unpeeled calabaza into 2-inch cubes. Scrape off and discard the seeds. Place the calabaza in a large saucepan and cover it with water. Bring it to a boil, reduce the heat, cover, and simmer until tender, about 20 minutes.

3. Drain the calabaza, reserving 2 cups of the cooking water.

4. When it is cool enough to handle, peel the calabaza and purée it. (I use a potato masher, but a food processor works as well.)

5. In a mixing bowl, combine the condensed milk with the 2 cups of reserved cooking water. Return half of this mixture to the saucepan.

Add the cinnamon stick and salt, and bring to a boil. Remove from the heat.

6. Stir together the remaining milk mixture, the pumpkin purée, cornstarch, and the remaining ½ cup of sugar. Combine this with the boiled milk mixture, place in the food processor, and process until well mixed.

7. Return the mixture to the saucepan and cook over medium heat, constantly stirring, until it has the consistency of custard.

8. Stir in the vanilla, pour the mixture into the caramelized mold, and refrigerate it until chilled.

9. When ready to serve, turn the flan over onto a serving plate that is deep enough to hold the caramel sauce. Slice it into portions and spoon the caramel over each serving.

NOTE: For a different but delicious result, substitute 2 cups of canned pumpkin for the calabaza, eliminate Steps 2 through 4, and use 2 cups of fresh milk in place of the cooking water.

DULCE DE LECHE
(SWEET MILK DESSERT)

6 servings

This very sweet and very Cuban dessert is often accompanied by cheese and crackers, but many Cubans eat it without any accompaniment. I prefer not to remove the cinnamon sticks before serving because I remember how much pleasure we children used to get when we happened to find them in our portion. The sticks, with dulce imbedded in each fold, were heavenly to lick.

4 cups milk
6 egg yolks, well beaten
2 cups sugar

2 cinnamon sticks
1 teaspoon vanilla extract

1. Stir together the milk, egg yolks, sugar, and cinnamon sticks in a heavy saucepan.

2. Cook this mixture over medium-low heat, stirring constantly,

for 30 minutes, until it turns amber-colored and has the consistency of frosting.

3. Remove from the heat and stir in the vanilla. Transfer the dulce to a serving dish and refrigerate it until chilled.

4. Spoon into individual bowls and serve with cheese and crackers on the side.

This classic custard may be served on its own—garnished with caramel sauce or cinnamon if desired—or used as a filling for Merengón con Natilla (page 230). This recipe was given to me by Loló Torres.

NATILLA
(SPANISH CUSTARD)

6 servings

¾ cup evaporated milk
1¼ cups fresh milk
Pinch of salt
2-inch piece of lime rind

3 egg yolks
2 tablespoons cornstarch
½ cup sugar
½ teaspoon vanilla extract

1. Combine the evaporated milk, fresh milk, salt, and lime rind in a heavy saucepan, bring just to a boil, and set aside to cool.

2. In a mixing bowl, beat the egg yolks until lemon-colored.

3. In a separate bowl, mix the cornstarch with enough of the cooled milk to make a light paste. Slowly add the rest of the milk and the egg yolks, stirring constantly.

4. Strain this mixture into another saucepan. Stir in the sugar and cook over low heat, constantly stirring, until the mixture thickens. Stir in the vanilla and set the custard aside to cool.

5. Spoon it into a serving bowl and refrigerate it until chilled.

MERENGÓN CON NATILLA

(MERINGUE RING WITH CUSTARD)

6 to 8 servings

The recipe for this spectacular dessert comes from my niece Ronnie Lluriá Zúñiga.

2¼ cups sugar
10 egg whites, at room temperature
¼ teaspoon cream of tartar

I teaspoon vanilla extract
I recipe Natilla (page 229), chilled

1. Use I cup of the sugar to caramelize a bundt pan as directed on page 225.

2. Preheat the oven to 400 degrees.

3. Beat the egg whites with the cream of tartar until soft peaks form. Gradually add the remaining I¼ cups sugar, 2 tablespoons at a time, beating until stiff peaks form. Fold in the vanilla.

4. Pour this meringue into the caramelized pan and place it in the oven. Close the oven, turn it off, and leave it undisturbed for at least 8 hours.

5. Let the meringue cool to room temperature, and then refrigerate it until chilled.

6. When ready to serve, run a knife around the meringue to loosen it. Set the bottom of the pan in hot water for a minute or two, and unmold the meringue onto a serving platter deep enough to hold the caramel sauce.

7. Cut the meringue into servings, and spoon natilla over each slice.

ARROZ CON LECHE VASCO

(BASQUE RICE PUDDING)

8 servings

My mother gave me this recipe as her own mother, who was Basque, had given it to her. It requires a lot of time and patience, but is well worth it.

½ cup Valencia (short-grain) rice
7 cups milk
¾ cup sugar
⅛ teaspoon salt
2 cinnamon sticks

Rind of ¼ Persian lime, cut in strips
⅛ teaspoon anise grains
Ground cinnamon

1. Rinse the rice, place it in a heavy saucepan, and add 4 cups of the milk. Cook gently over medium-low heat, uncovered, stirring occasionally, for about 2 hours, until the rice grains "open up."

2. Gradually stir in the remaining 3 cups of milk, and simmer over low heat for about another hour. When the rice is very tender, stir in the sugar, salt, cinnamon sticks, lime rind, and anise. Continue stirring and simmering until the texture is so creamy and smooth that the rice grains have practically disintegrated.

3. Spoon the pudding into a large glass bowl or individual serving bowls, and sprinkle it with ground cinnamon. Refrigerate it until chilled.

PUDÍN DIPLOMÁTICO
(CUBAN BREAD PUDDING WITH FRUIT)

8 to 10 servings

Where it is generally considered superior in this country to use fresh ingredients, many fancy old Cuban recipes call for canned or dried foods. There is a reason for that: Fruits such as apples, peaches, and apricots, and vegetables such as peas, mushrooms, and asparagus did not grow in Cuba's tropical climate. They had to be imported, and were therefore considered delicacies, even in canned or dried form. A large can of fruit cocktail, for instance, was a most elegant gift to bring the hostess when invited to a friend's home for dinner years ago. It was not until I was nearly grown, when foods began to be imported by airplane, that one could find a fresh peach in Cuba (outside of the ones my maternal grandfather miraculously grew in his Cárdenas yard), and by then recipes like pudín diplomático had become classics.

2 cups sugar
1 loaf (½ pound) Cuban or French
    bread, crust removed, sliced, and
    then torn into small pieces
2 cups milk
4 teaspoons butter
4 eggs
2 tablespoons dry white wine

¼ teaspoon ground cinnamon
¼ teaspoon ground nutmeg
½ teaspoon vanilla extract
½ teaspoon almond extract
⅛ teaspoon salt
1 cup canned fruit cocktail, well
    drained

1. Use I cup of the sugar to caramelize a loaf pan as directed on page 225.

2. Soak the bread slices in the milk.

3. Preheat the oven to 350 degrees.

4. In a food processor, pulse the remaining I cup of sugar with the butter until blended. Add the eggs, wine, the bread mixture, cinnamon, nutmeg, vanilla, almond extract, and salt, and process until well mixed.

5. Put the fruit cocktail in the caramelized mold, and pour the batter from the food processor over it.

6. Place the mold in a large pan. Add enough hot water to the larger pan to come halfway up the sides of the mold. Place the pan in the oven and bake the pudding for about 2 hours, until a knife inserted in the center comes out clean.

7. Remove the pudding from the oven and allow it to cool to room temperature on a wire rack. Turn the cooled pudding over onto a serving plate and refrigerate it until chilled. To serve, cut it into I-inch slices.

BONIATILLO
(SWEET POTATO DESSERT)

6 to 8 servings

This delightful dessert always brings to my mind the García "girls," three spinster sisters who lived in Varadero. They once brought a large dish of boniatillo to a party, and were thereafter known affectionately as "las Boniatillo."

Like many Cuban dishes, boniatillo is peasant fare that is fit for a king. If you enjoy the scintillating combination of cinnamon and citrus, be sure to try the variation.

2 pounds boniato (see Note)
I½ cups water
3 cups sugar
I cinnamon stick

4 egg yolks, beaten
2 tablespoons dry white wine
I teaspoon vanilla extract
I tablespoon ground cinnamon

I. Cut the unpeeled boniatos into chunks, place them in a large saucepan, and cover them with water. Bring them to a boil, reduce the heat, cover, and simmer until they are tender, about 30 minutes.

2. Drain the boniatos and, when cool enough to handle, peel them. Mash them by hand until smooth, or process them in a food processor until puréed (just a few pulses will do the job). Return the purée to the saucepan.

3. Combine the water, sugar, and cinnamon stick in another saucepan, bring to boil, and cook over medium heat until the mixture is thick enough to coat a spoon, about 6 minutes. Remove it from the heat.

4. Bring the boniato purée to a simmer and slowly pour in the hot syrup, stirring constantly. Continue to cook gently, stirring, until the purée tears away from the sides of the pan.

5. Stir in the egg yolks and then the wine and vanilla. Cook about 5 minutes more, always stirring.

6. Place the dessert in a serving dish, sprinkle it with the cinnamon, and refrigerate it until chilled.

NOTE: If you are not able to buy the tropical tuber known as boniato, substitute American sweet potatoes. The result, while not real boniatillo, will nevertheless be delicious.

VARIATION

Boniatillo con Naranja (Sweet Potato and Orange Dessert): Proceed as directed above, adding 2 tablespoons of grated orange rind in Step 4, and ¼ cup of orange juice in Step 5.

PUDÍN DE MALANGA

(MALANGA PUDDING)

6 to 8 servings

Malanga was considered so nutritious and easy to digest that, in purée form, it was the first solid food given to babies in my time. This ambrosial recipe, dressed with spices, is a tantalizing dessert.

One 8-ounce sponge cake, broken up into pieces
1 cup sweet white wine (such as Rhine wine)
8 tablespoons (1 stick) plus about 2 teaspoons butter
2 cups milk
¼ cup sugar
¼ teaspoon salt
2 whole cloves
1 cinnamon stick

¼ teaspoon ground nutmeg
Rind of ½ lime, cut into strips
5 malangas (2½ pounds total)
2 tablespoons freshly squeezed lime juice
2 eggs
2 tablespoons orange blossom water (see Note)
½ cup almonds, blanched and toasted
½ cup raisins

1. Soak the sponge cake in the wine. Butter a bundt pan or a 10-inch tube pan with about 2 teaspoons butter. Preheat the oven to 325 degrees.

2. In a heavy saucepan, stir together the milk, sugar, salt, cloves, cinnamon stick, nutmeg, and lime rind. Bring just to a boil and remove the mixture from the heat. Stir in the remaining butter and set it aside to cool.

3. Cut the unpeeled malanga into 1-inch rounds and peel each slice individually. Rub them with lime juice.

4. Place the malanga slices in a large saucepan and cover them with cold water. Bring to a boil, reduce the heat, cover, and simmer until the malanga is tender, about 20 minutes.

5. Discard all but ⅓ cup of the cooking water from the pot, and quickly mash the malanga with a potato masher until it has the consistency of mashed potatoes.

6. Beat the eggs, add them to the cooled milk mixture, and strain into a food processor bowl. Remove the lime rind and cinnamon stick before mixing in the food processor.

7. Add the orange blossom water, the wine-soaked sponge cake, and the malanga purée. Pulse in batches until well blended.

8. Fold in the almonds and raisins.

9. Pour the batter into the prepared pan. Bake for 1 hour, until a knife inserted into the pudding comes out clean.

10. Let the pudding cool to room temperature. Unmold it onto a serving platter and refrigerate it until chilled.

NOTE: Orange blossom water is available in some health food stores and pharmacies. You may substitute 1 tablespoon of water mixed with 1 tablespoon of white grape juice.

CASQUITOS DE GUAYABA

(GUAVA SHELLS)

8 servings

You can buy canned guava shells in the Latin section of many U.S. supermarkets and serve them with cream cheese for a typical Cuban dessert. But if you take the trouble to make yours from fresh guavas, you will find they are worth the effort.

This and other syrupy fruit desserts such as *dulce de hicacos* typically are served with hard cheeses such as Gruyère and Gouda, or with cream cheese on the side. This recipe was given to me by Lucy Fiallo.

24 ripe guavas
5 cups water
2 cups sugar

Red food coloring (optional; see Note)
8 ounces cream cheese, sliced

1. Peel the guavas, cut them in half, and scoop out the seeds.

2. Place the guava shells in a large saucepan and cover them with the water. Bring to a boil, reduce the heat, and simmer, uncovered, until tender.

3. Drain the guavas, reserving the cooking water, which should measure 4 cups. (Add more water if necessary.)

4. Return the cooking water to the saucepan, stir in the sugar, and bring to a boil. Lower the heat and cook gently, stirring occasionally, until the mixture becomes a thin syrup. Stir in the food coloring if needed, and let the syrup cool.

5. Add the guava shells to the syrup and bring to a boil again. Lower the heat and cook the mixture gently until the syrup coats a spoon.

6. Refrigerate the guava shells and syrup until chilled. Serve with the cream cheese on the side.

NOTE: Some guavas are rather pale, and since casquitos are expected to be ruby red, you may wish to add a few drops of food coloring.

DULCE DE HICACOS

(COCOPLUMS IN SYRUP)

4 to 6 servings

The beautiful beach where I grew up was on the Península de Hicacos, which took its name from the great number of hicaco, or cocoplum, trees that grew wild there. As a child I ate many a dish of this sweet dessert made from that succulent, cherrylike fruit.

I have never seen cocoplums in an American store, so you may substitute tart, fresh cherries. Leave the pits in the cherries and let each diner remove them himself.

This recipe is from my cousin Fifa Freire.

3 cups fresh, tart, unpitted cherries (or fresh cocoplums if available)
4 cups water
6 cups sugar
Sliced Gruyére, Gouda, or cream cheese

1. Place the cherries in a large saucepan, cover them with the water, and soak them for at least 8 hours.

2. Remove the fruit with a slotted spoon, reserving the soaking water. With a sharp knife, make 2 small cuts in the shape of an "X" in each cherry.

3. Stir the sugar into the reserved water and bring it to a boil. Continue boiling until the syrup is thick enough to coat a spoon, about 3 minutes.

4. Add the fruit and cook it gently without stirring for about 15 minutes. (The syrup will turn red.)

5. Transfer the fruit and sauce to a serving dish and refrigerate until chilled. Serve with cheese on the side.

This dessert, considered the most delectable of all delicacies, was a memorable part of an unforgettable dinner party at our Varadero home in 1925. Though Varadero was enjoyed principally by people from Cárdenas at the time, our beautiful beach was "discovered" in 1925 by one international figure—Irené du Pont of Wilmington, Delaware. When he decided to buy land there to build a vacation mansion, Mr. du Pont made inquiries and, learning that our family owned considerable property, asked my father to show him what was available. Though the land the billionaire chose (Las Peñas toward the end of the peninsula) belonged to the García family, he and my father hit it off famously. Before Mr. du Pont and his entourage left for the States that season, we had a farewell dinner for them at our house. As you can imagine, everything at that meal was to be the best our family had to offer. My father planned to make his famous paella, and Tía Guillermina Smith and Tía Mary La Rosa, my aunts by marriage, were delegated the task of making yemas dobles for dessert. I was only seven years old at the time, but I vividly remember how my aunts labored over the dish, and how they looked forward to lavish praise from our distinguished guests. But when dinner was served, the du Ponts spent all their compliments on the fabulous paella, and said not a word about the supreme dessert. Everyone in our family was puzzled—especially my poor tías!

YEMAS DOBLES
(MEDALLIONS OF EGG IN SYRUP)

6 servings

2 cups water
2 cups sugar
1 cinnamon stick
One 2-inch piece lime rind
1 teaspoon freshly squeezed lime juice

2 eggs
4 egg yolks
1 teaspoon baking powder
1 teaspoon vanilla

1. Combine the water, sugar, cinnamon stick, lime rind, and lime juice in a deep, heavy skillet. Bring it to a boil, reduce the heat to medium-low, and cook the syrup until it coats a spoon, about 30 minutes.

2. In a mixing bowl, beat together the eggs, egg yolks, and baking powder until lemon-colored.

3. Bring the thickening syrup to slow boil, and drop the egg mixture into it by tablespoonfuls. Let it cook for about 1 minute on one side and carefully turn them over to cook for the same amount of time on the other side. With a slotted spoon, transfer the poached yolks to a serving dish.

4. Remove the syrup from the heat, stir in the vanilla, and strain the syrup into the serving dish. Refrigerate until chilled. Serve in individual dishes.

PANETELA BORRACHA

(DRUNKEN SPONGE CAKE)

16 servings

Always a favorite in old-fashioned Cuban entertaining, panetela borracha is a very light sponge cake saturated with wine and syrup.

Butter or margarine
¾ cup flour (sifted twice before measuring), plus about 1 tablespoon
½ teaspoon baking powder
⅛ teaspoon salt
3 eggs, separated
¾ cup sugar

1 tablespoon water
½ teaspoon vanilla extract
1 cup port, sweet sherry, or Rhine wine
2½ cups Almíbar No. 1 (page 255)
Ground cinnamon

1. Preheat the oven to 325 degrees. Grease and flour an 8-inch-square cake pan, using about 1 tablespoon flour.

2. Sift ¾ cup flour together with the baking powder and salt.

3. In a mixing bowl, beat the egg whites, gradually adding the sugar until the meringue stands up in soft peaks.

4. In a separate bowl, beat the yolks until lemon-colored, and fold them into the meringue. Add the water and vanilla, and fold in the flour mixture.

5. Scrape the batter into the prepared pan. Bake for 25 minutes, or until a knife inserted in the center comes out clean. Cool on a rack.

6. Cut the cake into 2-inch squares and place them on a serving platter. Pour the port and the syrup over the cake, and sprinkle each piece liberally with ground cinnamon.

In South Florida, residents and visitors alike enjoy the ubiquitous Key lime pie without knowing its real origin. Key limes are Cuban *limoncitos criollos*, brought to Key West during the war for Cuban independence in 1868. The first Cuban settlers there developed this exquisite pie using their favorite limes (which now grow profusely throughout South Florida) and the sweetened condensed milk that is used so widely by Cubans.

The original Key lime pie crust was made with Cuban *galleticas de María*, which were very much like the Marie Lu crackers available in some Latin markets, but a graham cracker crust has become standard. The sweet, fluffy meringue is a wonderful counterpoint to the tart filling, but if you prefer, you may eliminate it and serve the pie with whipped cream instead.

PASTEL DE LIMONES CRIOLLOS DE CAYO HUESO

(KEY LIME PIE)

8 servings

One 14-ounce can sweetened
   condensed milk
2 egg yolks
½ cup Key lime juice
One 9-inch graham cracker pie
   crust

3 egg whites, at room temperature
⅛ teaspoon cream of tartar
6 tablespoons sugar
½ teaspoon vanilla

1. Preheat the oven to 350 degrees.

2. Mix the condensed milk, egg yolks, and Key lime juice together, blending well, and pour the mixture into the pie crust.

3. Beat the egg whites with the cream of tartar until soft peaks form. Gradually add the sugar and vanilla, beating until stiff peaks form. Spread this meringue over the pie.

4. Bake for 12 to 15 minutes, until the peaks of the meringue are lightly browned.

5. Allow the pie to cool to room temperature, and then refrigerate it until chilled.

PASTEL DE MANGO VERDE

(GREEN MANGO PIE)

8 servings

My mother's dear American friend, Melva Guthrie, lived in Cuba for many years, and was so fond of mangoes that she refused to take her yearly vacation in the States during mango season. Melba loved mangoes at every stage of their development. She even enjoyed green, unripe ones, from which she made delicious desserts. This recipe is one that she passed on to Mamá, who in turn passed it on to me.

FOR THE PIE CRUST:

2¼ cups flour plus more for rolling
1 teaspoon salt
¾ cup lard
5 tablespoons cold water

FOR THE FILLING:

5 cups thinly sliced green mango
⅔ cup light raw sugar (see Note) plus 1 teaspoon for garnish
⅛ teaspoon salt
2 tablespoons water
1 tablespoon cornstarch
2 tablespoons butter
1 teaspoon nutmeg (optional)

MAKE THE CRUST:

1. Sift the flour and salt into a mixing bowl.

2. Add the lard, and work the dough with a pastry cutter or 2 knives, crossed scissorlike, until the mixture looks like pebbles or beans.

3. Add the water, a spoonful at a time, stirring until the dough holds together. (Keep the dough light; do not knead it.)

4. Gently divide the dough into 2 equal balls and place each on a piece of floured wax paper.

5. With a floured rolling pin, roll out each piece, from the center toward the edge, until it is ¼ inch thick and about 1 inch larger than your pie plate.

6. Line the pie plate with one circle of dough. Refrigerate the other until needed.

COMPLETE THE PIE:

1. Preheat the oven to 375 degrees.

2. Place the mango slices in layers in the dough-lined pie plate, sprinkling each layer liberally with the sugar.

3. Mix together the salt, water, and cornstarch, and spread it over the sugared mango layers.

4. Cut the butter into slivers and spread them over the filling.

5. Cover the pie with the top crust, crimping and trimming the edges. Make a few decorative cuts in the center of the pie to allow the steam to escape.

6. Mix together the remaining 1 teaspoon of sugar and the nutmeg, and sprinkle it on top.

7. Bake for 40 minutes.

8. Serve warm or at room temperature.

NOTE: If raw sugar is not available, regular granulated sugar is perfectly acceptable.

MASA REAL DE GUAYABA
(GUAVA PIE WITH ROYAL CRUST)

12 servings

Dulce de guayaba, or guava paste, was one of the most widely available and inexpensive sweets in Cuba, and it can be found in this country in most Latin markets. This simple and delicious recipe was given to me by Marilyn Calienes Fernández.

16 tablespoons (2 sticks) butter or margarine, softened, plus extra for the pan
4 cups flour (sifted before measuring), plus enough for the pan
2 teaspoons baking powder
¼ teaspoon salt
2 cups sugar
2 eggs
2 tablespoons cold water
2 teaspoons vanilla extract
1 pound guava paste, cut into thin slices

1. Preheat the oven to 350 degrees. Grease and flour a 9-by-13-inch cake pan.

2. Sift the flour with the baking powder and salt.

3. In a large mixing bowl, beat the butter with the sugar and eggs. Gradually beat in the flour mixture, then the water and vanilla. You will have a stiff dough, not a batter.

4. Divide the dough in half. On a floured surface, roll each half into a rectangle the size of your pan. Press one half into the pan, covering the bottom.

5. Spread slices of guava paste over the crust, thoroughly covering it.

6. Place the remaining crust on top, again spreading it with your fingers until the guava is completely covered.

7. Bake for 45 to 50 minutes, until lightly brown on top.

8. When it is cool, cut the pie into 3-inch squares and serve.

COSUBÉS

(YUCCA COOKIES)

12 cookies

This recipe goes back to colonial times in Cuba, when Spanish colonists and their slaves were learning to use the yucca flour they had inherited from the native Siboneyes.

I tablespoon plus I teaspoon lard or vegetable shortening
I½ cups yucca flour (see Note)
I cup confectioners' sugar

¼ teaspoon ground anise
⅛ teaspoon salt
I tablespoon dry white wine
I egg

1. Preheat the oven to 375 degrees. Lightly grease a cookie sheet with the teaspoon of lard.

2. Sift the flour, sugar, anise, and salt into a bowl. Add the wine, egg, and the remaining tablespoon of lard. Knead the dough, adding more flour if necessary, until it no longer sticks to your fingers.

3. Roll out the dough on a floured surface to a ¼-inch thickness. With a knife, cut it into 12 triangles, adding some decorative marks if you like.

4. Place the cosubés on the cookie sheet and bake them until golden, about 12 minutes.

NOTE: Yucca flour is available in some Latin markets. You may substitute potato flour, or cake flour that has been sifted 3 times.

Esta noche es Nochebuena, noche de comer buñuelos. En mi casa no se comen por falta de harina y huevos. (Tonight is Christmas eve, a night to eat buñuelos. In my house they are not eaten for lack of flour and eggs.)

BUÑUELOS
(TROPICAL BUNUELDS)

8 servings

This song goes back to my grandparents' time—the late 1800s, the time of Cuba's thirty-year war for independence from Spain. Then, as now under Castro's dictatorship, food was scarce, and it was difficult, if not impossible, to find the ingredients for buñuelos. But Cubans in exile remember a time when food of every kind was plentiful in their homeland, and enjoy the abundance of tropical produce in this country. This recipe is from Lucy Fiallo.

I pound (2 medium) fresh or frozen yucca
½ pound (¼ medium) calabaza
½ pound (I medium) boniato
2 eggs

I teaspoon ground anise
¼ cup flour
1½ to 2 cups vegetable oil
2½ cups Almíbar No. 2 (page 255)

I. Slit the yucca lengthwise and peel off the barklike skin. Cut it into chunks. (If using frozen yucca, follow the package directions.) Wash the calabaza and the boniato under cold running water and cut them into chunks.

2. Place the vegetables in a large pot and cover them with water. Bring to a boil, lower the heat, cover, and simmer until tender.

3. Drain the vegetables, saving the cooking water. When they are cool enough to handle, peel the calabaza and boniato.

4. Mash the vegetables by hand or in a food processor, adding 2 or 3 tablespoons of cooking water, until they have the consistency of mashed potatoes. Add the eggs and anise, and mix well.

5. Spread the flour on a countertop or kneading board and knead the yucca mixture into a smooth dough, adding more flour if necessary to prevent stickiness.

6. Form the dough into balls about 2 inches in diameter, and roll each one out into the shape of a thin bread stick. Twist them into figure eights.

7. Line a large, freezerproof container with waxed paper and dust it with flour. Place the buñuelos in the container in layers separated by more floured wax paper. Seal it tightly and freeze the buñuelos.

8. Just before serving, heat the oil in a deep, heavy skillet or a deep fryer until fragrant (about 375 degrees). Drop the frozen buñuelos into the hot oil, no more than 4 at a time, and fry them until golden on all sides (about 5 minutes).

9. Drain the fried buñuelos on paper towels. Serve them with the syrup, hot or at room temperature.

CHURROS
(SPANISH DUNKING PASTRIES)

12 to 15 pastries

Churros are a winter thing. In Spain they are the number one choice for dunking into a steaming cup of Hot Chocolate (page 268). In Cuba, despite our warm climate, we liked the same thing.

I cup water
½ teaspoon salt
I cup flour

1½ cups vegetable oil
½ cup superfine sugar

1. Place the water and salt in a saucepan and bring to a boil.

2. Quickly add the flour to the boiling water, stirring until the dough is thick and smooth. Set it aside.

3. Heat the oil in a deep, heavy skillet or a deep fryer until fragrant (about 375 degrees).

4. Place the dough in a *churrera* (a gadget for making churros) or a cake decorator with a wide enough opening to form dough strips about I inch in diameter.

5. Press the dough out directly into the hot oil in strips about 6 inches long, cooking 5 or 6 strips at a time. When the churros are swollen and golden, transfer them to paper towels to drain.

6. Sprinkle the churros with the sugar while they are still hot and serve immediately.

These light little cakes are so fragile they literally turn to *polvo* or "dust" when handled.

There are several ways to make polvorones. This one was in my mother's collection of recipes; it called for lard, but I prefer using butter.

16 tablespoons (2 sticks) plus about 2 teaspoons unsalted butter, softened

½ cup confectioners' sugar plus more for rolling

2½ cups flour (sift before measuring)

¼ teaspoon salt

I teaspoon vanilla extract

1. Cream the 2 sticks of butter with the sugar until it is lemon-colored.

2. Beat in the flour, salt, and vanilla, making a stiff dough.

3. Refrigerate until well chilled.

4. Preheat the oven to 400 degrees. Grease a cookie sheet with the remaining butter.

5. Roll the dough into balls about 1 inch in diameter. Place them on the cookie sheet and press them down a bit with the back of a spoon.

6. Bake them for about 14 minutes, until lightly golden.

7. As soon as you remove them from the oven, roll the polvorones in confectioners' sugar and set them on a wire rack. When they are cool, roll them in the sugar again.

8. Serve at room temperature.

FRANGOLLO

(LITTLE ROLLS OF
PLANTAINS,
MOLASSES, AND
PEANUTS)

24 rolls

EL MANICERO (The Peanut Vendor)

Maní, maní…
si te quieres con el pico divertir
cómete un cucuruchito de maní

Cerca de tí, que rico está
ya no se puede pedir más.

Ay! Caserita, no me dejes ir
porque después te vas a arrepentir
y va a ser muy tarde ya.
El manicero se va, el manicero se va…

Caserita no te acuestes a dormir
sin comer un cucurucho de maní.

Cuando la calle sola está
casera de mi corazón,
el manicero entona su pregón
y si la niña escucha su cantar
llama desde su balcón.

Dáme de tu maní,
dáme de tu maní,
que esta noche no voy a poder dormir
sin comerme un cucurucho de maní.

—Moisés Simon

THE PEANUT VENDOR

Peanuts, peanuts…
If you want to have some fun with your beak
eat a little cone-full of peanuts.
Close to you, how sweet it is
who could ask for anything more

Oh, little housewife, don't let me go
because later you'll regret it
and then it will be too late.
The peanut vendor is leaving, the peanut vendor is leaving...
Little housewife, don't go to sleep
without having a little cone-full of peanuts.

When the street is deserted,
housewife of my heart,
the manicero sings his ditty
and if the girl listens to his singing
she calls from her balcony.
Gimme peanuts
Gimme peanuts
because tonight I won't be able to fall asleep
without first eating a cone-full of peanuts

This song, one I sang as a child, reminds me of the toasted and salted *maní*, or peanuts, that were sold in the markets and on the streets in Cuba in little paper cones called *cucuruchos*. They were also used in sweets such as this one, which combines peanuts with molasses, a product of the sugarcane. In the old days, the first step to making this tasty treat was to make the plantain chips, but today you can buy them in any Latin market.

One 5-ounce package unsalted
   plantain chips
½ cup molasses
I egg white

2 tablespoons sugar
½ cup finely chopped unsalted
   peanuts
Butter or margarine

I. Place the plantain chips in the food processor and pulse them until they are reduced to a powder.

2. Line a colander with cheesecloth and set it over a bowl.

3. In a saucepan, stir the molasses together with the egg white and heat it over medium-high heat. Remove it from the heat when it begins to boil, and strain it through the colander.

4. Return the molasses mixture to the saucepan and stir in the plantain powder. Bring to a boil, reduce the heat, and simmer, stirring constantly, for about 10 minutes, until you can see the bottom of the pan while stirring and the mixture does not stick to the sides.

5. Pour the molasses mixture out onto a marble surface or into a large glass baking dish or platter. Let it cool just enough to handle.

6. Put the sugar and the peanuts in small bowls within reach. Preheat the oven to 325 degrees. Lightly grease a cookie sheet.

7. Grease your hands with butter and form the molasses mixture into balls about 1 inch in diameter.

8. Roll the balls first in the sugar and then in the peanuts, placing them on the cookie sheet as you go.

9. Bake the frangollos for 15 to 20 minutes, until golden.

Salsas (Sauces)

Mojo Criollo (Cuban Garlic Sauce) 253

Salsa Española (Spanish Sauce) 253

Salsa Bechamela con Cebolla (Béchamel Sauce with Onion) 254

Salsa Ajillo Especial (Special Garlic Sauce) 255

Almíbar No. 1 (Dessert Syrup) 255

Salsas (Sauces)

"Ese está como el perjíl: en todas las salsas." ("That one is like parsley: in all the sauces."—Something that is said about a person who is seen everywhere all the time.)

Cuban sauces are not as varied as French sauces, but they can be, to quote Julia Child, "the splendor and glory" of a dish. Here are a few basic ones—not all of which, in fact, contain parsley!

Used for marinating meats and vegetables alike, this tangy garlic sauce is a staple of Cuban cooking. It is available bottled in Latin markets, but homemade is much better.

MOJO CRIOLLO

(CUBAN GARLIC SAUCE)

2 cups

10 garlic cloves, peeled
I teaspoon salt
I cup sour orange juice

(or a 50-50 mixture of sweet orange juice and lime juice)
I cup vegetable oil

1. Mash the garlic and salt into a paste. (A mortar and pestle works best, but you may mince the garlic finely with a knife or put it through a garlic press and mash the seasonings in with a fork.) Stir in the orange juice.

2. In a saucepan, heat the oil just to the boiling point and remove it from the heat. Whisk in the orange juice mixture until well blended.

3. Use right away; homemade mojo criollo does not keep well.

This sauce, second only to mojo criollo in its importance in Cuban cuisine, is used on fish, vegetables, meatballs, croquettes, eggs, and even pasta. It is best to make this fresh when you need it, but it will keep for a few days in the refrigerator.

SALSA ESPAÑOLA

(SPANISH SAUCE)

About 3 cups

I½ cups Spanish olive oil
2 large onions, peeled and chopped
I medium green bell pepper, cored, seeded, and chopped
6 garlic cloves, peeled and minced
½ cup fresh tomato sauce, or use canned

½ cup dry white wine
I bay leaf
½ teaspoon salt
½ teaspoon freshly ground pepper
¼ cup chopped parsley

1. Warm the oil in a large skillet over medium heat. Sauté the onions and green pepper until the onions are translucent, about 3 minutes. Stir in the garlic and cook for 2 minutes more.

2. Stir in the tomato sauce, wine, bay leaf, salt, and pepper. Bring to a boil, reduce the heat, and simmer for 5 minutes.

3. Remove the sauce from the heat and stir in the parsley.

SALSA BECHAMELA CON CEBOLLA

(BÉCHAMEL SAUCE WITH ONION)

☙

1 cup

Cubans, so influenced by European culture, were fond of au gratin dishes made with béchamel sauce. A heavy béchamel was used for croquettes, canelones, and other dishes that required a binding sauce, while a light béchamel was used as a base for other sauces, and to make creamy au gratin dishes.

Here are recipes for both, along with a blender method from my sister-in-law Carmita Diaz, who uses it when making her Chicken-stuffed Cannelloni (page 109).

HEAVY BÉCHAMEL

2 tablespoons butter
1 small onion, peeled and finely
    chopped
1 cup milk

2 tablespoons flour
¼ teaspoon salt
⅛ teaspoon ground nutmeg

1. In a heavy saucepan, melt the butter over low heat. Sauté the onion until translucent, about 5 minutes.

2. In another saucepan or a microwave, heat the milk to just below the boiling point.

3. Stir the flour, salt, and nutmeg into the butter mixture, forming a smooth paste. Gradually add the scalded milk, stirring all the while with a whisk so that no lumps form. Keep stirring until the sauce thickens.

VARIATIONS

Light Béchamel: Reduce the flour to 1½ tablespoons and proceed as directed above.

Blender Method: Omit the onion. Process the milk, flour, salt, and nutmeg in a blender until smooth. Pour the mixture into a saucepan. Add the butter and cook over low heat, stirring constantly, until the sauce thickens.

This sauce, from Miami's excellent Málaga Restaurant, is superb on all kinds of seafood. It is what puts the garlic in the dishes listed as "al ajillo" on the Málaga menu. Co-owner and manager Teresa Fernández kindly shared the recipe.

3 cups Spanish olive oil
10 heads of garlic, cloves separated and peeled
10 medium onions, peeled and coarsely chopped
16 tablespoons (2 sticks) butter, melted
2 cups chopped parsley
4 cups extra dry white wine
Salt

1. Working in batches, combine the olive oil, garlic, onion, butter, parsley, and wine in a blender and process until smooth.

2. Pour the sauce into a large glass container and shake well to combine. Check for seasoning and add salt to taste. Store in the refrigerator for up to 6 weeks. The butter will harden after it is refrigerated. To use a portion of the mixture, set the glass container in hot water until the butter softens and the mixture can be shaken to blend, then measured.

This sweet syrup is used extensively in Cuban desserts.

2 cups sugar
1½ cups water
¼ cup freshly squeezed lime juice
2-inch strip lime rind
1 cinnamon stick
1 teaspoon vanilla extract

1. Combine the sugar, water, lime juice, lime rind, and cinnamon stick in a heavy saucepan, and bring to a boil. Boil for about 30 minutes, until the syrup is thick enough to coat a spoon.

2. Remove the syrup from the heat and stir in the vanilla. Set it aside to cool.

VARIATION

Almíbar No. 2: Omit the lime juice, lime rind, cinnamon stick, and vanilla. Add 2 teaspoons of anise powder.

Bebidas (Beverages)

BEBIDAS (Beverages)

*C*ubans, as a rule, are not heavy drinkers, but that does not mean they seldom drank in the old days. People very much enjoyed their *traguitos* ("little" cocktails), and we had our famous rum and *aguardiente*, another kind of hard liquor made from sugarcane, as well as excellent beers.

One had to be wealthy, however, to drink wine regularly, for it was imported and therefore expensive. My paternal grandfather is said to have had a fabulous wine collection in Cárdenas, but by the time I was growing up, we were no longer rich, and it was only Chicha, my great-grandmother, who drank wine in our house. A glass of *vino tinto*, Spanish red wine, decanted from a huge carafe, was served to her at every meal.

Spanish sangría was served on special occasions in those well-to-do households that had vino tinto. Now in exile, Cubans drink sangría more often, I dare say, than they ever did in our native land.

One party beverage that was very popular in my time was *bul*, a weak mixture of limeade and beer made with lots of sugar and ice. Everyone drank it, down to the children, and in my youth I thought it was the ultimate in delicious drinks. I have lost my taste for *bul*, just as I have for *malta*, a dark, heavy malt drink with a low alcohol content that was considered most efficacious as a tonic. Mixed into a shake with sweetened condensed milk, it was considered just the thing to help a skinny child gain weight.

At parties, weddings, christenings, girls' fifteenth birthday parties, and other special occasions, it was customary to drink *sidra*, imported Spanish hard cider, and, depending on the wealth of the family, French Champagnes.

You will also find in this chapter recipes for nonalcoholic beverages—potent café, refreshing batidos or shakes made of tropical fruit, and nourishing elixers such as *horchata* or almond nectar, to name a few—that were and are an essential and delicious part of Cuban entertaining and family life.

Tú me dijiste a mí, tú me dijiste a mí que no tomabas. Y en la cantina te ví, en la cantina te ví, tomándote un ron Bacardí. (You said to me, you said to me that you did not drink. And in the bar I saw you, in the bar I saw you, drinking a Bacardí rum.)

CUBA LIBRE

("FREE CUBA" RUM AND COKE)

I serving

So went a popular song of many years ago in Cuba. Bacardí rum was the most popular hard liquor on the island. Now Bacardí rum is manufactured in Puerto Rico, but it is still the only rum as far as Cubans in exile are concerned.

A Cuba libre is simply rum mixed with Coca-Cola over ice. Since Castro took over in 1959, Cuba has been far from free, and this drink has come to be known sarcastically in the exile community as *mentirita,* or "little lie." (In my opinion, *mentirota,* or "big lie.")

Ice cubes or cracked ice	2½ ounces (more or less) Coca-Cola
2 ounces white Bacardí rum	I lime wedge (optional)

Place ice in a tall glass and pour the rum over it. Fill the glass with Coca-Cola, and add lime if you wish.

DAIQUIRÍ CLÁSICO

(CLASSIC DAIQUIRI)

I serving

Here is the original daiquiri, Ernest Hemingway's favorite drink, as it was served at La Floridita, the Havana bar that claimed to have been its cradle. But the drink, which is at least as popular in this country as it was in Cuba, was actually invented by an American named Jennings Cox who was a mining engineer in Daiquirí, a coastal town in the province of Oriente.

There are innumerable variations on the daiquiri theme, some of which are given below. The old method of making the drink involved the laborious crushing of ice by hand and the vigorous shaking of the contents in a cocktail shaker. Nowadays the procedure is immeasurably simplified by the use of a blender.

2 ounces white Bacardí rum	I teaspoon sugar
I teaspoon freshly squeezed lime juice	About ½ cup cracked ice

Put all the ingredients into a blender and blend on high speed until the drink becomes frappé. Pour it into a cocktail glass.

VARIATIONS

Daiquirí de Naranja (Orange Daiquiri): Reduce the lime juice to ½ teaspoon, and add 1 teaspoon orange juice and 1 teaspoon Curaçao.

Daiquirí de Toronja (Grapefruit Daiquiri): Increase the lime juice to 1 tablespoon and add ¼ cup grapefruit juice and 1 teaspoon Marrasquino syrup.

Daiquirí de Piña (Pineapple Daiquiri): Increase the lime juice to 1 tablespoon and add ¼ cup pineapple juice.

MOJITO
(THE ORIGINAL MOJITO COCKTAIL)

1 serving

Here is another of Ernest Hemingway's favorite cocktails. When I think of mojito, however, I think not of Hemingway but of my father. There, in our Varadero house, he would perform his evening ritual: Holding a cocktail shaker swathed in a starched linen napkin, he offered his mojito around for everyone to sample. Even we children were given a taste. The classic Cuban mojito is made with rum. My father's favorite variation, which he jokingly claimed to have invented and patented, was made with gin.

¼ cup freshly squeezed lime juice
2 ounces white Bacardí rum
2 teaspoons sugar
Plenty of finely cracked ice

2 or three sprigs of fresh peppermint
4 ounces seltzer or club soda

Put the lime juice, rum, sugar, ice, and peppermint in a cocktail glass. Add the desired amount of seltzer and stir, or shake in a cocktail shaker.

VARIATION

Mojito Matriculado (Papa's "Patented" Mojito Cocktail): Substitute gin for the rum and reduce the sugar to 1 teaspoon. Serve with a twist of lime.

Sidra, hard Spanish cider, is widely available in American liquor stores.

1 pound (2¼ cups) sugar
8 ounces dry sherry
4 ounces crème de cacao
4 ounces bitters

32 ounces imported Spanish cider
Three 32-ounce bottles sparkling
   water, chilled
2 limes, cut into wedges

Mix together the sugar, sherry, crème de cacao, bitters, and cider, and chill well. Add the sparkling water and serve in a punch bowl, garnished with lime wedges.

PONCHE FUERTECITO PARA 35
(STRONG PUNCH FOR 35)

As Ricky Ricardo of "I Love Lucy" fame, Desi Arnaz introduced Americans to "Babalú," a song by Margarita Lecuona. Little did viewers of that classic 1950s television show know that Ricky was singing about making offerings, including a jug of aguardiente or "firewater," to Babalú, a *Santería* deity. Santería is Cuban "black magic," a folk religion that grew out of the African religions brought to the island by slaves. It is forbidden by the Catholic Church.

Aguardiente, which literally means "burning water," was never served in polite society; it was the sort of beverage that men took on fishing trips. Drunk by itself, aguardiente was like pure alcohol, but *compuesto*, or seasoned, it was pleasant if potent. This is the way my father prepared the beverage that kept him and his fishing buddies in perfectly warm, healthy, and happy condition.

5 quarts water
8 cups sugar
40 orange skins, hung out to dry
   for several days (see Notes)

12 quarts aguardiente
   (see Notes)

1. Combine the water and sugar in a large pot. Bring to a boil, reduce the heat to medium, and cook, uncovered, until it is a very thick syrup. Set it aside to cool.

AGUARDIENTE COMPUESTO
(SEASONED "FIREWATER")

2. Cut the dried orange skins into 1-inch pieces.

3. In a *garrafón* (4-gallon carafe), combine the syrup, orange skins, and aguardiente.

4. Cork the carafe and let it rest for 40 days, shaking it occasionally to mix the ingredients. Then strain the aguardiente compuesto and pour it into bottles.

NOTES: In Cuba, oranges were always peeled before eating. With a sharp knife, one would start at the top, circling around to the orange's other "pole" and ending up with one long strip of skin. We children liked to throw the peel on the floor to see what letter it would form. (It usually was an "S.") We did eat a lot of oranges, so Papá was never short of dry skins.

At least one company, Century Cellars Inc. of Miami, which is owned by Pedro Luis Alzola, whose parents came from my hometown of Cárdenas, makes aguardiente in this country. Ask for it at a liquor store that caters to a Latin clientele.

AGUA DE COCO
(COCONUT WATER)

Hay vistas que tumban cocos. (There are sights which can knock down coconuts.) —An old Cuban saying

The water from the green coconuts that grow throughout the tropics is as versatile as it is delicious. Coconut water is known to be a highly effective diuretic, and in Cuba it was given to people with kidney trouble. It was also used as a tonic for anemia.

On some Caribbean islands, coconut water was mixed with liquor as a cocktail, but in Cuba we drank it pure as it came out of a fresh coconut. Whether served at room temperature or chilled, there are few drinks more refreshing. While vacationing on the island of Bali many years ago, we drank nothing but fresh coconut water for ten days. I cannot think of another time when I was so glad that the local water was unsafe to drink!

How to Open a Green Coconut

With a strong, sharp knife, cut a hole about 2 inches in diameter around the stem of the coconut (the center top) where it is softest. Then simply insert a straw and drink the coconut water, or empty it into a glass. (You may, of course, chill the coconut water, or simply chill the coconut before opening it.)

If you like, insert a spoon through the hole once the coconut is empty and eat the sweet meat, which in a green coconut has a custardlike consistency.

BATIDOS
(TROPICAL FRUIT SHAKES)

2 servings

The fertile soil of Cuba provided us with an almost unlimited array of tropical fruits all year long. From the pulp of those sweet, succulent fruits the most delicious batidos or shakes were made. Today in this country, one can purchase the frozen pulp of many tropical fruits in the supermarket. My favorite batido is mango, and much as I enjoy the convenience of frozen pulp, I still believe there is no fruit more delicious than a ripened mango fallen from a tree in your own backyard. Whatever their form, you will find that papaya is so bland and *guanábana* so tart that you will want to add sugar when using them in shakes.

I use nonfat dry milk for my batidos. Without ice cream, the shake is thick and rich, and has only about 80 calories per serving.

BATIDO DE MANGO (MANGO SHAKE)

1 cup mango pulp   Sugar (optional)
⅔ cup cold milk

BATIDO DE ANONES (ANONES SHAKE)

1 cup custard apple pulp   1 tablespoon sugar
½ cup cold milk

Batido de Fruta Bomba (Papaya Shake)

1 cup papaya pulp
2 scoops vanilla ice cream
   (optional)

½ cup cold milk
1 teaspoon sugar, or more to taste

Batido de Guanábana (Guanábana Shake)

1 cup frozen guanábana pulp
½ cup cold milk

2 scoops vanilla ice cream (optional)
¼ cup sugar

In a blender, combine all the ingredients for the shake of your choice, and blend them on high until smooth and frothy.

CHAMPOLA DE GUANÁBANA

(GUANÁBANA
REFRESHMENT)

6 servings

This is another one of the many tropical drinks that Cubans love. Guanábana's rather peculiar, exotic taste is not for everyone. Be sure to strain it first if trying to convert someone to its pleasures, for its gelatinous texture can put off a newcomer.

1 fresh guanábana (about 3
   pounds)
About 2 cups sugar

1 quart milk
Cracked ice

1. Peel the guanábana. Cut it in half and discard the heart, then cut up the rest in small pieces.

2. Place the guanábana in a large bowl and sprinkle it with 2 cups of sugar, or more to taste. (The pulp of this fruit is very tart.) Set it aside for at least 1 hour.

3. Strain the mixture through a colander, discarding the seeds and the cottony substance. Stir in 1 cup of milk for each cup of guanábana pulp and mix well.

4. Chill, and serve over cracked ice.

VARIATIONS

Juice Extractor Method: Put the peeled and cleaned guanábana in the machine, extract the pulp, mix the remainder with milk and sugar, and serve it very cold over cracked ice.

With Frozen Pulp: Put the pulp in a blender with the milk and sugar, and blend until smooth. Serve cold over cracked ice.

CAFÉ
(CUBAN COFFEE)

10 servings

The saying goes that the four letters of café stand for its most essential qualities: *caliente* (hot), *amargo* (bitter), *fuerte* (strong) and *escaso* (scanty). Cuban coffee is served at the end of a meal in tiny *tacitas* that are smaller than demitasse cups. And any time of day or night at the countless little Cuban restaurants that dot Miami, people line up for "jolts" of café cubano served in thimble-size paper cups.

Here is the old-fashioned way to make Cuban coffee, though the truth is that Cubans in this country make their coffee in Italian espresso makers.

1 quart water
4 tablespoons Cuban coffee (Bustelo,
    La Estrella, Pilón, El Pico, etc.)

Sugar

1. Bring the water to a boil in a saucepan. Add the coffee, and let it boil for 2 or 3 minutes.

2. Strain the coffee through a cone-shaped strainer lined with cotton flannel. (The strainer and flannel are sold in many Latin markets.) Add sugar to taste.

CAFÉ CON LECHE

(COFFEE WITH MILK)

1 serving

Café con leche should be called *leche con café*, for it really is milk with coffee. A steaming cup of this sweet, soothing brew served with toasted bread or Cuban crackers is a typical Cuban breakfast.

The milk in Cuba when I was young was brought each *madrugada*, the time before dawn, by a *lechero* or milkman riding a donkey. A maid would boil it in a big pail as everyone was getting up, and the aroma of the boiling milk and brewing coffee would encourage even the sleepiest heads to start the day.

Now that raw milk is no longer used, the boiling stage is not strictly necessary, but I recommend it nevertheless. Real café con leche tastes better boiled. The pinch of salt gives it a special *gracia* reminiscent of old Cuba, so do not be tempted to omit it.

Cubans on the go in this country often pour themselves a mug of milk, put it in a microwave for 2 minutes on high, and then add a teaspoon each of sugar and instant coffee. The result is a pleasant drink that vaguely resembles but cannot compare with authentic café con leche.

Pinch of salt   ¼ cup strong brewed Cuban coffee
¾ cup milk   Sugar

I. Add the salt to the milk and bring it to a boil. Stir in the coffee and add sugar to taste.

CHOCOLATE ESPAÑOL

(SPANISH-STYLE HOT CHOCOLATE)

4 to 6 servings

Las cuentas claras y el chocolate espeso.

This old Spanish proverb recommends that one keep one's accounts clear but one's chocolate thick and murky. And so it is with Spanish chocolate, which contains cornstarch and, when made right, is almost like pudding in consistency.

Although hot chocolate could never compete in popularity with café con leche, it was served for breakfast in some homes of old Cuba along with *bizcochos*, cookies similar to lady fingers, for dunking.

Four or five 1-ounce pieces	1 quart milk
Spanish-style chocolate (see	¼ cup sugar
Note)	

1. Grate the chocolate into fine shreds and place it in a saucepan with the milk and sugar.

2. Bring the mixture to a slow boil, constantly stirring it with a whisk or a *batidor de chocolate,* a wooden chocolate beater. Beat the cooking chocolate until it melts and becomes perfectly smooth. Continue to beat it more vigorously until the chocolate is frothy and thick.

3. Pour the chocolate into mugs and serve immediately.

NOTE: In Cuba, we used imported Spanish brands of chocolate such as La Estrella and Menier, which contained cinnamon as well as cornstarch. In this country, various Latin American brands are widely available. Check the label to make sure it contains cornstarch.

HORCHATA
(ALMOND NECTAR)

4 servings

Cuban horchata is made from crushed, blanched almonds. It looks like the Spanish version, which is made of tiger nuts, but tastes a bit different. In Cuba, horchata was given to nursing mothers because it was thought to be very nutritious. Never mind that it was highly caloric: Mothers were supposed to be fat; the important thing was to have rich milk for the babies. I remember Chicha, my great grandmother, making horchata for my mother when she was nursing my second baby brother, Pili. Though only five feet three inches tall, Mamá weighed 200 pounds at the time!

Calories aside, horchata is such a fabulously delicious drink that no one should miss trying it at least once. Although I have given the old-fashioned method of grinding and straining the almonds, there is no reason why horchata cannot be made with a juice extractor after the almonds have been peeled.

1 pound raw almonds
1 pound sugar

1. Bring a large pot of water to a boil. Put the almonds in it and remove the pot from the heat. Let the almonds soak for about 30 minutes, until their skins are swollen and wrinkled.

2. Drain the almonds and slip their skins off with your fingers. Grind them into a fine paste with a hand grinder or food processor.

3. Mix the ground almonds and the sugar into a thick paste. (The mixture looks like marzipan and can be eaten like candy.)

4. Roll the paste into a cylinder about 2 inches in diameter and 8 inches long. Wrap it in waxed paper and refrigerate.

5. Cut off about 2 inches of the almond paste per serving, and combine it in a blender with 1 cup per serving of cold water. Blend it on high until the horchata is smooth and frothy. Chill it well and serve it in a tall glass.

A portion of the north beach of Varadero, circa 1930. The beach of fine white sand, old Victorian houses (the Club Náutico is in the center), and crystal clear water extended for more than twenty miles. *Juan Castro Larrieu*

INDEX